IBSEN

Volume III: Four Plays

Smith and Kraus *Books for Actors*

GREAT TRANSLATIONS FOR ACTORS SERIES

Mercadet by Honoré de Balzac, tr. by Robert Cornthwaite

Zoyka's Apartment by Mikhail Bulgakov, tr. by N. Saunders & F. Dwyer

Chekhov: Four Plays, tr. by Carol Rocamora

Chekhov's Vaudevilles, tr. by Carol Rocamora

The Sea Gull by Anton Chekhov, tr. by N. Saunders & F. Dwyer

Three Sisters by Anton Chekhov, tr. by Lanford Wilson

The Wood Demon by Anton Chekhov, tr. by N. Saunders & F. Dwyer

The Coffee Shop by Carlo Goldoni, tr. by Robert Cornthwaite

Villeggiatura: The Trilogy by Carlo Goldoni, tr. by Robert Cornthwaite

The Summer People by Maxim Gorky, tr. by N. Saunders & F. Dwyer

Ibsen: Four Major Plays, tr. by R. Davis & B. Johnston

Ibsen Volume II: Four Plays, tr. by Brian Johnston

Spite for Spite by Agustin Moreto, tr. by Dakin Matthews

Cyrano de Bergerac by Edmond Rostand, tr. by Charles Marowitz

A Glass of Water by Eugene Scribe, tr. by Robert Cornthwaite

Marivaux: Three Plays, tr. by Stephen Wadsworth

If you require pre-publication information about upcoming Smith and Kraus books, you may receive our semi-annual catalogue, free of charge, by sending your name and address to *Smith and Kraus Catalogue, P.O. Box 127, Lyme, NH 03768. Or call us at (603) 922-5105, fax (603) 922-3348.*

IBSEN

Volume III: Four Plays

translated by Brian Johnston

with Rick Davis

Great Translations for Actors

SK

A Smith and Kraus Book

A Smith and Kraus Book
One Main Street, PO Box 127, Lyme, NH 03768
603.795.4331

Cover illustration *On the Sailboat* by Caspar David Friedrich
Cover and Book Design By Julia Hill

First Edition: July 1998
9 8 7 6 5 4 3 2 1

Library of Congress Cataloging-in-Publication Data
Ibsen, Henrik, 1828–1906.
[Plays. English. Selections.]
Ibsen: four plays / translated by Brian Johnston with Rick Davis. —1st ed.
p. cm. — (Great translations for actors)
Contents: The Lady from the Sea — Little Eyolf — John Gabriel Borkman — When We Dead Awaken.

ISBN 1-57525-145-0
I. Johnston, Brian, 1932- . II Title. III. Scrics.

PT8854.D38   1995
839.8'226—dc20   95-13632
CIP

CONTENTS

THE REALITY OF
IBSEN'S DRAMAS

Ibsen's twelve realist dramas, from *Pillars of Society* to *When We Dead Awaken,* invite directors, actors, and actresses to extend the terms of the modern theatre. The plays do not imitate the reality we encounter in the world outside the theater: they create a liberating alternative to that reality. His theater "gives liberty of action to forces and possibilities to which life does not grant the chance of coming into their rights," proclaimed Ibsen's son, Sigurd, when describing the function of art. Ibsen's dramatic characters are moved to actions, utterances, and encounters, within very strictly regulated terms of stage time and space, which are more fateful, more consequential, and imaginatively more expansive than the terms of our everyday existence. One might say these characters earn a place in Ibsen's Cycle only when they are capable of carrying archetypal, rather than strictly naturalistic, significance. Each character sustains, in ensemble with the others, a wide-ranging and imaginative vision, which is further extended by the metaphoric surroundings Ibsen devises for them. Though each of his character studies is interesting "in itself," it is the interaction of these individual characters, as an ensemble within the environments they are placed, that makes his plays so wide ranging and so tantalizing. Ibsen called his plays "poems," and they are best explored in the way we explore major poetry: as creating imaginative metaphoric structures we never will completely know but will continue to re-explore and re-experience in ever new ways. Not only each generation will discover a new Ibsen, each new performance will do so—for directors, actors, and designers are the primary interpreters of the plays.

IBSEN'S CHARACTERS

Ibsen's characters inhabit a histrionic world of carefully shaped three, four, or five act structures, subject less to the compulsions and limitations of "real life" circumstances than to those of the demanding art form: a fundamental principle of any art but one frequently forgotten by interpreters of realist drama. These characters must act and speak only those lines that build up the dialectic structure of each act that, as in Greek drama, will move to its crises of *anagnorisis* (perception) and *peripeteia* (reversal). Like the characters of poetic drama they speak a language loaded with imagery that reaches far beyond the immediate moment. However, any experience of the plays reveals how their characters take possession of our imaginations and our sympathies as living, complex, multilayered individuals in whose intricate destinies we become emotionally involved. We are challenged to recognize the theatrical and aesthetic beauty of these texts, but also to make them come alive as compelling, moving, or disturbing human experiences. They live and move in a "pressurized" space of causes moved to extremes of effect; of demands pushed to limits that will have devastating consequences. But it is always the stuff of our own experience that is in this way heightened and clarified by the action. The plays give us extensions, not distortions, of our own lives.

IBSEN'S INVENTION OF A METAPHORIC NORWAY

Ibsen did not imitate the Norway of these plays: he *invented* it. The "everyday" Norway that confronted Ibsen (and which, until late in life, he took great care, through twenty-seven years of self-imposed exile, actually not to inhabit) was not a "Truth" to be imitated, but a muddled and bungled work of art—a fallen and imprisoned world that had evolved through long historical time. Our unhappy, unfree, human consciousness, the result of centuries of blundering history "on the wrong track" in Ibsen's words, is unaware of the spiritual legacy it has forfeited or distorted and needs not to be "reproduced" but "awakened," both to the extent of its loss and to the possibility of recovery. Ibsen dramatized his reinvented Norway as a subversive and charged theatric space into which can erupt "forces and possibilities" that the modern world has forgotten or repressed.

However valid this vision of things as a philosophy, as a *theatric metaphor* it superbly extends the human gesture on the stage from the particular to the universal—as all great drama must do. With its action of two or three hours only, within the limited few feet of stage space, all major drama needs a form of metaphoric shorthand—creating "infinite riches in a little room," which enables drama to match the range of reference of more expansive literary forms, such as the epic or novel. In such a drama, the actor, aided by the director and designer, will lure the audience beyond the familiar and everyday to the perception of a larger, more universal or archetypal range of reference. It is the constant challenge of a role such as Oedipus, Electra, Hamlet, Ellida Wangel, or

John Gabriel Borkman, for which each generation will devise new solutions. It does not matter that we may not wholly understand what the poet is up to in such plays: they are there to be re-explored, again and again, with new possibilities of meaning and significance still waiting for us to discover. The greatest art always ultimately eludes us, which is why we need continually to revisit it.

OUR RESPONSIBILITY AS INTERPRETERS

Therefore, I believe we should approach an Ibsen play with no preconceptions as to its meaning but with a readiness to respond, as if for the first time, to its metaphoric structure and imagery. A controlling metaphor in *The Lady from the Sea*, for example, which might lead us into the world of this richly imaginative play, is that of an ever-widening *division* between competing realms of reality: the comfortingly familiar but confining on the one side and the alarming and unlimited on the other. The division begins innocently as the division, in the Wangel garden, between the verandah, on which the daughters sit, and the arbour or summer house of Ellida, with Wangel shuttling between the two—a compromise that conceals an actual gulf between the two. It then expands into the division between the garden in the foreground and the distant fjord and mountains in the background; then between the confined carp pond and the limitless sea; then between the Wangel home and the coastal town Wangel envisages returning Ellida to and shuttling between; then between the world of Wangel's decorous domesticity and the anarchic sea world of the Stranger—who, presumably returning from the dead, seems to operate outside the categories of all human consciousness. The world of the Stranger sets the limitless and ineffable against the confined and familiar world Ellida finds herself trapped in.

This sequence of ever-expanding *external* oppositions is *internalized* in the schizophrenic condition of Ellida's mind, hovering fearfully, to the point of madness, over the horrifying yet alluring realm of the limitless that beckons beyond the confinement of her everyday condition. This condition is only the extreme expression of the consciousness of the whole play, its female characters in particular sensing the infinite distance between their confined and limited world and the limitless reality beckoning them. The play is unique in the Cycle, until the last four plays, in taking place almost entirely *al fresco* (outdoors), with huge vistas of distant landscape. In Act II the play ascends to The Prospect's (Udsigten) height, with huge overviews of the open fjord, islands, headlands and distant mountain peaks. A scenography in which, as in a Caspar David Friedrich canvas, the mysterious world seems offered up to the characters' pensive contemplation. By contrast, Act III opens with these characters hovering over and peering into the confined carp pond, as into the mind itself, fascinated by its dark interior life.

Ibsen's notes in the draft manuscript of the play emphasize this theme of external and internal division, between the limited and the limitless and the Romantic yearnings it provokes:

> Life is apparently a happy, easy and lively thing up there in the shadow of the mountains and in the monotony of this seclusion. Then the suggestion is thrown up that this kind of life is a life of shadows . . . This is how life is lived in the brief light of summer. And afterwards—into the darkness. Then longings are roused for the life of the great world outside. But what would be gained from that? With changed surroundings and with one's mind developed, there is an increase in one's longings and desires. A man or a woman who has reached the top desires the secrets of the future, a share in the life of the future and communication with distant planets . . . .

I once took part in a symposium following a performance of the play where one of the panelists insisted the play was about a woman's unhappy marriage and a husband's chastened recognition of his unsatisfactory role in the matter. The play, then, was yet another nail in the coffin of detestable male chauvinism, and Ibsen brought the Stranger from the depths of the sea and perhaps from the realm of the infinite to perform the task of a competent (and feminist) marriage counsellor. In response, I murmured, with Horatio in *Hamlet,* "There needs no ghost, my lord, come from the grave to tell us this!" We should keep this admonition in mind when approaching any Ibsen play. Ibsen did not submit himself to an arduous, imaginatively extensive, aesthetically audacious, and complexly crafted dramatic artistry to convey "meanings" that might more effectively be set out in a polemical pamphlet! This is not to say that such issues are not present in the play as part of its design, just as the need to make adequate provision for superannuated monarchs is part of the design of *King Lear.* But these are departure points for the dramatic explorations, not the goals. It is better to be baffled by a play, experiencing its immensity of intention, than to settle for a meaning that renders it familiar, politically correct, and banal.

The plays in this volume, therefore, challenge directors, actors and designers to come up with performance strategies that can encompass all their possible dimensions of significance: To match the audacity of Ibsen in stretching all the elements of drama—scene, character, action, dialogue, and props—to their imaginative limits. Against soaring landscapes stretching into the infinite, the characters are moved by larger than life emotions, aspirations, sorrows, and guilts. Yet while these plays expand immensely outward, they also journey deep into the interior, to "the heart of darkness" within individuals, to areas where the psyche seems locked in the condition of *aporia* (literally "the impassable path"). This is particularly true of *Little Eyolf, John Gabriel Borkman,* and *When We Dead Awaken,* but *The Lady from the Sea* also prefigures this condition of the four last plays, both in its external scenic metaphor of the extended landscape and in its exploration of depths within the psyche that Ellida and Wangel term the horrible (*grufulde*)—the terrifying that at the same time, appallingly 'attracts' (*drager*). Over these depths Ellida's consciousness hovers, paralyzed, unable to inhabit either the immediate everyday world or commit herself to the terrifying limitless realm into which the Stranger invites her. It might be because *The Lady from the Sea* already looks ahead to the third group that a character from the play, Hilde Wangel, opens the dialectic action of that group when she enters the world of *The Master Builder.*

In the last play in the Cycle, WHEN WE DEAD AWAKEN, this internal condition of aporia is directly presented, in Act Three, as an onstage situation: it is what Ulfhejm calls being *bergfast*—rock-trapped—caught in the 'sticking place' in which there seems no going forward or back. All the major characters in the final four plays are 'bergfast'—aware of having arrived at a spiritual impasse in their lives from which there seems to be no escape. Halvard Solness, in *The Master Builder,* paralyzed by guilt and fear of retribution from the young, broods obsessively over the past, finding no joy in creativity yet jealously preventing it in others. Alfred and Rita Allmers, in *Little Eyolf,* are daily tormented by the presence of the little crippled boy, Eyolf, whose death forces them to circle hopelessly round their guilt and the failure of their marriage. The Borkman household long has been locked in a condition of near manic noncommunication, both Gunhild and Borkman clinging to a completely unrealizable dream of 'redemption'—she for the restoration of Honor, he for that of Power. *When We Dead Awaken* opens with the conclusion of a meaningless railway journey, the boredom and ennui of a marriage at the end of its tether, and the exhaustion of creative powers.

The major characters of these plays thoroughly know their situations. They have brooded on them for years, are trapped in their multilayered complexes of guilt and betrayal, and there seems no possible way forward for them. Into this condition of agonized spiritual stagnation there erupt startling unexpected visitors (the Stranger, the Rat-Wife, the dying Ella, and the resurrected Irene), whose arrival will enforce an even deeper exploration of the past, a profounder acknowledgment both of destructive transgression and of betrayed possible fulfilment. The plays search into the heart of loss. The characters rouse themselves for a final, transcendent action that will bind up both lost possibility and past guilt into a redemptive action in the present. John Gabriel Borkman's Lear-like rush into the dark night and the storm manages to survive the hilarious comic deflation threatened by Foldal's parodic version of it—Ibsen's comedy can suddenly erupt in even his most serious plays—to achieve the visionary and poignant poetry of his last speeches on the heights. Rubek and Irene's speeches, as they ascend, act by act, to the mountain peak, are harsh dissonances that resolve into painful harmonies of reconciliation with themselves and with their tortured pasts.

There is a desire on the part of the guilty elders to escape from the condition of aporia by means of a horizontal movement out into the world of action and of the future, to rejoin the human communty in a resurrection of former powers. This, they learn painfully, is ruled out: there is no place for them in the present or the future. That belongs either to a younger generation who will survive them, or to younger couples (Asta and Borgheim, Ulfhejm and Maja) who are free of the constricting dialectic of the guilty pairs. In the sequence of the last plays, scenic metaphors of "vertical liberation" from the "sticking place" are enacted within increasingly elevated last act endings: Solness's tower in *The Master Builder,* the hillock elevation of *Little Eyolf,* the higher hilltop of *John Gabriel Borkman,* and the mountain top of *When We Dead Awaken*—a *spatial* progression that is accompanied by the *temporal* sequence of the last acts: *evening, late evening, night,* and *dawn before the sunrise.*

All the plays in the Cycle enact an interplay between the seemingly reduced text of our everyday reality and a larger supertext of archetypal and metaphoric perspectives subversively (dialectically) brought to bear upon that reality. In perhaps the most familiar example, we watch Torvald and Nora Helmer's doll house disintegrate before our eyes as the realities it tried poignantly to ignore, invade and overwhelm their bower of domestic bliss. *The Lady from the Sea* and the last four plays extend this dialectic to its limits. The familiar is challenged by the terrifyingly strange: a stifling alienated reality is invaded by unexpected visitors who open up huge prospects or abysses unsuspected within the worlds of the protagonists. In performance, the results can be enthralling. Both *John Gabriel Borkman* and *Little Eyolf* were major hits of the London 1996–97 seasons. Robert Brustein and Robert Wilson collaborated in a memorable production of *When We Dead Awaken* in Boston in 1990. *The Lady from the Sea,* powerfully revived by Eleonora Duse, later by Vanessa Redgrave, and more recently in a brilliantly imaginative production in 1988 at Center Stage, Baltimore, continues to attract directors, performers, and scene designers eager to extend the terms of their art. Though Ibsen's plays challenge our notions of naturalist theater they have proved their success with the public. They are invitations to imaginative exploration, mysterious and exhilarating journeys to destinations our theater still has to discover.

— *Brian Johnston*

IBSEN'S PROSE CYCLE

IBSEN

Volume III: Four Plays

THE LADY
FROM THE SEA

1888

CHARACTERS

DR. WANGEL, district doctor
ELLIDA WANGEL, his second wife
BOLETTE, older daughter by his first wife
HILDE, younger daughter by his first wife
ARNHOLM, a head schoolteacher
LYNGSTRAND
BALLESTAD
A STRANGER
YOUNG TOWNSPEOPLE
TOURISTS
SUMMER GUESTS

TIME AND PLACE

The action takes place during the summer in a little town by a fjord in northern Norway. All scene directions are from the audience's point of view.

ACT ONE

Dr. Wangel's house with a large covered veranda to the left. A garden in front and around it. Below the veranda is a flagpole. In the garden to the right is an arbour with a table and chairs. A hedge with a little gate in the background. Behind the hedge a road beside the shore. An avenue of trees beside the road. Between the trees can be glimpsed the fjord and high mountains and peaks in the distance. It is a warm and brilliantly clear summer morning.

BALLESTED, a middle-aged man, dressed in an old velvet jacket and a broad-brimmed artist's hat, is standing under the flagpole and attending to the cords. The flag is lying on the ground. Close by is an easel with a canvas spread upon it. Beside it a camp stool, paintbrushes, palette, and a paintbox.

BOLETTE WANGEL enters from the garden-room door to the veranda. She is carrying a large vase of flowers, which she sets on the table.

BOLETTE: So, Ballestad, is it going to work all right?

BALLESTED: Oh yes, Miss. No problem at all. But may I ask if we're expecting visitors[1] today?

BOLETTE: Yes, we're expecting Mr. Arnholm here this morning. He got into town last night.

BALLESTED: Arnholm? Wait a moment— Wasn't he called Arnholm—who was tutor here some years back?

BOLETTE: Right, that's the man.

BALLESTED: I see. So he's back in these parts again.

BOLETTE: Yes, it's why we're raising the flag.

BALLESTED: It seems the right thing to do.

BOLETTE goes back through the garden-room door. Soon after, LYNGSTRAND enters from the road, right, and comes to a halt, interested, when he sees the easel and the painting objects. He is a slender young man, poorly but neatly dressed, and of a delicate appearance.

LYNGTRAND: *(On the other side of the hedge.)* Good morning!

BALLESTED: *(Turning.)* What—! Good morning. *(Raises the flag.)* There we are—up like a balloon. *(Fastens the cord then goes over and occupies himself by the easel.)* Good morning, my dear sir—I really haven't had the pleasure—

LYNGTRAND: So you're actually a painter.

BALLESTED: Yes, naturally. Why shouldn't I be a painter, as well?

LYNGTRAND: Of course, I can see you are. May I come in a moment?

BALLESTED: Maybe you'd like to have a look?

LYNGTRAND: Yes, I'd like to very much.

BALLESTED: There's really not that much to see just yet. But if you really wish—step in closer.

LYNGSTRAND: Many thanks. *(He comes in through the garden gate.)*

BALLESTED *(Painting.)* It's the fjord there between the islands I'm trying to catch.

LYNGSTRAND: So I see.

BALLESTAD: But it still lacks the figure. There's no model for it here in town.

LYNGSTRAND: There's to be a figure as well?

BALLESTED: Yes. Lying right by the reef here in the foreground—a dying mermaid

LYNGSTRAND: Why should she be dying?

BALLESTED: She's strayed in from the sea and can't find her way out again. So, you see, she lies here, wasting away in the brackish water of the fjord.

LYNGSTRAND: Really, so that's why.

BALLESTED: It was the lady of the house, here, who got me thinking of the subject.

LYNGSTRAND: What will you call the picture once it's finished.

BALLESTED: I've thought of calling it "The Death of a Mermaid."

LYNGSTRAND: That will do nicely. You can really make something good out of this.

BALLESTED: A fellow artist, perhaps?

LYNGSTRAND: You mean a painter?

BALLESTED: Yes.

LYNGSTRAND: No, not exactly. But I'm going to be a sculptor. My name's Hans Lyngstrand.

BALLESTED: So, you're going to be a sculptor. Well, sculpture's a fine, elegant art, too. I believe I've seen you a couple of times in the street. Have you been with us long?

LYNGSTRAND: No, just a fortnight. But I'm going to see about staying here the whole summer.

BALLESTED: To enjoy all the amenities of our bathing resort? Is that it?

LYNGSTRAND: Yes, to see if I can get some of my strength back.

BALLESTED: You're not at all ill?

LYNGSTRAND: Just a little ill, yes. But nothing very serious. Just some kind of shortness of breath.

BALLESTED: Oh, that's nothing at all! What you should do, however, is talk to a decent doctor.

LYNGSTRAND: I've thought of asking Dr. Wangel for advice.

BALLESTED: Yes, do that. *(Looking to the left.)* There comes another steamer—packed full of passengers. There's been an incredible increase in tourist trade here in the last few years.

LYNGSTRAND: I've certainly noticed a lot of tourist traffic.

BALLESTED: We're brimful with summer guests, too. I'm often afraid our town will lose its character with all these strangers about.

LYNGSTRAND: You were born here in town?

BALLESTED: Not exactly. But I've accla-acclimatized myself to it. I feel I'm tied to the place—bonds of time and custom, I suppose.

LYNGSTRAND: Then you've lived here long?

BALLESTED: About seventeen-eighteen years. I came here with Skive's theatre company. But then we ran into financial difficulties. So the company dissolved and scattered to the four winds.

LYNGSTRAND: But you stayed behind?

BALLESTED: I stayed. And settled in very nicely. You see, at the time I was working mostly as a scene painter.

(BOLETTE comes out with a rocking chair, which she sets down on the veranda.)

BOLETTA *(Calling into the garden room.)* Hilda, see if you can find the embroidered footstool for Father.

LYNGSTRAND: *(Going toward the veranda and calling out.)* Good morning, Miss Wangel!

BOLETTA: *(By the railing.)* Why, so it's you Mr. Lyngstrand? Good morning. Do excuse me a moment—I just have to—*(Going into the house.)*

BALLESTED: Do you know the family here?

LYNGSTRAND: Not very well. I've just run into the young ladies in company here and there. And I've spoken a little to Mrs. Wangel—the last time when there was music up at Prospect Park. She said I should feel free to come and visit them.

BALLESTED: Well, you know what—you should cultivate that acquaintance.

LYNGSTRAND: Yes, I've also thought of paying them a visit. Calling on them, as it were. If only I could come up with an excuse to—

BALLESTED: Why an excuse? *(Looking out to the left.)* Damn and blast! *(Gathering his things together.)* The steamer's docked in at the pier. I must get down to the hotel. Some of the new arrivals might be needing me. I also work as a barber and hairdresser, you see.

LYNGSTRAND: You're certainly very versatile.

BALLESTED: In a small town one must learn to accla-acclimatize oneself in various fields. Anyway, should you be needing something or other for your hair—a little pomade or suchlike, just ask after dance instructor Ballested.

LYNGSTRAND: Dance instructor—?

BALLESTED: Leader of the wind ensemble, if you prefer. We're giving a concert up at Prospect Park this evening. Goodbye—goodbye! *(He exits with the painting things through the door in the fence and goes off to the left.) (HILDA comes out with the footstool. BOLETTA brings more flowers. LYNGSTRAND, down in the garden, bows to HILDA.)*

HILDA: *(By the railing, not returning the greeting.)* Boletta said you'd invited yourself in here today.

LYNGSTRAND: Yes, I took the liberty of coming in here for a while.

HILDA: You've been out on a morning tour, I suppose?

LYNGSTRAND: Oh no, there wasn't much of a tour today.

HILDA: You've been bathing, then?

LYNGSTRAND: Yes, I was in the sea for a little while. I saw your mother down there. Going into her bathing hut.

HILDA: Who did you see?

LYNGSTRAND: Your mother.

HILDA: Really? *(She sets the footstool before the rocking chair.)*

BOLETTA: *(At the same time, breaking in.)* You didn't happen to see Father's boat out on the fjord?

LYNGSTRAND: Yes, I believe I saw a sailing boat making for shore.

BOLETTA: That's bound to be father. He was out on a sick call to the islands. *(She arranges things on the table.)*

LYNGSTRAND: *(A step higher toward the veranda.)* That's really a magnificent display of flowers—

BOLETTA: Yes, doesn't it look good?

LYNGSTRAND: Really splendid. It looks like some family celebration's going on.

HILDA: That's just what's happening.

LYNGSTRAND: I think I can guess. It must be your father's birthday today.

BOLETTA: *(Warningly, to HILDA.)* Hm—hm!

HILDA: *(Paying no attention.)* No, mother's.

LYNGSTRAND: Really—so it's your mother's.

BOLETTA: *(Quietly, angry.)* But, Hilda—!

HILDA: *(In the same tone.)* Leave me alone! *(To LYNGSTRAND.)* Now you'll be going back to have your breakfast?

LYNGSTRAND: *(Retreating down the steps.)* Yes, I should see about getting something to eat.

HILDA: I take it you're really comfortable over at the hotel.

LYNGSTRAND: I'm not staying at the hotel any more. It's too expensive for me.

HILDA: So where are you staying now?

LYNGSTRAND: I'm now at Mrs Jensen's.

HILDA: Which Mrs. Jensen?

LYNGSTRAND: The midwife.

HILDA: Excuse me, Mr. Lyngstrand, but I really have other things to attend to—

LYNGSTRAND: Ah, I really shouldn't have mentioned that.

HILDA: Mentioned what?

LYNGSTRAND: What I just said.

HILDA: *(Measuring him, disdainfully.)* I've really no idea what you mean.

LYNGSTRAND: Well, well. But now I must say goodbye to you both.

BOLETTA: *(Coming down the steps.)* Goodbye, Mr. Lyngstrand. You really must excuse us, today. But another occasion—when you've time—and if you feel like it—you definitely must call on Father—and on all of us, too.

LYNGSTRAND: Many thanks. I'll be very happy to. *(He bows to them and leaves through the garden gate. As he goes along the road to the left, he bows to the veranda once more.)*

HILDA: *(Half aloud.)* Adieu, monsieur. And give my regards to mother Jensen.

BOLETTA: *(Quietly, shaking her arm.)* Hilda—! You wicked brat. Are you quite crazy! He could have heard you!

HILDA: Huh! Do you think I care about *that!*

BOLETTA: *(Looking to the left.)* Here comes Father.
(DR. WANGEL, dressed for travelling and carrying a valise, comes up the footpath to the right.)

WANGEL: See, children, I'm back again!

BOLETTA: *(Going down to meet him in the garden.)* Oh, it's so good you've come.

HILDA: *(Also going down to him.)* Are you free now, Father, for the rest of the day?

WANGEL: Not just yet. I must go down to the office for a while. Tell me—do you know if Mr. Arnholm's arrived yet?

BOLETTA: Yes, he got here last night. We've heard from the hotel.

WANGEL: So you've not seen him yet?

BOLETTA; No, but he's sure to come here this morning.

WANGEL: Yes, he'll be here by then for certain.

HILDA: *(Tugging at him.)* Father, you've just got to look around you.

WANGEL: *(Looking at the veranda.)* Yes, I can see it very well. Very festive you've made it.

BOLETTA: Yes, don't you think we've made it look fine?

WANGEL: Yes, I must hand it to you. Are we—are we alone in the house just now?

HILDA: Yes, she's gone to—

BOLETTA: *(Hastily breaking in.)* Mother's gone down to bathe.

WANGEL: *(Looking affectionately at Boletta and patting her on the head. Then he continues, a little hesitantly.)* Now listen, children—are you going to have this set up here all day? And the flag raised the whole day, too?

HILDA: You know very well that's how it is, Father.

WANGEL: Hm—all right. But don't you see—

BOLETTA: *(Nodding, with a twinkle in her eye.)* You see we've done all this for Mr. Arnholm's sake. When such a good friend comes to visit you for the first time—

HILDA: *(Smiling and shaking him.)* After all, Father—he was Boletta's tutor.

WANGEL: *(Half smiling.)* You really are a pair of sly ones. Well, good Lord, I suppose it's only natural we should remember her—who's no longer with us. Just the same—Take this, Hilda *(Giving his bag.)* Down to the office with it! No, girls, I don't like this at all. Not in this way, you understand. And we do this every year. But—what can one say! I suppose it can't be any other way.

HILDA: *(About to go through the garden to the left with the bag, but stops and turns, looking before her.)* Do you see that man approaching over there. That must be your tutor.

BOLETTA: *(Looking there.)* Him, *there?* Really, Hilda! You actually imagine that middle-aged fellow is Mr. Arnholm!

WANGEL: No, wait a moment my child. I truly do believe it is him! Yes, it definitely is!

BOLETTA: *(Staring ahead, quietly surprised.)* Good lord, if I don't think so too!

(ARNHOLM, in elegant morning dress, with light spectacles and a thin cane, enters on the road from the left. He has a somewhat weary appearance. He looks into the garden, gives a friendly greeting, and comes through the gate.)

WANGEL: *(Going to meet him.)* Welcome, my dear friend, welcome back to the old place.

ARNHOLM: Thank you, thank you, Doctor. So kind of you. *(They shake hands and walk together across the garden.)* And there are the girls. *(Shaking their hands while surveying them.)* I'd hardly have recognized them.

WANGEL: No, I can well believe it.

ARNHOLM: Well—maybe Boletta. Yes, I'd have recognized Boletta.

WANGEL: Barely, I should think. It must be about eight or nine years since you saw her last. Ah yes, things here have changed a great deal in that time.

ARNHOLM: *(Looking about him.)* Oh, I don't really think so. I admit the trees have grown up quite a bit—and you've put in that arbour there—

WANGEL: Well, its true that on the surface—

ARNHOLM: *(Smiling.)* And then, of course, you've now two marriageable daughters about the house.

WANGEL: Well, only one's marriageable so far.

HILDA: *(Half audibly.)* Oh *really*, Father!

WANGEL: And now I think we should sit on the veranda. It's cooler there. After you.

ARNHOLM: Thank you, Doctor.

(They go up to the veranda. WANGEL offers ARNHOLM the rocking chair.)

WANGEL: There. Now you must just sit quietly and rest yourself. You're looking rather tired after your journey.

ARHNOLM: Oh, it's nothing, really. Back in these surroundings—

BOLETTA: *(To WANGEL.)* Shall I bring some soda water and lemonade? It'll soon be getting too warm out here.

WANGEL: Yes, do that Boletta. Soda water and lemonade. And maybe a little cognac.

BOLETTA: Cognac as well?

WANGEL: Just a little. In case someone wants it.

BOLETTA: Very well, then. Hilda, you take the valise down to the office.

(BOLETTA goes into the garden room, closing the door after her. HILDA goes with the valise down through the garden, left, to the back of the house.)

ARNHOLM: *(Who has been following BOLETTA with his eyes.)* What a fine-looking—what fine-looking girls they've grown into!

WANGEL: *(Sitting.)* Yes, I think they have, too.

ARNHOLM: Boletta, quite amazingly so. And Hilda, too. But what about yourself, my dear Doctor. Are you thinking of living here for the rest of your life.

WANGEL: Almost certainly so. Here I was born and bred, as they say. It was here I was so deeply happy with her—who left us so early. Whom you knew when you were here last, Arnholm.

ARNHOLM: Yes, yes—

WANGEL: And now I'm happy with my second wife. Yes, I must say, on the whole, fate's been very good to me.

ARNHOLM: But no children from your second marriage?

WANGEL: We had a little boy two—two and a half years ago. But we didn't keep him long. He died when he was some four or five months old.

ARNHOLM: Isn't your wife home today?

WANGEL: Yes, she should be back very soon. She's gone down to bathe. She does so almost every day at this time of year, whatever the weather.

ARNHOLM: Anything wrong with her?

WANGEL: Not wrong, exactly. It's just that she's been remarkably nervous this last couple of years. That is, on and off. I've really no clue what's the matter with her. But bathing in the sea—that's what she mostly lives for, it seems.

ARNHOLM: Yes, so I remember from before.

WANGEL: *(With a barely noticeable smile.)* Of course, you knew Ellida that time you were teaching out there in Skjoldvik.

ARNHOLM: That's right. She often came to the rectory.[2] And then I'd often meet her when I called on her father at the lighthouse.[3]

WANGEL: You can understand how those days have left a deep impression on her. It's something the people here can't understand. They call her the "Lady from the Sea."

ARNHOLM: They do?

WANGEL: Yes, and that's why— Talk with her about the old days, Arnholm. It will do her so much good.

ARNHOLM: *(Looks doubtingly at him.)* You really have some reason for thinking that?

WANGEL: I'm certain of it.

ELLIDA'S VOICE: *(Heard from outside the garden, to the right.)* Are you there, Wangel?

WANGEL: *(Getting up.)* Yes, dear.

(ELLIDA WANGEL in a large, light robe, her hair wet and falling over her shoulders, enters from through the trees by the arbor. ARNHOLM gets up.)

WANGEL: *(Smiling and reaching out his hands to her.)* Now you get to see our mermaid.

ELLIDA: *(Going hurriedly to the veranda and grasping his hands.)* Thank God to see you again. When did you arrive?

WANGEL: Just now—a short while ago. *(Pointing to ARNHOLM.)* But aren't you going to greet an old friend—?

ELLIDA: *(Extending her hand to ARNHOLM.)* So, here you are, with us again. Welcome. And do forgive me for not being at home—

ARNHOLM: Please, don't feel under any obligation—

WANGEL: The water was nice and fresh today?

ELLIDA: Fresh! When is the water here ever fresh? So sluggish and tepid. The water's feeble, here in the fjord.

ARNHOLM: Feeble?

ELLIDA: Yes, it's feeble. And I believe it makes us feeble, too.

WANGEL: Well, that's a fine recommendation for the spa.

ARNHOLM: More likely, Mrs. Wangel, you're deeply tied to the sea and all that belongs to it.

ELLIDA: Yes, maybe so. I almost believe that myself. But see how fine the girls have made everything for your sake!

WANGEL: *(Embarrassed.)* Hm— *(Looking at his watch.)* I really have to be off now—

ARNHOLM: Is all this really for my sake—?

ELLIDA: You can be sure of it. We don't put up all this display every day. Oh—how stifling it is here under this roof! *(Goes down into the garden)* Come over here! At least the air's fresh here. *(She sits in the arbor.)*

ARNHOLM: *(Starting to join her.)* I think the air up here is quite fresh.

ELLIDA: Ah, yes! You're used to the stale city air. I hear it can be quite dreadful in the summer.

WANGEL: *(Who similarly has walked to the garden.)* And now, Ellida dear, it's up to you to entertain our good friend for a while.

ELLIDA: You've got work to do?

WANGEL: Yes, down at the office. And then a change of clothes. But I won't be long—

ARNHOLM: *(Sitting in the arbor.)* No need to hurry yourself, my dear Doctor. Your wife and I will know how to pass the time.

WANGEL: *(Nodding.)* Ah yes, I'm sure about that. Well—until later! *(He goes through the garden to the left.)*

ELLIDA: *(After a short pause.)* Don't you find it pleasant, sitting here?

ARNHOLM: I find it very pleasant.

ELLIDA: This is called my summerhouse because it was I who got it built. Or rather Wangel did—for my sake.

ARNHOLM: And it's here you usually like to sit?

ELLIDA: That's right. I sit here most of the day.

ARNHOLM: With the girls, I suppose?

ELLIDA: No, the girls prefer the veranda.

ARNHOLM: And what about Wangel?

ELLIDA: Well, he goes to and fro. For while he's over here and then, for a while, over there with the children.

ARNHOLM: Is that the way you want it?

ELLIDA: I think all parties concerned find it the best solution. We can always call over to each other—if we ever feel we've anything to say.

ARNHOLM: *(After a moment's reflection.)* The last time our paths crossed— out there in Skjoldvik, I mean— Hm. That's a long time ago, now.

ELLIDA: It's a good ten years since you were out there with us.

ARNHOLM: Yes, roughly that. But when I think about you out there at the lighthouse—! The pagan—that's what the old priest called you. Because your father had you baptized with a ship's name instead of a Christian one.

ELLIDA: Well, what of it?

ARNHOLM: The last thing I'd have expected would have been seeing you here as Mrs. Wangel.

ELLIDA: No, at that time Wangel wasn't— At that time the girls' mother was still alive. Their real mother, I mean.

ARNHOLM: True. True. But even if that hadn't been— Even if he'd been completely free— I'd still never have thought this could come about.

ELLIDA: Nor me, either. Never in the world—at that time.

ARNHOLM: Wangel is so fine. So honorable. So thoroughly good and kind to everyone.

ELLIDA: *(Warmly and heartfelt.)* Yes, he truly is!

ARNHOLM: But you two must be poles apart, I can't help thinking.

ELLIDA: You're right, there. There's that, as well.

ARNHOM: Then how could this come about? How did it happen?

ELLIDA: Ah, my dear Arnholm, don't ask me that. I couldn't explain it to you—and even if I could, you'd never be able to understand the least part of it.

ARNHOLM: Hm. *(A little quieter.)* Have you ever confided anything to your husband about me? I mean, of course, that fruitless proposal I let myself blunder into.

ELLIDA: No, how could you think so! I've not said a single word to him about—about that matter.

ARNHOLM: I'm glad. It was a little embarrassing for me to think that—

ELLIDA: There was really no need for that. I merely told him what is the truth—that I was extremely fond of you and that you were the truest and best friend I had out there.

ARNHOLM: Thanks for that. But tell me now—why did you never write to me after I went away?

ELLIDA: I thought it might cause you pain to hear anything from someone who—who couldn't be for you what you wished me to be. I felt it would be like reopening an already painful wound.

ARNHOLM: Yes, yes. You could be right in that.

ELLIDA: And why didn't you write yourself?

ARNHOLM: *(Looking at her and smiling half reproachfully.)* I? Make the opening move? Maybe have you think I was pestering you all over again? After the reception I was given?

ELLIDA: No, I can understand. Have you never since thought of another commitment?

ARNHOLM: Never. I stay faithful to my memories.

ELLIDA: *(Half joking.)* Whatever for? Let the old, sad memories go their own way. Instead, think about being a happily married man—that's my opinion.

ARNHOLM: It will have to be pretty soon, Mrs. Wangel. Remember, I'm already—I'm ashamed to admit—past thirty-seven.

ELLIDA: Well, all the more reason to make haste now. But listen, Arnholm, now I'm going to tell you something I couldn't have told you then even to save my life.

ARNHOLM: What's that?

ELLIDA: When you made what just now you called your fruitless proposal, I couldn't have answered you any other way than I did.

ARNHOLM: I know. You had nothing other to offer me but friendship. I'm aware of that.

ELLIDA: But what you don't know is that at that time my whole being and all my thoughts were given to someone else.

ARNHOLM: At that time?

ELLIDA: Precisely.

ARNHOLM: But that's completely impossible! You're wrong about the time. I'm positive you didn't know Wangel in those days.

ELLIDA: It isn't Wangel I'm talking about.

ARNHOLM: Not Wangel? But in those days—out there in Skjoldvik— I can't call to mind anyone at all you could possibly have been interested in.

ELLIDA: No, no—I can believe you. Because it was all so wildly insane—all of it!

ARNHOLM: Let me hear more about this.

ELLIDA: Isn't it enough to know I was bound to someone else at that time? And that now you know it?

ARNHOLM: And if you hadn't been bound to someone at that time?

ELLIDA: Then what?

ARNHOLM: Would your answer to my letter have been any different?

ELLIDA: How can I know? My answer was different when Wangel appeared.

ARNHOLM: Then what was the point in telling me you weren't free?

ELLIDA: *(Getting up, nervously restless.)* Because I have to confide in someone. No, no, don't get up.

ARNHOLM: Your husband knows nothing at all about this matter?

ELLIDA: I told him at the start I once belonged to someone else. But he never wanted to know more. And we never brought it up again. It had all been nothing but a kind of madness, anyhow. And it was all over so suddenly—at least, in a way.

ARNHOLM: *(Rising.)* Only in a way? Not completely!

ELLIDA: Yes, completely! Good lord, my dear Arnholm, it's not at all what you think. It's something so utterly incomprehensible. I don't know how to describe it to you. You'd only think that I was ill. Or that I was completely mad.

ARNHOLM: My dearest Ellida, you must and you shall tell me everything.

ELLIDA: Very well, then. I'll try to. But how you, as a reasonable man, could make sense of— *(Looking round and breaking off.)* Wait a moment— someone's coming.

(LYNGSTRAND enters from the road to the left and comes through the garden. He has a flower in his buttonhole and carries a large, fine bouquet wrapped in paper and silk ribbon. He stands, waiting a little uncertainly, by the veranda.)

ELLIDA: *(From the arbor.)* Is it the girls you are looking for, Mr. Lyngstrand?

LYNGSTRAND: *(Turning.)* Ah, there you are, Mrs. Wangel. *(Bows and comes nearer.)* No, actually not. I'm not looking for the girls. It's you, Mrs. Wangel. You told me I could come and call on you—

ELLIDA: That's right. You're welcome anytime.

LYNGSTRAND: Thank you. And as I happened to learn there's a celebration here today—

ELLIDA: Oh, so you know about it?

LYNGSTRAND: Oh yes. And that's why I'm glad to take the liberty of presenting you with these— *(Bowing and offering the bouquet.)*

ELLIDA: *(Smiling.)* But Mr Lyngstrand, wouldn't it be better if you gave your lovely flowers to Mr. Arnholm himself? For actually he's the one—

LYNGSTRAND: *(Looking uncertainly at them both.)* Please excuse me, but this gentleman's a stranger to me. It's just that— It's for the birthday, Mrs. Wangel.

ELLIDA: Birthday? You're mistaken, Mr. Lyngstrand. There's no birthday here today.

LYNGSTRAND: *(Smiling knowingly.)* Ah, but I know there is. I didn't realize it was to be such a secret.

ELLIDA: What is it you know?

LYNGSTRAND: That it's—that it's your birthday, Mrs. Wangel.

ELLIDA: Mine?

ARNHOLM: *(Looking inquiringly at her.)* Today? No, surely not.

ELLIDA: *(To Lyngstrand.)* Whatever gave you that idea?

LYNGSTRAND: It was Miss Hilda who gave it away. I was here a little earlier today. And I asked the young ladies why they were putting up the decorations, with flowers and the flag—

ELLIDA: And then?

LYNGSTRAND: —and then Miss Hilda said, "Today is Mother's birthday."

ELLIDA: Mother's—I see.

ARNHOLM: Aha! *(He and Ellida exchange an understanding glance.)* Well, since the young man's found out, Mrs. Wangel—

ELLIDA: *(To Lyngstrand.)* Yes, now you've found out—

LYNGSTRAND: *(Presenting the bouquet once more.)* May I take leave to congratulate you—

ELLIDA: *(Taking the flowers.)* Thank you very much. Won't you please sit down a moment, Mr. Lyngstrand. *(ELLIDA, ARNHOLM, and LYNGSTRAND sit in the arbor.)* All this—about my birthday—was meant to be a secret, Mr. Arnholm.

ARNHOLM: So that was it. Not something for us outsiders.

ELLIDA: *(Placing the bouquet on the table.)* Just so. Not for outsiders.

LYNSTRAND: I won't mention it to a living soul.

ELLIDA: Oh, it's really of no importance. But how are things with you? I think you're looking better than before.

LYNGSTRAND: Yes, I really think I'm getting on fine. And then, next year, when maybe I'll be going to the south—

ELLIDA: And you *will* be going, the girls said.

LYNGSTRAND: Yes, because I have a patron in Bergen who's looking after my interests. And he's promised he'll help me go next year.

ELLIDA: How did you manage to meet him?

LYNGSTRAND: It all happened so splendidly. I once went out to sea on one of his ships.

ELLIDA: You did? Were you drawn to the sea in those days?

LYNGSTRAND: No, not in the least. But after my mother died, my father didn't want me hanging around the house any more. So he arranged for me to go to sea. Then, on the home voyage we were wrecked in the English channel—which was a piece of luck for me.

ARNHOLM: How was that?

LYNGSTRAND: Because that's how I got my problem. In my chest here. I'd been so long in the icy water before they rescued me. So I had to quit the sea. Yes, it was a great piece of luck.

ARNHOLM: Really? You believe that?

LYNGSTRAND: Yes, because the problem's not very serious. And now I can become a sculptor, as I really long to be. Imagine! To be modeling in that lovely clay—as it submits so softly to one's fingers.

ELLIDA: What would you model? Mermen and mermaids? Or would it be the old Vikings?

LYNGSTRAND: No, nothing like that. As soon as I'm ready, I'll attempt a major work. In the form of a "group"—as it's called.

ELLIDA: Really. What will the group consist of?

LYNGSTRAND: It will be something I've experienced myself.

ARNHOLM: That's right, always stick to that.

ELLIDA: Yes, but what's it going to be?

LYNGSTRAND: Well, I've imagined there'd be a young sailor's wife, lying asleep and strangely restless. And dreaming. I think I could work it so you'd see she's dreaming.

ARNHOLM: Will there be anything else?

LYNGSTRAND: Yes, there'll be one other figure. More a *shape*—or *gestalt*— as it's called. It will be her husband, who she's been unfaithful to while he was away. And he's been drowned at sea.

ARNHOLM: What's that you say—?

ELLIDA: He's been drowned?

LYNGSTRAND: Yes, drowned on a voyage. But the uncanny thing is—he's returned home, all the same. It's night time. And there he'll be, standing by the bed, gazing on her. He'll stand, dripping wet, like a man dragged up from the sea.

ELLIDA: (*Leans back in her chair.*) That's really an extraordinary image. (*Closing her eyes.*) Yes, I can see it quite vividly in front of me.

ARNHOLM: But, how in the world, Mr.—er—! You definitely said it was to be something you'd experienced.

LYNGSTRAND: Ah, but then I have experienced it. In a *kind* of way.

ARNHOLM: Experienced a dead man—?

LYNGSTRAND: Well, I don't quite mean *actually* experienced. At least, not directly experienced, you understand. But just the same—

ELLIDA: (*Eager and excited.*) Tell me all you know—all you can recall! I'd really like a full account of it.

ARNHOLM: (*Smiling.*) Yes, this is just the subject for you. Something to do with the sea.

ELLIDA: How did it happen, Mr. Lyngstrand?

LYNGSTRAND: It happened when our ship was due to sail for home from a place called Halifax. We had to leave our boatswain behind in a hospital, so we signed on an American in his place. This new boatswain—

ELLIDA: The American?

LYNGSTRAND: Yes—well, one day he borrowed a bunch of old newspapers from the captain which he then began reading—constantly. Because he wanted to learn Norwegian, he said.

ELLIDA: Really! Go on!

LYNGSTRAND: Well, one evening there was a powerful storm. All the men were on deck—apart from the boatswain and me. He'd sprained his ankle and couldn't walk on it, and I was feeling sick and lying in my bunk. Well, he was sitting there in the cabin, once again reading one of those old newspapers—

ELLIDA: And then! And then!

LYNGSTRAND: And while he was sitting there I heard a sort of howl come from him. And when I looked at him I saw he'd gone white as chalk. Then he went on to crush and twist the paper, and then tear it into a thousand little pieces. But he did all this so quietly, so quietly.

ELLIDA: Did he say anything at all? Didn't he speak?

LYNGSTRAND: Not right away. But a little later he said to himself: "Married. To another man. While I was away!"

ELLIDA: *(Closing her eyes and saying, half audibly.)* He said that?

LYNGSTRAND: Yes. And imagine—he said it in perfectly good Norwegian. He must have had a real gift for learning languages, that man.

ELLIDA: And after that? What else happened?

LYNGSTRAND: Well, now followed something so extraordinary I'll never be able to forget. Not in all this world. For he went on, still quite calmly, "But she's mine and she'll stay mine. And she'll come with me, even if I have to return and fetch her like a drowned man from the depths of the sea."

ELLIDA: *(Pours herself a glass of water. Her hand shakes.)* Uff! How stifling it is today.

LYNGSTRAND: And he said it with such determination, I felt he'd be the man to do it, too.

ELLIDA: Do you know anything more—know what became of him?

LYNGSTRAND: Well, he's definitely no longer alive, Mrs. Wangel.

ELLIDA: *(Quickly.)* What makes you think that?

LYNGSTRAND: Because it was straight after that we were wrecked in the English Channel. I got away in the longboat with the captain and five others. The mate went in the dinghy, together with the American and another man.

ELLIDA: And nothing's been heard of them since?

LYNGSTRAND: Not an earthly thing, Mrs. Wangel. My patron recently wrote me about it in a letter. But that's just why I've such a desire to make a sculpture of it. The sailor's faithless wife—I can see it so vividly before me! And then the avenger, drowned, who yet comes back from the sea. I can see them both, so clearly.

ELLIDA: So can I. *(Getting up.)* Come, let's go inside. Or, rather, let's go down and join Wangel. It's getting so close and stifling here. *(She comes out of the arbor).*

LYNGSTRAND: *(Who also has risen.)* For my part, I must take my leave. I just wanted to call to honor your birthday.

ELLIDA: Well, if you must. *(Shaking his hand.)* Goodbye, and thank you for the flowers.

(LYNGSTRAND bows and exits through the door, left in the wicket fence.)

ARNHOLM: *(Gets up and goes over to ELLIDA.)* I can see this has struck you to the heart.

ELLIDA: Oh yes, you could put it that way, although—

ARNHOLM: Although, in the nature of things, you should have been prepared for it.

ELLIDA: *(Looks at him an amazement.)* Prepared for it!

ARNHOLM: Yes, I think so.

ELLIDA: Prepared for someone coming back—coming back in such a way!

ARNHOLM: But what on earth—! Is it that ridiculous sculptor's sea story—?

ELLIDA: Maybe he's not so ridiculous after all, my dear Arnholm.

ARNHOLM: Is it this talk of a dead man that's shaken you so? And all the time I thought—

ELLIDA: What did you think?

ARNHOLM: Naturally, I thought it was all a masquerade on your part. That you were sitting here and suffering because you discovered a family celebration was being kept secret from you. That your husband and his children live a private life you have no part in—

ELLIDA: Oh no, no. That must be as they wish. I've no right to claim my husband all to myself.

ARNHOLM: I should have thought you had.

ELLIDA: Yes—but all the same I haven't. That's a fact. I myself have a life the others are kept out of.

ARNHOLM: *You? (More quietly.)* Am I to understand you—you really don't love your husband!

ELLIDA: Oh yes, I do—with all my heart I've come to love him. And that's just why it's so terrible—so inexplicable—so completely unthinkable—

ARNHOLM: Now you must confide in me. Tell me all that's distressing you. Won't you do that, Mrs. Wangel?

ELLIDA: I can't, my dear friend. Not now, at any rate. Maybe later.

BOLETTA: *(Comes out on the veranda and goes down into the garden.)* Father's coming back from the office. Shouldn't we all go and sit in the garden room?

ELLIDA: Yes, let's do that.

WANGEL: *(Having changed his clothes, enters with HILDA from behind the house on the left.)* There! Here I am, free at last. Now it will be nice to have a good glass of something cool.

ELLIDA: Just a moment. *(She goes into the arbor and fetches the bouquet.)*

HILDA: Ooh, look! All those lovely flowers. Where did you get them?

ELLIDA: I got them from Mr. Lyngstrand, Hilda dear.

HILDA: *(Startled.)* From Lyngrstrand.

BOLETTA: *(Uneasily.)* Was Lyngstrand here—again?

ELLIDA: *(With a half-smile.)* Yes, he came back with these—in honor of the birthday, you understand.

BOLETTA: *(Glancing to HILDA.)* Ah!

HILDA: *(Muttering.)* The beast!

WANGEL: *(Painfully embarrassed, to ELLIDA.)* Hm! Yes, well you see— Ellida, my dear, let me explain—

ELLIDA: *(Interrupting.)* Come along, girls. Let's put these flowers in water along with the others. *(She goes up on to the veranda.)*

BOLETTA: *(Quietly, to HILDA.)* You see, she's really very nice after all.

HILDA: *(Half aloud.)* It's just a charade. She's only out to impress Father!

WANGEL: *(Up on the veranda, presses ELLIDA'S hand.)* Thanks, thanks. My deepest thanks for that, Ellida

ELLIDA: *(Arranging the flowers.)* Whatever for? Shouldn't I also take part in celebrating—Mother's birthday?

ARNHOLM: Hm.

(He goes up to WANGEL and ELLIDA. BOLETTA and HILDA remain below in the garden.)

END OF ACT ONE

ACT TWO

Up at Prospect Park, a wooded height behind the town. A little to the back is a cairn with a weathervane. Large stones, used as sitting places, have been laid round the cairn and in the foreground. Deep below in the background is the fjord, with its islands and jutting headlands. The open sea is not visible. It is a summer evening at dusk. A golden-red haze hangs in the air and over the mountain peaks far off in the distance. The faint sound of part-singing can be heard in the background, below to the right.

Young men and women from the town enter in couples from the right, walk past the cairn, engaging in intimate conversation, and go out to the left. Soon after, BALLESTAD enters as a guide to a party of foreign tourists and their ladies. He is loaded down with shawls and travel bags.

BALLESTAD: *(Pointing up with his stick.)* Sehen Sie, meine Herrschaften, dort lieger eine andere peak. Das willen wir alsobesteigen und now herunter— *(He continues in English and leads the party off to the right. HILDA climbs briskly up the slope to the right, pauses and looks back. Soon after, BOLETTA climbs up the same way.)*

BOLETTA: But, Hilda, why are we running away from Lyngstrand?

HILDA: Because I can't stand climbing the hills so slowly. Look—look how he's crawling up.

BOLETTA: Now you know how ill he is.

HILDA: Do you think it's very serious?

BOLETTA: Yes, I know for sure.

HILDA: He was with Father this afternoon. I'd like to know what *he* thinks of him .

BOLETTA: Father told me there's a hardening in both lungs—or something like that. He won't live very long, Father said.

HILDA: No, did he really! You know, that's exactly what I'd guessed.

BOLETTA: But for God's sake don't let him notice anything.

HILDA: How can you imagine such a thing! *(Half aloud:)* Look! Hans has now managed to crawl up. Hans— Can't you tell just by looking at him his name is Hans?

BOLETTA: *(Whispering.)* Now behave yourself. I'm warning you!

(LYNGSTRAND enters from the right with a parasol in his hand.)

LYNGSTRAND: You girls will have to bear with me for not keeping up with you.

HILDA: So you've found yourself a parasol now?

LYNGSTRAND: It's your mother's. She told me to use it as a stick since I didn't bring one with me.

BOLETTA: Are they still down there? Father and the others?

LYNGSTRAND: Yes, your father went into the restaurant for a while. The others are sitting outside listening to the music. But your mother said they'll all be up here later.

HILDA: *(Who is standing and looking at him.)* You must be very tired now.

LYNGSTRAND: Yes, I rather think I am a bit tired. I suppose it would be best for me to sit down for a while. *(He sits on a stone in the foreground to the right.)*

HILDA: *(Standing in front of him.)* Did you know there'll be dancing down at the concert place?

LYNGSTRAND: Yes, I heard talk of it.

HILDA: Don't you think it's lovely, going dancing?

BOLETTA: *(Who is gathering wild flowers in the heather.)* Now Hilda, give Mr. Lyngstrand a chance to catch his breath!

LYNGSTRAND: *(To Hilda.)* Yes, Miss Hilda, I'd love to dance—if only I could.

HILDA: I see. Didn't you ever learn, then?

LYNGSTRAND: No, actually, I never did. But that wasn't what I meant. I mean I can't because of my chest.

HILDA: Because of the "problem" you say you have?

LYNGSTRAND: Yes, for that reason.

HILDA: Are you very unhappy having this problem?

LYNGSTRAND: No, I can't say that, really. *(Smiling.)* Because I think that's why everyone's so nice and friendly and helpful toward me.

HILDA: Yes, and then it's not really serious, either.

LYNGSTRAND: No, not the least bit serious. That's what I gathered from your father.

HILDA: And it will all be cleared up as soon as you go abroad.

LYNGSTRAND: That's right. It'll all clear up.

BOLETTA: *(With the flowers.)* Here you are, Mr. Lyngstrand. This is for your buttonhole.

LYNGSTRAND: Thanks ever so much, Miss Wangel. This really is too nice of you.

HILDA: *(Looking down over to the right.)* Here come the others up the path.

BOLETTA: *(Also looking down.)* As long as they know where to turn off. No, they're going the wrong way.

LYNGSTRAND: *(Getting up.)* I'll run down to the turning and call out to them.

HILDA: You would have to call very loud.

BOLETTA: No, it's not worth it. You'd only tire yourself out again.

LYNGSTRAND: Oh, downhill's so easy. *(He goes out to the right.)*

HILDA: Downhill, yes. *(Watching him.)* He's even jumping. Not thinking that he's got to climb up again.

BOLLETA: Poor boy—

HILDA: If Lyngstrand proposed to you, would you accept him?

BOLETTA: Have you gone mad?

HILDA: I mean, of coure, if he didn't have this "problem." And if he wasn't going to die soon, would you take him then?

BOLETTA: I think it would be best if *you* took him.

HILDA: There's no way I would. He hasn't a penny. Not even enough to keep himself.

BOLETTA: Then why do you go about with him all the time?

HILDA: I do it only because of his "problem."

BOLETTA: I've not noticed you pitying him much for that.

HILDA: No, I don't particularly. But I think it's so fascinating.

BOLETTA: How?

HILDA: Well, watching him. Getting him to say it isn't serious. That he'll be travelling abroad, and how he's going to be an artist. He goes around believing all this and he's filled with joy. Yet none of it will ever happen. Never in the world. Because he won't live long enough. I think it's so thrilling to think about.

BOLETTA: Thrilling!

HILDA: Yes, I do find it thrilling. I admit it.

BOLETTA: Uff, Hilda, you really are an abominable brat!

HILDA: It's what I want to be. For spite! *(Peering downward.)* Well, at last! Arnholm doesn't take too well to climbing. *(Turning.)* Oh, by the way, do you know what I noticed about Arnholm at lunch?

BOLETTA: Well?

HILDA: Imagine—he's going bald—here, on top, in the middle.

BOLETTA: Nonsense, that's really not true.

HILDA: It is. And he's got wrinkles round his eyes. Good Lord, Boletta, to think you could have been so in love with him when he was your tutor.

BOLETTA: *(Smiling.)* Yes, can you imagine? I remember crying my eyes out once because he said he thought Boletta was an ugly name.

HILDA: Yes, just imagine. *(Looking downward again.)* Well, will you just look at that! There goes the "Lady from the Sea" chattering away with him. Not with Father. I wonder if those two have eyes for each other.

BOLETTA: You ought to be ashamed of yourself, you really ought! How can you stand there saying such things about her? Just as we're getting along so well together.

HILDA: Go ahead—just carry on fooling yourself, my girl! Oh no, no good's going to come of trying to get along with her. She's not our sort. And we're not hers, either. God knows why Father dragged her into the house. I shouldn't be surprised if one fine day she went raving mad on us.

BOLETTA: Mad! How can you say such a thing?

HILDA: Oh, it wouldn't be so strange. Her mother went mad, too. She died mad. I know for a fact.

BOLETTA: God, what haven't you got your nose into! Just don't go talking about it. Be a nice girl, for Father's sake. Do you hear, Hilda?

(WANGEL, ELLIDA, ARNHOLM, and LYNGSTRAND come up from the right.)

ELLIDA: *(Pointing over to the background.)* There it lies, right out there!

ARNHOLM: That's right. It has to be in that direction.

ELLIDA: Out there's where the sea lies.

BOLETTA: *(To Arnholm.)* Don't you think it's very pleasant up here?

ARNHOLM: I think it's marvellous—a magnificent view.

WANGEL: Yes. Have you never been up here before?

ARNHOLM: No, never. In my day this area was barely explored at all—there was no footpath then.

WANGEL: And no park, either. We've gained all this in the last few years.

BOLETTA: Over there, on Lodskoll, the view's even more impressive.

WANGEL: Shall we go there, Ellida?

ELLIDA: *(Sitting on a stone to the right.)* No thanks, I'd rather not. But you others go along. Meanwhile, I'd just as soon be sitting here.

WANGEL: Then I'll stay here with you. The girls can show Mr. Arnholm around.

BOLETTA: Would you like to join us, Mr. Arnholm?

ARNHOLM: Yes, very much. Is there a path going up there, too?

BOLETTA: Oh yes, a good wide one.

HILDA: The path's so wide it can easily fit two people walking arm in arm.

ARNHOLM: *(Playfully.)* I wonder if that's so, my little Hilda. *(To BOLETTA.)* Shall we find out if she's right?

BOLETTA: *(Suppressing a smile.)* Why not. Let's do it. *(They go off arm in arm to the left.)*

HILDA: *(To LYNGSTRAND.)* Shall we go too?

LYNGSTRAND: Arm in arm?

HILDA: Why ever not? It's fine with me.

LYNGSTRAND: *(Taking her arm and laughing happily.)* This really is terrific fun.

HILDA: Fun?

LYNGSTRAND: Yes, because it looks exactly as if we were engaged.

HILDA: Well, it's clear you've never walked arm in arm with a lady before, Mr. Lyngstrand.

(They go out to the left.)

WANGEL: *(Standing close by the cairn.)* Now we've some time to ourselves, Ellida dear.

ELLIDA: Yes. Come and sit here beside me.

WANGEL: *(Sitting.)* It's quiet and peaceful here. We've a chance to talk.

ELLIDA: What about?

WANGEL: About you. And then about our life together, Ellida. I see clearly it can't go on in this way.

ELLIDA: How should it be instead, do you think?

WANGEL: Complete trust and confidence, my dear. A true life together—as before.

ELLIDA: Oh, if it only could be. But it's so utterly impossible.

WANGEL: I believe I understand you. From certain things you've let fall, from time to time, yes, I think I do.

ELLIDA: *(Vehemently.)* But you don't! Don't say you understand—!

WANGEL: I do. You've an honest nature, Ellida. Such a loyal heart—

ELLIDA: Yes, I have that.

WANGEL: For you to feel really secure and happy in any relationship it would have to be complete and unconditional.

ELLIDA: *(Looking tensely at him.)* So—what then?

WANGEL: You are not made to be a man's second wife.

ELLIDA: Why do you think that now?

WANGEL: The suspicion's often flashed though my mind. Today made it clear to me. The children's anniversary celebration— You saw me as a kind of accomplice— Perhaps it's so—a man's memories can't just be wiped away. At least, not in my case. I'm not like that.

ELLIDA: I know that. Oh, I know that so well.

WANGEL: But you're mistaken, just the same. To you, it's as if the children's mother was still living. As if she were invisibly present, here among us. You believe my heart's divided between you and her. It's these imaginings that agitated you, making you see something immoral in our relationship. And that's why you no longer can—or no longer want—to live with me as my wife.

ELLIDA: *(Rising.)* Have you seen all this, Wangel? Searched into all of this?

WANGEL: Yes, today I've searched and at last fathomed it all. Right to the depths.

ELLIDA: Right to the depths, you say. Oh, you musn't believe that.

WANGEL: *(Rising.)* I realize very well there's more to it than that, my dear Ellida.

ELLIDA: *(Fearfully.)* You know there's more?

WANGEL: Yes. The fact is you can't bear this part of the world. The mountains press and weigh on your spirit. There's not enough light for you here. The sky's not wide enough. There's no energy and life in the motion of the air.

ELLIDA: Yes, your totally right there. Night and day, winter and summer, it fills me—this homesickness for the sea.

WANGEL: I completely understand, my dear Ellida. *(Places his hand on her head.)* That's why this poor, sick child shall go back home to where she belongs.

ELLIDA: What do you mean?

WANGEL: Just what I said. We'll go away.

ELLIDA: Go away!

WANGEL: Yes. To somewhere out by the open sea—someplace where you can find a home truly after your own heart.

ELLIDA: Ah, dearest, don't even think of it. It's quite impossible. You could never be happy living anywhere in the world but here.

WANGEL: That must take care of itself. In any case, do you think I could be happy living here—without you?

ELLIDA: But I *am* here. And I shall stay here. So I'm with you.

WANGEL: Are you, Ellida?

ELLIDA: Oh, let's not talk about that. Everything you live for and believe in is here. Your whole life's mission is here—alone.

WANGEL: That must take care of itself, I said. We're leaving here. Going somewhere else. It's settled irrevocably, Ellida.

ELLIDA: What do you expect we'd gain doing this?

WANGEL: You'd gain your health and peace of mind once more.

ELLIDA: I hardly think so. But what about you? Think of yourself as well. What would you gain?

WANGEL: I'd win you back again, my dear.

ELLIDA: But that's what you can't do. No, no, you won't be able to, Wangel! That's just what's so terrible to think of, so heartbreaking.

WANGEL: Well, we must find out. If you're going around here with ideas like this, then there's simply no way out for you then—to go away. The sooner the better. It's settled—irrevocably, do you hear?

ELLIDA: No! In heaven's name, I'd much rather tell you everything, just as it happened.

WANGEL: Yes, yes—just tell me.

ELLIDA: Because you're not to make yourself miserable on my account. Especially since it won't help us in any way.

WANGEL: And I have your word you'll tell me everything, just as it happened.

ELLIDA: I'll tell you as best I can. And so far as I think I understand it. Come and sit beside me.

(The sit on one of the stones.)

WANGEL: Well, Ellida?

ELLIDA: That day you came out there and asked me if I could bring myself to marry you, you spoke so frankly and openly about your first marriage. It had been such a happy one, you said.

WANGEL: And it was, too.

ELLIDA: Yes, yes, I really believe it was, dear. So that's not why I bring it up now. I only want to remind you that, on my side, I was just as frank with you. I told you quite unreservedly that at one time I'd been in love with someone else and we'd become engaged—in a way.

WANGEL: In a way—

ELLIDA: Yes, something of the sort. Oh, it lasted only a short while. He went away. And afterwards I ended it. I told you all that.

WANGEL: But my dear Ellida, why are you bringing all this up again? It's something that really doesn't concern me. I've never so much as asked you who he was.

ELLIDA: No, you haven't. You're always so considerate toward me.

WANGEL: *(Smiling.)* Well, in this case—I could come up with a shrewd guess at his name.

ELLIDA: His name!

WANGEL: Out in Skjoldvik and thereabouts there weren't so many to choose from. Or, more correctly, there was really only one.

ELLIDA: You believe it was Arnholm

WANGEL: Yes. Wasn't it?

ELLIDA: No.

WANGEL: Not him? Then I'm completely lost.

ELLIDA: Do you remember once, late in autumn, a big American ship put in to Skjoldvik for repairs?

WANGEL: Yes, I remember it well. It was on that ship the captain was found murdered in his cabin. I was there to do the autopsy.

ELLIDA: Yes, so you were.

WANGEL: It was the second mate who'd murdered him.

ELLIDA: No one can say that for sure. It was never proved.

WANGEL: There's not much doubt about it, just the same. Why else would he go and drown himself as he did?

ELLIDA: He didn't drown himself. He got away on a ship going north.

WANGEL: *(Surprised.)* How do you know that?

ELLIDA: *(With difficulty.)* You see, Wangel, that second mate was the man I was engaged to.

WANGEL: *(Starting up.)* What are you saying? Can it be possible?

ELLIDA: Yes, it's true. He was the one.

WANGEL: But Ellida, how in the world—! How could you do such a thing? Getting engaged to a man like that? A complete stranger! What was his name?

ELLIDA: At the time he called himself Friman. Later, he signed his letters Alfred Johnston.

WANGEL: Where was he from?

ELLIDA: From up in Finnmark, he said. But he was born over in Finland— crossing over as a child—with his father, I believe.

WANGEL: He was a Quain, then?

ELLIDA: That's what they're called, yes.[1]

WANGEL: What else do you know about him?

ELLIDA: Only that he went to sea very young. And that he'd sailed on long voyages.

WANGEL: Otherwise nothing else at all?

ELLIDA: No. We never talked about such things.

WANGEL: What did you talk about then?

ELLIDA: Mostly we talked about the sea.

WANGEL: Ah yes. About the sea.

ELLIDA: About its storms and its stillnesses. About dark nights at sea. And we talked of the days when the sea glittered in the sunshine. But most of all we talked about the whales and dolphins and the seals that lie out on the rocks in the noonday heat. And we talked about the gulls and sea eagles and all the other seabirds. And—it was most extraordinary—when we spoke of these things, it seemed to me that both the seabirds and the creatures of the sea shared their world with him.

WANGEL: And you, yourself?

ELLIDA: Yes, I almost believed that I, too, shared their world with them.

WANGEL: I see. And that's how you became engaged?

ELLIDA: Yes. He said I had to.

WANGEL: Had to? Didn't you have a will of your own?

ELLIDA: Not when I was with him. Oh, afterwards, it all seemed so completely incredible.

WANGEL: Were you often with him?

ELLIDA: No, not very often. One day he came to see round the lighthouse. After that we'd meet once or twice. And then followed that business with the captain and he had to go away.

WANGEL: Yes, let me hear more about that.

ELLIDA: It was early one morning, when the light was still gray, that I got a note from him telling me to meet him out at Bratthammer. You know, the headland between the lighthouse and Skjoldvik.

WANGEL: Yes, yes, I know it very well.

ELLIDA: He wrote I was to go out to him at once as he had to speak to me.

WANGEL: And you went?

ELLIDA: Yes, I couldn't do otherwise. Well, then he told me he'd stabbed the captain that night.

WANGEL: He actually said that himself? Just like that?

ELLIDA: Yes. But he'd only done what was right and proper, he said.

WANGEL: Right and proper! Why had he stabbed him, then?

ELLIDA: He wouldn't tell me why. He said it was not something for me to hear.

WANGEL: And you believed him on his own bare word?

ELLIDA: Yes, there was nothing else I needed. Well, now he had to go away, but, just as he was going to say goodbye— No, you'd never imagine what he did then.

WANGEL: Well, let me hear.

ELLIDA: He took a key chain out of his pocket and pulled from his finger a ring he always wore. Then he took a little ring from me. He slipped these two rings on the key chain. Then he said that now we two must be married to the sea.

WANGEL: Married—?

ELLIDA: Yes, that's what he said. And then, with all his strength, he threw the chain and the two rings as far as he could out into the sea.

WANGEL: And you, Ellida? Did you go along with that?

ELLIDA: Yes, just imagine—at the time it seemed it had to be that way. Then, thank God, he went away.

WANGEL: And after he'd gone away—?

ELLIDA: Oh, you can be sure I soon came to my senses again. Came to understand how completely insane and meaningless the whole thing had been.

WANGEL: But earlier you spoke about letters. That means you've heard from him since.

ELLIDA: Yes, I've heard from him. First, I received a few short lines from Archangel simply stating he was going to America and advising me where I could send an answer.

WANGEL: And did you?

ELLIDA: Immediately. Naturally, I wrote that everything was over between us. That he mustn't think of me anymore, just as I would never think of him.

WANGEL: But he wrote to you again in spite of that?

ELLIDA: Yes, he wrote again.

WANGEL: And how did he respond to what you'd told him?

ELLIDA: Not a word about it. It was just as if I'd never broken with him. He wrote quite firmly and calmly that I should wait for him. When he could provide for me, he'd let me know, and I was to go to him at once, he wrote.

WANGEL: So he wouldn't release you?

ELLIDA: No. So I wrote again. Almost word for word what I wrote before—only, if anything, more strongly.

WANGEL: And then did he give up?

ELLIDA: Oh no, not in the slightest. He wrote just as calmly as before. Not a word about my breaking with him. So then I saw it was useless, and I never wrote to him again.

WANGEL: And never heard from him again?

ELLIDA: Yes, I've had three letters from him since. Once he wrote me from California and another time from China. The last letter was from Australia, saying he was going to the goldmines. But I haven't heard from him since.

WANGEL: That man has an uncanny power over you, Ellida.

ELLIDA: Yes, yes. That horror of a man.

WANGEL: But you mustn't think about him anymore. Never! Promise me that much, my dear, precious Ellida! Now we'll seek out another cure for you. Air fresher than here in the fjord—the bracing, salt sea air. What do you say to that?

ELLIDA: Don't talk of such a thing! Or even think of it! There's no help for me there, I feel sure of it. I could never shake this from me, even out there.

WANGEL: What? My dear, what do you mean?

ELLIDA: The horror, I mean. The inexplicable power he has over my mind.

WANGEL: But you've cast it from you, a long time back. That day you broke with him. It's been long since it was over with.

ELLIDA: (Starting up.) No, that's the point—it isn't.

WANGEL: Not over with!

ELLIDA: No, Wangel, not over with. And I'm afraid it will never be. As long as I live.

WANGEL: *(In a choked voice.)* Are you saying that, deep down, you've never been able to forget this man?

ELLIDA: I had forgotten him. But then it was as if he'd come back again.

WANGEL: How long ago was that?

ELLIDA: It was about three years ago. Or a little more. It was while I was expecting the child.

WANGEL: Ah! It was at that time then? Yes, Ellida, now I'm beginning to understand so many things.

ELLIDA: You're wrong, my dear. This—that has happened to me—I believe no one in the world can account for it.

WANGEL: *(Looking at her with a pained expression.)* To think—that here, for three whole years, you've gone about feeling love for another man. Not for me—but for another!

ELLIDA: Ah, you're so completely mistaken. I love no one else but you.

WANGEL: *(Quietly.)* Then why is it in all this time you've not wanted to live with me as my wife?

ELLIDA: It's because of the terror that lies in that strange man.

WANGEL: Terror—?

ELLIDA: Yes, terror. A terror so horrible that only the sea possesses. Because now, Wangel, you must know—
(The young people from the town come back from the left, greet them, and go out to the right. With them come ARNHOLM, BOLETTA, HILDA, and LYNGSTRAND.)

BOLETTA: *(While they are passing.)* Well, you two still wandering about up here?

ELLIDA: Yes, up here it's so cool and pleasant.

ARNHOLM: For our part we're on our way down to dance.

WANGEL: Good, good. We'll be coming down soon.

HILDA: Goodbye for now, then.

ELLIDA: Mr. Lyngstrand, could you wait a moment. *(LYNGSTRAND waits. ARNHOLM, BOLETTA, and HILDA go off to the right.)* Will you be dancing?

LYNGSTRAND: No, Mrs. Wangel, I'd better not risk it.

ELLIDA: No, it's better to be careful. That chest trouble of your's—you've not got over it yet, have you?

LYNGSTRAND: Not completely, no.

ELLIDA: *(Somewhat hesitantly.)* How long is it since you made that voyage?

LYNGSTRAND: When I got my problem?

ELLIDA: Yes, that voyage you were telling me about this morning.

LYNGSTRAND: Oh, it was about—let me see— Yes, it must have been a good three years now.

ELLIDA: Three years, then.

LYNGSTRAND: Or just a little more. We left America in February and we were wrecked in March. We ran into the equinoctial storms.

ELLIDA: *(Looking at WANGEL.)* And it was just at that time that—

WANGEL: But Ellida, dear—

ELLIDA: But don't let us keep you, Mr. Lyngstrand. Go now—but no dancing!

LYNGSTRAND: No, I'll just be watching. *(He goes off to the right.)*

WANGEL: Ellida, dear, why were you asking him about that voyage?

ELLIDA: Johnston was on that same ship—I'm quite sure of it.

WANGEL: What leads you to think so?

ELLIDA: *(Without answering.)* It was on board he found out I'd married someone else while he was away. And—it was at that same time all this overwhelmed me!

WANGEL: All this terror?

ELLIDA: Yes. All at once, I suddenly find myself seeing him, clearly, there before me. Or rather, a little to one side. He never looks at me. He's just there.

WANGEL: How do you imagine he looks?

ELLIDA: Exactly as I saw him last.

WANGEL: Ten years ago—

ELLIDA: Yes. Out there at Bratthammer. But what I see most clearly is his tie-pin with a great, bluish-white pearl in it like the eye of a dead fish. As if staring at me.

WANGEL: In God's name—! You are more ill that I thought. More ill than you realize yourself, Ellida.

ELLIDA: Yes, yes—help me if you can! I can feel it closing in on me, more and more.

WANGEL: And you've been going about like this for three whole years. Suffering in secret and never confiding in me.

ELLIDA: But that's just what I couldn't do. It's only now I have to—for your own sake! If I'd confided all of this before, I would have had to tell you the—the unspeakable thing.

WANGEL: The unspeakable—?

ELLIDA: *(Evading him.)* No, no, no! Don't ask me! Just one other thing, and that's all. Wangel—how account for the mystery of the child's eyes—?

WANGEL: My dear—my precious Ellida, I assure you it was only your imagination. The child had exactly the same eyes as other normal children.

ELLIDA: No, no, he didn't! How could you not have seen it? The child's eyes changed color with the sea. When the fjord lay calm in the sunlight, so were his eyes. And then, when it was stormy— Oh, I saw it clearly enough even if you couldn't.

WANGEL: *(Indulging her.)* Well, if you say so. But then, what if it's true? What of it?

ELLIDA: *(Softly, approaching.)* I've seen eyes like that before.

WANGEL: Oh? And where—?

ELLIDA: Out at Bratthammer. Ten years ago.

WANGEL: *(Recoiling a step.)* What does this—

ELLIDA: *(Whispering fearfully.)* The child had the stranger's eyes.

WANGEL: *(Crying out involuntarily.)* Ellida—!

ELLIDA: *(In distress, striking her head with her hands.)* Now you can understand why I never can—never *dare*—live with you as your wife! *(She turns quickly and rushes down the slope to the right.)*

WANGEL: *(Hurrying after her and calling.)* Ellida—Ellida! My poor, unhappy Ellida!

END OF ACT TWO

ACT THREE

A remote corner of Dr. Wangel's garden. The place is damp, marshy, and overshadowed with huge old trees. To the right, the edge of a dark pond can be seen. A low picket fence separates the garden from a footpath. The fjord is in the background. On the other side of the fjord rise mountain ridges and peaks. It is late afternoon—almost evening.

BOLETTA is sitting, sewing, on a stone seat to the left. On the seat lie a few books and a sewing basket. HILDA and LYNGSTRAND, both with fishing tackle, go the the edge of the pond.

HILDA: *(With a gesture to LYNGSTRAND.)* Keep still! I can see a big one.

LYNGSTRAND: *(Looking.)* Where?

HILDA: *(Pointing.)* Can't you see—it's right down there. And look! There's another one for God's sake! *(Peering through the trees.)* Uff, here he comes, to frighten them away.

BOLETTA: *(Looking up.)* Who's coming?

HILDA: Your headmaster, old girl.

BOLETTA: Mine?

HILDA: Well, he's never been mine, thank God.

ARNHOLM: *(From the right, emerging through the trees.)* Are there still fish in the pond?

HILDA: Yes, there's some really old carp.

ARNHOLM: No! So those old carp are still alive!

HILDA: Yes, they're a tough lot, all right. But now we're going to see if we can't finish off a couple of them.

ARNHOLM: You'd do better out on the fjord.

LYNGSTRAND: No, the pond's—it's more secretive and mysterious in a way.

HILDA: Yes, it's more thrilling here. You've just been in the water?

ARNHOLM: That's right. I'm just back from the bathing hut.

HILDA. You stuck pretty close to the shore, then?

ARNHOLM: Well, I'm not a particularly good swimmer.

HILDA: Can you swim on your back?

ARNHOLM: No.

HILDA: I can. *(To LYNGSTRAND.)* Let's try over there on the other side. *(They go around the pool to the right.)*

ARNHOLM: *(Drawing closer to BOLETTA.)* You're sitting all by yourself, Boletta?

BOLETTA: Yes, I generally do.

ARNHOLM: Isn't your mother down here in the garden?

BOLETTA: No, I expect she's gone for a walk with Father.

ARNHOLM: How is she this evening?

BOLETTA: I don't really know. I forgot to ask.

ARNHOLM: What books have you got there?

BOLETTA: Well, one's about botany and the other's geography.

ARNHOLM: You like reading that sort of thing?

BOLETTA: Yes, when I can find time. But first of all I have to look after the housework.

ARNHOLM: But doesn't your mother—your stepmother—doesn't she help you with that?

BOLETTA: No, it's up to me. I had to do it the two years Father was on his own. And that's how it's been ever since.

ARNHOLM: But you've the same great love of reading?

BOLETTA: Yes, I read all the serious books I can get hold of. It's so important to know something of what's going on in the world. You see, here we're so cut off from everything that's happening. Well, almost everything.

ARNHOLM: My dear Boletta, you mustn't say that.

BOLETTA: It's true. I don't think we live all that differently from the carp down there in the pond. They've got the fjord close by them, where the great shoals of fish stream in and out. But the poor tame domesticated fish know nothing about it. And they can never join them.

ARNHOLM: It wouldn't do them much good if they found themselves out there.

BOLETTA: Oh, I think it would come to much the same thing.

ARNHOLM: In any case, you can't really say you're so cut off from the world, at least not in the summers. This place, nowadays, has become a sort of meeting place for the whole world. It's almost a hub of activity. There's so much life passing through it.

BOLETTA: (Smiling.) Yes, when you're one of those just passing through, it's easy to make fun of us.

ARNHOLM: I make fun of you? What makes you think that?

BOLETTA: You see, all this talk about a meeting place and hub of the whole world, it's just something you've heard people in town saying. That's the way they carry on.

ARNHOLM: Yes, I must admit I've noticed that.

BOLETTA: But actually, there's not a word of truth in what they say—at least not for us who must live here all the year round. How does it help us that the great, unknown world comes here on its way to see the midnight sun? We can't go with them ourselves. We don't get to see the midnight sun. Oh no, we must go on living here in our fish pond.

ARNHOLM: *(Sitting beside her.)* Tell me now, Boletta, isn't there something or other—something special, I mean—you go around here longing for?

BOLETTA: Yes, maybe there is.

ARNHOLM: What, in particular, are you longing for?

BOLETTA: Most of all, to get away.

ARNHOLM: More than anything else at all?

BOLETTA: Yes. And then to learn so much more—to really get to know about everything.

ARNHOLM : That time I was teaching you, your father often said you'd go on to college.

BOLETTA: Ah, poor Father—he says so many things. But when it comes to the point— There's no real willpower in Father.

ARNHOLM: No, unfortunately, you're right, there. Have you talked with him about this? I mean seriously and thoroughly.

BOLETTA: No, I haven't, really.

ARNHOLM: Well, you really should, you know. Before it's too late, Boletta. Why don't you?

BOLETTA: I expect it's because there's not much willpower in me, either. It's something I must get from Father.

ARNHOLM: Hm. Aren't you possibly being unfair to yourself?

BOLETTA: No, I'm not, unfortunately. And then, Father's got so little time to think about me or my future—or much inclination to, either. He keeps his distance from things like that if he can. He's so completely taken up with Ellida—

ARNHOLM: With her—? How—?

BOLETTA: I mean that he and my stepmother— *(Breaking off.)* You see, Father and Mother live just for each other.

ARNHOLM: Then it's all the more reason for you to get away from here.

BOLETTA: Maybe, but I don't think I've a right to do that—not to desert him.

ARNHOLM: But, my dear Boletta, you'll have to do that someday. So I really think, the sooner the better—

BOLETTA: Yes, I suppose there's no other way. I have to think about myself, too. I'll have to look for some position or other. When Father dies, there'll be no one to turn to. But, poor Father, I dread leaving him.

ARNHOLM: Dread?

BOLETTA: Yes, for his own sake.

ARNHOLM: But, good lord, what about your stepmother? She'll be with him.

BOLETTA: Yes, that's true. But she's just not capable of doing all the things Mother was so good at. There's so much here she just doesn't *see*. Or, perhaps, she *won't* see—or doesn't care about. I don't know which it is.

ARNHOLM: Hm. I think I know what you mean.

BOLETTA: Poor Father—in some ways he's quite weak. I expect you've noticed that. He really doesn't have enough work to fill up his time. And then she's so completely incapable of giving him any support. Though, as far as that goes, he's only himself to blame.

ARNHOLM: In what way, do you mean?

BOLETTA: Well, Father likes to see happy faces around him. He says there must be sunshine and a pleasant atmosphere in the house. So I'm afraid he often gives her medicine that isn't good for her in the long run.

ARNHOLM: You really think so?

BOLETTA: I can't help thinking so, because she's so strange at times. *(Vehemently.)* But it's so unfair that I should have to stay here at home! Because it's of no earthly use to Father. And I've got duties to myself, too, I believe.

ARNHOLM: You know what, Boletta, we must talk seriously about this subject.

BOLETTA: Oh, it won't come to anything. I suppose I'm meant to stay here in my carp pond.

ARNHOLM: In no way. It's entirely up to you.

BOLETTA: *(Animatedly.)* Do you think so?

ARNHOLM: Yes, believe me. The whole thing's entirely in your own hands.

BOLETTA: If it were only true—! Would you put in a good word for me with Father?

ARNHOLM: I'll do that, too. But most of all, I want to speak frankly and openly with you, Boletta. *(Looks out to the right.)* Shh, don't let them notice anything. We'll come back to this later.

(ELLIDA enters from the left. She is without a hat but has a large shawl over her head and shoulders.)

ELLIDA: *(In uneasy animation.)* Ah, it's good here. Really lovely!

ARNHOLM: *(Getting up.)* Have you been out for a walk?

ELLIDA: Yes, a long, long, marvellous tour with Wangel. Now we're going sailing.

ARNHOLM: Won't you sit down?

ELLIDA: No thank you. I won't sit.

BOLETTA: *(Moving along the seat.)* There's a good place here.

ELLIDA: *(Walking about.)* No, no, no. I couldn't sit—couldn't sit.

ARNHOLM: Your walk seems to have done you good. You're looking so lively.

ELLIDA: Yes, I really feel so completely refreshed—so inexpressibly happy! So safe! So safe—! *(Looks out to the left.)* What's that large steamship just coming in?

BOLETTA: *(Getting up and looking.)* It must be the big English one.

ARNHOLM: It's putting in at the moorings. Does it usually stop here?

BOLETTA: Just for half an hour. Then it goes on up the fjord.

ELLIDA: And then tomorrow—out again. Out into the great open sea. Far across the sea. Imagine going along, too! To be able to do that! Just be able to!

ARNHOLM: Have you never been on a long sea voyage, Mrs. Wangel?

ELLIDA: No, never once. Only little trips here in the fjord.

BOLETTA: *(With a sigh.)* No, we must make do with dry land.

ARNHOLM: Well, it's our home—where we truly belong.

ELLIDA: No, I don't think we do at all.

ARNHOLM: Not belong to dry land?

ELLIDA: No, I don't think so. I believe that, if right at the beginning, mankind had chosen to live on the sea—or even in the sea—we would have evolved more completely—as both better and happier than we are.

ARNHOLM: Do you really believe that?

ELLIDA: Yes, I can't see why not. I've often talked with Wangel about it.

ARNHOLM: And he—

ELLIDA: He thinks it could be true.

ARNHOLM: *(Jokingly.)* Well, maybe. But what's done is done. We've taken the wrong path once and for all and have become land creatures instead of sea creatures. In the circumstances, it's a bit late trying to correct the mistake.

ELLILDA: Yes, what you say is true—unhappily. I think people sense it too, and it haunts us like a secret sorrow and regret. Believe me, *there's* the deepest source of human melancholy. Yes, take my word for it.

ARNHOLM: But my dear Mrs. Wangel, I've not noticed humanity was all that melancholy. On the contrary, I believe most people live their lives cheerfully and pleasantly—with great, quiet and instinctive joy.

ELLIDA: No, no, that isn't true. This joy—it's only like the joy we feel in the long, light summer days. Over it all is the reminder of the approaching darkness and that casts its shadow on all human happiness—just as the drifting clouds cast their shadows over the fjord. It lies there, so clear and blue, and then—

BOLETTA: You shouldn't give way to such sad thoughts. You were so bright and cheerful just a moment ago.

ELLIDA: Yes, yes, so I was. It's foolish of me to go on like this. *(Looking uneasily about her.)* If only Wangel would come. He promised me so firmly, yet still he doesn't come. Dear Mr. Arnholm, won't you see if you can find him for me?

ARNHOLM: I'd be glad to.

ELLIDA: Tell him he must come right away. Because now I can't see him—

ARNHOLM: Can't see him—?

ELLIDA: You don't understand. When he's not near me I often can't remember what he looks like. And then it's as if I'd lost him completely. And that tortures me terribly. But please—just go! *(She wanders over to the pond.)*

BOLETTA: *(To ARNHOLM.)* I'll go with you.

ARNHOLM: Don't worry, I know where—

BOLETTA: *(Quietly.)* No, no, I'm worried. I'm afraid he's on board the steamer.

ARNHOLM: Afraid?

BOLETTA: Yes. He likes to see if there's anyone he knows. And as there's a bar in the restaurant—

ARNHOLM: Ah—come along then. *(He and BOLETTA go out to the left.)*

(ELLIDA stands for a moment staring into the pool, now and then talking softly to herself in broken phrases. Beyond, on the footpath behind the garden fence to the left, a STRANGER in travelling clothes appears. He has bushy red hair and a beard. He wears a Scottish cap and carries a travelling bag on a strap over his shoulder.

STRANGER goes slowly along the fence and stares into the garden. When he catches sight of ELLIDA he stops, looks fixedly at her.)

STRANGER: *(In a low voice.)* Good evening, Ellida!

ELLIDA: *(Turning and crying out.)* Oh, my love—you've come at last!

STRANGER: Yes, at last.

ELLIDA: *(Looking at him in surprise and fear.)* Who are you? Are you looking for anyone here?

STRANGER: You know very well I am, my dear.[1]

ELLIDA: *(Startled.)* *What* did you say? How dare you address me like that. Who are you looking for?

STRANGER: I'm looking for you.

ELLIDA: *(Starting.)* Ah—! *(Stares at him, then staggers back and gives a stifled cry.)* The eyes! The eyes!

STRANGER: So, at last you're beginning to recognize me. I knew you at once, Ellida.

ELLIDA: The eyes! Don't look at me like that! I shall call for help!

STRANGER: Hush, hush! Don't be afraid. I won't do anything to harm you.

ELLIDA: *(Covers her eyes with her hand.)* Don't look at me like that, I tell you.

STRANGER: *(Leaning his arms on the fence.)* I came here on the English steamer.

ELLIDA: *(Shooting a fearful glance at him.)* What do you want with me?

STRANGER: I promised you I'd come again as soon as I could.

ELLIDA: Go away! Go back again! Never—never come back here! I wrote you that it was all over between us—completely! You know that!

STRANGER: *(Unperturbed, not answering.)* I wanted to come before but wasn't able to. Now at last I can, so here I am, Ellida.

ELLIDA: What do you want with me? What are you thinking of? What have you've come here for?

STRANGER: You know very well I've come to fetch you.

ELLIDA: *(Retreating in terror.)* To fetch me? Is *that* what you're thinking of?

STRANGER: Yes, that's right.

ELLIDA: But you must know that I'm married.

STRANGER: Yes, I know that.

ELLIDA: And yet just the same—! Just the same, you've come her to—to—fetch me!

STRANGER: Yes, that's what I'll do.

ELLIDA: *(Clasping her hands to her head.)* Oh, this terrible—this horrible, horrible—!

STRANGER: You don't want to come?

ELLIDA: *(Wildly.)* Don't look at me like that!

STRANGER: I'm asking—don't you want to?

ELLIDA: No, no, no! I won't! Never, in all eternity. I won't, I tell you. I neither can nor will. *(More quietly.)* Nor dare to.

STRANGER: *(Climbing over the fence into the garden.)* Very well, Ellida. Then just let me say one thing before I go away.

ELLIDA: *(Wants to escape but cannot. She stands as if transfixed with terror and supports herself on a tree stump by the pond.)* Don't move! Keep away from me—don't come near me! Keep away, I tell you!

STRANGER: *(Cautiously taking a few steps toward her.)* You needn't be afraid of me, Ellida.

ELLIDA: *(Her hands before her eyes.)* Don't look at me like that!

STRANGER: Just don't be afraid. Don't be afraid.

(WANGEL comes through the garden on the left.)

WANGEL: *(Still among the trees.)* You've certainly had to wait far too long for me.

ELLIDA: *(Rushing toward him, clinging tightly to his arm and crying.)* Ah Wangel—save me! Save me—if you can!

WANGEL: Ellida—what is it, in God's name—!

ELLIDA: Save me, Wangel! Can't you see him? Standing over there!

WANGEL: *(Looking at him.)* That man there? *(Approaching.)* May I ask who you are and what you're doing in this garden?

STRANGER: *(Nodding toward ELLIDA.)* I want to speak with *her.*

WANGEL: I see. So it was you—? *(To ELLIDA.)* I heard a stranger had been at the house asking after you.

STRANGER: Yes, that was me.

WANGEL: So, what do you want with my wife? *(Turning.)* Do you know him, Ellida?

ELLIDA: *(In a low voice, wringing her hands.)* Do I know him? Oh yes, yes, yes.

WANGEL: *(Quickly.)* Well!

ELLIDA: It's *him,* Wangel. This is the man himself—the one I told you—

WANGEL: What! What are you saying? *(Turning.)* Are you the Johnston who once—?

STRANGER: You can call me Johnston. It's all one to me—though it's not my name.

WANGEL: It isn't?

STRANGER: Not any longer, no.

WANGEL: What can you want with my wife? Because you must know the lighthouse keeper's daughter has been married for some time. And whom she married—you must know *that,* too.

STRANGER: I've known for over three years.

ELLIDA: *(Tensely.)* How did you find out?

STRANGER: I was on my way home to you. Then I came across an old newspaper—from these parts—and there, in it, was your wedding.

ELLIDA: *(Looking straight in front of her.)* The wedding— So that was what—

STRANGER: I thought it so strange. Because, with those rings—*that* was a wedding too, Ellida.

ELLIDA: *(Her hands covering her face.)* Ah—!

WANGEL: How dare you—!

STRANGER: Had you forgotten?

ELLIDA: *(Sensing his gaze and crying out.)* Don't stand looking at me like that!

WANGEL: *(Placing himself before him.)* You must address yourself to me, not to her. So, in short, since you know the situation, what possible business can you have here? Why have you come seeking out my wife?

STRANGER: I promised Ellida I'd come for her as soon as I could.

WANGEL: Ellida! Again you dare—!

STRANGER: And Ellida promised solemnly to wait for me till I came.

WANGEL: You continue to use my wife's first name. That kind of familiarity is not appreciated here.

STRANGER: I know that. But since she belongs to me first of all—

WANGEL: To you! You still—?

ELLIDA: *(Hiding behind WANGEL.)* Oh, he'll never let go of me!

WANGEL: You claim she belongs to you?

STRANGER: Has she told you about the two rings—mine and Ellida's?

WANGEL: Yes, but what of it? She put an end to that long since. You got her letters, so you know that yourself.

STRANGER: Ellida and I both agreed that joining those rings would have all the binding strength and force of a wedding vow.

ELLIDA: But I don't want this, I tell you. I don't want to know you, never in this world! Stop looking at me like that! I don't want to!

WANGEL: You must be deranged if you think you can come here basing your claim on such a childish prank.

STRANGER: That's true. I've no claim—not the way you mean it—none at all.

WANGEL: Then what do you intend doing? You surely don't imagine you can take her from me by force, against her own will?

STRANGER: No, what good would that do. If Ellida goes with me, she must do so of her own free will.

ELLIDA: *(Starting and crying out.)* My own free will—!

WANGEL: And do you really imagine—?

ELLIDA: *(To herself.)* My own free will　!

WANGEL: You must be out of your mind. Go your way! We've nothing more to do with you.

STRANGER: *(Looking at his watch.)* Soon it'll be time for me to be on board again. *(A step closer.)* Well, Ellida—so now I've done what I came to do. *(Still nearer.)* I've kept my promise to you.

ELLIDA: *(Pleading, shrinking away.)* Oh, don't touch me!

STRANGER: And you have tomorrow night to think it over.

WANGEL: There's nothing here to think over. Just see to it you clear out.

STRANGER: *(Continuing to ELLIDA.)* I'm now going up the fjord with the steamer. Tomorrow night I'll come back and see you again. You must wait for me here in the garden because I'd rather settle this matter with you alone, you understand.

ELLIDA: *(Softly, trembling.)* Oh, do you hear, Wangel?

WANGEL: Just stay calm. We'll know how to prevent that visit.

STRANGER: Goodbye—for the present, Ellida. Tomorrow night, then.

ELLIDA: *(Pleading.)* Oh no, no, don't come tomorrow. Don't ever come back again!

STRANGER: And if by that time you're willing to follow me over the sea—

ELLIDA: Don't look at me like that!

STRANGER: I only mean should you make yourself ready to go.

WANGEL: Go up to the house, Ellida.

ELLLIDA: I can't. Oh help me! Save me, Wangel!

STRANGER: Because remember this—if you don't come with me tomorrow, it will be all over.

ELLIDA: *(Looking at him, trembling.)* It will be all over? Forever?

STRANGER: *(Nodding.)* It can never be changed after that, Ellida. I'll never come back to this country. You'll never see nor hear from me again. I'll be as if dead and lost to you forever.

ELLIDA: *(Catching her breath.)* Ah—!

STRANGER: So consider carefully what you do. Goodbye. *(He climbs over the fence, stops and says.)* Yes, Ellida, be ready to leave tomorrow night. Because then I'll be here to fetch you. *(He goes leisurely and calmly along the path to the right.)*

ELLIDA: *(Looking after him for a while.)* My own free will, he said. To think—! He said I would go with him of my own free will.

WANGEL: Keep calm, he's gone now. And you need never see him again.

ELLIDA: How can you say that? He's coming back here tomorrow night.

WANGEL: Let him come. There's no need for you to meet him, whatever happens.

ELLIDA: *(Shaking her head.)* Oh, Wangel, don't imagine you can stop him.

WANGEL: Don't worry, dearest, just leave it all to me.

ELLIDA: *(Pondering, not listening to him.)* When he's been here—tomorrow night—? And when he's sailed over the sea with the steamer—?

WANGEL: Yes, what then?

ELLIDA: Can we be sure he will never—never more come back?

WANGEL: Yes, Ellida, you can be quite sure. What would he have to do here after that? When he's heard from your own lips you want nothing more to do with him? That puts an end to the whole thing.

ELLIDA: *(To herself.)* Tomorrow then. Or never.

WANGEL: And if he should decide to come here again—

ELLIDA: *(Tensely.)* What then?

WANGEL: It lies in our power to render him harmless.

ELLIDA: Oh, don't believe that.

WANGEL: I say it lies in our power! If you can't get free of him by any other means, he must still answer for the murder of the captain.

ELLIDA: *(Fiercely.)* No, no, no. Never! We know nothing about the murder of the captain. Absolutely nothing!

WANGEL: Nothing? He confessed it to you himself!

ELLIDA: No, we know nothing about it! If you say anything, I'll deny it. He's not to be shut in! He belongs out there on the open sea—out there!

WANGEL: *(Looking at her and says slowly.)* Ah, Ellida, Ellida!

ELLIDA: *(Clinging desperately to him.)* On my dearest, my faithful love—save me from that man!

WANGEL: *(Gently freeing himself.)* Come! Come with me!

(LYNGSTRAND and HILDA, both with fishing tackle, enter from the right by the pond.)

LYNGSTRAND: *(Quickly approaching ELLIDA.)* Oh Mrs. Wangel, you're about to hear the most amazing thing!

WANGEL: What is it?

LYNGSTRAND: Only imagine—we've seen the American!

WANGEL: The American?

HILDA: Yes, I saw him, too.

LYNGSTRAND: He went round behind the garden to go on board the big English steamer.

WANGEL: How could you know who he was?

LYNGSTRAND: I was on a voyage with him once. I thought for sure he'd been drowned but here he is—completely alive.

WANGEL: Do you know anything else about him?

LYNGSTRAND: No. But he must have come back to be revenged on his faithless wife.

WANGEL: What are you saying?

HILDA: Lyngstrand's going to use him for a sculpture.

WANGEL: I don't understand a word—

ELLIDA: You'll hear about it later.

(ARNHOLM and BOLETTA enter from the left from the footpath beyond the garden fence.)

BOLETTA: *(To those in the garden.)* Come over here and look! The English steamer's sailing up the fjord.

(A great ship glides slowly by in the distance.)

LYNGSTRAND: *(To HILDA, by the fence.)* Tonight he'll be standing over her for sure.

HILDA: *(Nodding.)* Over the sailor's faithless wife, yes.

LYNGSTRAND: Imagine—just at midnight.

HILDA: I think it must be so thrilling.

ELLIDA: *(Looking after the ship.)* Tomorrow, then—

WANGEL: And then never again.

ELLIDA: *(Softly, trembling.)* Oh, Wangel—save me from myself!

WANGEL: *(Looking anxiously at her.)* Ellida! I can sense something behind all this.

ELLIDA: Yes, behind, the tide pulls and attracts.

WANGEL: The tide—?

ELLIDA: That man is like the sea.

> *(She goes slowly and thoughtfully through the garden and out to the left. WANGEL walks uneasily by her side, observing her closely.)*

END OF ACT THREE

ACT FOUR

DR. WANGEL'S garden room, with doors right and left. In the background, between two windows, a glass door opening onto the veranda. Below this, part of the garden can be seen. A sofa with a table in front of it to the left. To the right, a piano, and further back a large stand for plants and flowers. In the center of the floor a round table surrounded with chairs. On the table a rosebush in bloom and other pots of plants around it. It is morning.

    BOLETTA is sitting on the sofa by the table, occupied with embroidery. LYNGSTRAND sits on a chair at the upper end of the table. Down in the garden BALLESTAD is sitting, painting. HILDA stands and watches beside him.

LYNGSTRAND: *(His arms on the table, sits for a moment in silence and watches* BOLETTA *at work.)* It must be very difficult, to sew a border like that, Miss Wangel.

BOLETTA: Oh no, not so difficult. As long as you remember to count correctly.

LYNGSTRAND: To count? You have to count, too?

BOLETTA: Yes, the stitches. Look.

LYNGSTRAND: So I see. Fancy that! Then it's almost a kind of art. Can you make your own designs?

BOLETTA: If I have a pattern to work from.

LYNGSTRAND: Not otherwise?

BOLETTA: No, not otherwise.

LYNGSTRAND: So it's not really an art, after all.

BOLETTA: No, it's more like—a handicraft.

LYNGSTRAND: But I expect you could actually learn an art.

BOLETTA: Even if I don't have the gift for it?

LYNGSTRAND: All the same—if you could spend some time with a real artist—

BOLETTA: You really think I could learn from him?

LYNGSTRAND: Not exactly learn in the usual sense. But I think it would come to you little by little. In a way, rather like a miracle, Miss Wangel.

BOLETTA: That would be wonderful.

LYNGSTRAND: *(Soon after.)* Have you ever thought closely—? I mean, have you ever thought really seriously about marriage, Miss Wangel?

BOLETTA: *(Glancing at him.)* About—? No.

LYNGSTRAND: I have.

BOLETTA: Really? You have?

LYNGSTRAND: Oh yes—I often think about things like that. Above all, about marriage. I've read a good many books on the subject, too. I think marriage has to be considered some kind of miracle—the way a woman gradually comes to resemble her husband.

BOLETTA: Takes up his interests, you mean?

LYNGSTRAND: Yes, precisely.

BOLETTA: And what about his abilities—his gifts and his talents?

LYNGSTRAND: Well, yes—I dare say all of those, too.

BOLETTA: Then perhaps you believe that everything a man has studied—or has thought out for himself—all that can become part of his wife, too?

LYNGSTRAND: Yes, that as well, little by little. Just like a miracle. But I believe that can only happen in a marriage that is faithful, loving, and truly happy.

BOLETTA: Has it never occurred to you that a man might be drawn to his wife in the same way. Become like her, I mean.

LYNGSTRAND: A man? Oh no, I've never thought of that.

BOLETTA: But why shouldn't the one case be just like the other?

LYNGSTRAND: Well, because a man has a vocation to live for. And it's *that* which gives him strength and purpose, Miss Wangel. He has a calling in life.

BOLETTA: Every man?

LYNGSTRAND: Oh no. I'm thinking mostly of artists.

BOLETTA: Do you think it's right for an artist to get married?

LYNGSTRAND: Yes, I do think so. If he can find someone he deeply loves, then—

BOLETTA: All the same, I think he really should live for his art alone.

LYNGSTRAND: Yes, of course he should. But he can do that just as well if he's married.

BOLETTA: Yes, but what about her?

LYNGSTRAND: Her? In what way—?

BOLETTA: The one he marries? What should she live for?

LYNGSTRAND: She will live for his art, too. I'd imagine a woman would feel really happy doing that.

BOLETTA: I Im. I'm really not so sure

LYNGSTRAND: Yes, take my word for it, Miss Wangel. It's not just all the honor and esteem she acquires through him—for I'd imagine that's the least concern. It's that she gets to help him create, that she can make his work easier—by being with him, making him comfortable, taking care of his needs and making his life pleasant. I should think that must be really delightful for a woman.

BOLETTA: Oh, you don't realize how egotistical you are!

LYNGSTRAND: I! Egotistical! Great heavens, no—! If only you knew me a

little better than you do. *(Bending more closely to her.)* Miss Wangel—
when I'm gone—and that will be quite soon—

BOLETTA: *(Looking at him sympathetically.)* Now don't start thinking sad
thoughts.

LYNGSTRAND: There's nothing very sad about it really, I think.

BOLETTA: What do you mean, then?

LYNGSTRAND: I'm going away in about a month. First, just from here.
Then afterwards I'll be going to the south.

BOLETTA: Oh that—of course.

LYNGSTRAND: Will you be thinking of me sometimes, Miss Wangel.

BOLETTA: Yes, I'll be glad to.

LYNGSTRAND: *(Pleased.)* You promise me?

BOLETTA: Yes, I promise.

LYNGSTRAND: Your word of honor?

BOLETTA: My word of honor. *(Changing her tone.)* But what's the point?
Nothing in the world will come of it.

LYNGSTRAND: How can you say that? For me, it will be so wonderful to
know that here at home you were thinking of me.

BOLETTA: Yes, but then what?

LYNGSTRAND: Well, I really don't know for sure what would follow—

BOLETTA: Nor do I. So much stands in the way. Everything in the world
stands in the way, I think.

LYNGSTRAND: Oh, some miracle or other just might happen—a lucky turn
of fortune, something like that. For I really believe I *have* luck on my side.

BOLETTA: *(Eagerly.)* Yes, isn't that true? You *do* believe that?

LYNGSTRAND: I absolutely believe it. And so, in a few years, when I come
home again as a famous sculptor, well off and in good health—

BOLETTA: Yes, yes, that's what we're all hoping for.

LYNGSTRAND: You've good reason to hope. Only think about me, loyally
and warmly, while I'm away there, down in the south. And so I have your
word for it?

BOLETTA: You have. *(Shaking her head.)* But nothing will come of this, just
the same.

LYNGSTRAND: Oh yes, Miss Boletta. At the very least it means that I'll set
about my work so much more easily and quickly.

BOLETTA: Is that what you think?

LYNGSTRAND: Yes, I feel it instinctively. And I'm convinced it will be
inspiring for you as well—knowing that here in this backwater—you,
yourself, in a way are helping me in my creative work.

BOLETTA: *(Looking at him.)* Yes, but what about you, on your part?

LYNGSTRAND: I—?

BOLETTA: *(Looking out to the garden.)* Hush!—let's talk about something else. Here comes the headmaster.

(ARNHOLM can be seen in the garden to the left. He is standing talking to BALLESTAD and HILDA.)

LYNGSTRAND: Are you fond of your old teacher, Miss Boletta?

BOLETTA: Am I fond of him?

LYNGSTRAND: I mean, do you think really well of him?

BOLETTA: Oh yes, I do. He's such a wonderful man to have as a friend and adviser. And he's always ready to be helpful when he can.

LYNGSTRAND: But isn't it odd that he never married?

BOLETTA: You think that's so odd?

LYNGSTRAND: Yes, because he's really quite well off, so I gather.

BOLETTA: I suppose he must be. But it can't be easy for him to find anyone who'll have him.

LYNGSTRAND: Why do you say that?

BOLETTA: Well, he's been the tutor of almost all the young girls he knows. He says so himself.

LYNGSTRAND: What difference does that make?

BOLETTA: Good lord, you don't marry someone who's been your tutor.

LYNGSTRAND: You don't think a young girl could love her tutor?

BOLETTA: Not after she's really grown up.

LYNGSTRAND: Well—imagine that!

BOLETTA: *(Warningly.)* Ssh! Ssh!

(BALLESTAD, meanwhile, has collected his things and carries them through the garden to the right. HILDA helps him, while ARNHOLM goes up to the veranda and comes into the room.)

ARNHOLM: Good morning, my dear Boletta. Good morning Mr. er—hm!

(He looks displeased and nods coldly to LYNGSTRAND, who rises and bows.)

BOLETTA: *(Getting up and going to ARNHOLM.)* Good morning, Mr. Arnholm.

ARNHOLM: How are all of you today?

BOLETTA: Fine, thank you.

ARNHOLM: Has your stepmother gone down to bathe as usual?

BOLETTA: No, she's sitting upstairs in her room.

ARNHOLM: She isn't ill?

BOLETTA: I can't say. She's locked herself in.

ARNHOLM: Hm— Has she?

LYNGSTRAND: Mrs. Wangel was very upset about that American yesterday.

ARNHOLM: What do *you* know about it?

LYNGSTRAND: I told her I'd seen him large as life walking past the garden.

ARNHOLM: Ah, so that's it.

BOLETTA: *(To ARNHOLM.)* You and Father were sitting up late together last night.

ARNHOLM: Yes, fairly late. We had serious things to talk about.

BOLETTA: Did you get to talk to him about me and my situation, too?

ARNHOLM: No, Boletta dear, I didn't manage to. He was so taken up with something else.

BOLETTA: *(Sighing.)* Ah yes, he always is.

ARNHOLM: *(Looking meaningfully at her.)* But later today we two must go into this more closely. Where is your father just now? Not at home, perhaps?

BOLETTA: Yes, he must be down at the office. I'll go and fetch him.

ARNHOLM: No, don't bother. I'd rather go down to him.

BOLETTA: *(Listening to the left.)* Wait a little, Mr. Arnholm. I think Father's coming downstairs. Yes. He must have been up there looking after her. *(DR. WANGEL enters through the door on the left.)*

WANGEL: *(Offering ARNHOLM his hand.)* My dear friend, so you're here already. It was good of you to come so early. Because I need to talk some more with you.

BOLETTA: *(To LYNGSTRAND.)* Perhaps we should go and join Hilda in the garden.

LYNGSTRAND: Yes, let's do that, Miss Wangel. *(He and BOLETTA go down to the garden and through the trees in the background.)*

ARNHOLM: *(Who has been following them with his eyes, turns to WANGEL.)* Do you know that young man very well?

WANGEL: No, hardly at all.

ARNHOLM: Don't you think he spends rather a lot of time with the girls?

WANGEL: Does he? I hadn't really noticed.

ARNHOLM: I think you ought to keep an eye on that sort of thing.

WANGEL: Yes, you're quite right. But, good lord, what's a poor fellow supposed to do? The girls by now are so used to fending for themselves. They won't listen to a word I or Ellida say.

ARNHOLM: Not to her, either?

WANGEL: No. And in any case, I can't really expect her to get involved in things like that. It's not in her nature. *(Breaking off.)* But that's not what we're here to talk about. So tell me—have you thought any more over this business—of all that I told you?

ARNHOLM: I've thought of nothing else since we parted last night.

WANGEL: And what's to be done, do you think?

ARNHOLM: My dear Wangel, I think you, as a doctor, must know better than I.

WANGEL: Ah, if you only realized how difficult it is for a doctor to diagnose correctly about a sick person he deeply loves! And this is no ordinary sickness, either. No ordinary doctor—and no ordinary medicine—can help here.

ARNHOLM: How is she today?

WANGEL: I was with her just now and she appeared quite calm. But behind all her moods there was something hidden that's impossible for me to fathom. And then she's so changed, so unpredictable and unstable.

ARNHOLM: That's to be expected in her morbid state of mind.

WANGEL: Not entirely. It's deepest source is something she was born with. The truth is, Ellida belongs with the sea people.

ARNHOLM: What exactly do you mean by that, my dear Doctor?

WANGEL: Haven't you noticed the people out there by the open sea are a race apart? It's almost as though they lived the sea's own life. The motions of the waves—the ebbs and flows, too—are there in their thoughts and feelings. They can't bear to be transplanted. Oh, I should have thought of that before. It was a crime against Ellida to take her away from there and bring her here inland.

ARNHOLM: Is that what you really believe?

WANGEL: Yes, more and more. And I should have acknowledged it before. Because really I knew but couldn't bring myself to admit it. I loved her so much, you see, and was thinking only of myself. I was unforgivably selfish at the time.

ARNHOLM: Hm—every man is a little selfish in those circumstances. All the same I've never noticed that failing in you to a marked degree, Doctor.

WANGEL: (Pacing restlessly.) Oh yes! And I've gone on that way ever since. I'm so much older than she is. I should have been like a father to her—guiding her. I should have done my best to cultivate and develop her mind. Unfortunately, nothing was done in that regard. I never had the will power, you see, because I loved her as she was. So things got worse and worse for her, and I went about not knowing what to do. (More quietly.) And that's why, in my desperation, I wrote and asked you to come to us.

ARNHOLM: (Looking at him in surprise.) What's that? Is that why you wrote?

WANGEL: Yes. But don't let on to anyone.

ARNHOLM: But what in the world—what good did you think I would be? I just don't understand.

WANGEL: No, that's only reasonable. Because I was on the wrong track. I thought Ellida's heart was given over to you at one time, and that secretly, part of it still was. I thought it would do her good to see you again and talk with you about home and those days in the past.

ARNHOLM: So it was your wife you meant when you wrote there was someone here waiting for me—perhaps longing for me?

WANGEL: Yes, who else?

ARNHOLM: *(Quickly.)* No, no, you're right. I just misunderstood.

WANGEL: Quite naturally, as I said. I was completely on the wrong track.

ARNHOLM: And you call yourself selfish!

WANGEL: There's so much I had to atone for, I dared not reject any remedy that might in the slightest way relieve her mind.

ARNHOLM: How do you explain the power this stranger has over her?

WANGEL: Ah, dear friend, there may be aspects of this case that don't admit an explanation.

ARNHOLM: Something inexplicable in itself, you mean? That can't be explained?

WANGEL: Not at present, at any rate.

ARNHOLM: Do you believe in such things?

WANGEL: I neither believe nor disbelieve. I just don't know. Therefore, I leave it open.

ARNHOLM: But tell me one thing—that extraordinary, uncanny assertion that the child's eyes—

WANGEL: *(Vehemently.)* I don't believe that about the eyes in the slightest! I won't believe such a thing! That must be pure imagination on her part. Nothing else.

ARNHOLM: Did you notice the man's eyes when you saw him yesterday?

WANGEL: Yes, I did indeed.

ARNHOLM: And you saw no kind of resemblance?

WANGEL: *(Evasively.)* Hm—good lord, what shall I say? The light wasn't very good when I saw him, and then Ellida had so insisted on the likeness beforehand— I don't think I could have looked at him objectively.

ARNHOLM: No, no, that could be true. But what about the other matter— that all this fear and unrest came over her just at the time the stranger seems to have been on his way home.

WANGEL: Well, you see—*that* is also something she may have imagined and dreamt up since the day before yesterday. It didn't happen to her so suddenly—all at once—as she now claims. But since she heard from this young Lyngstrand that Johnston—or Freeman—or whatever he's now called—was on his way home three years ago—in March—she apparently believes that the mental unrest seized hold of her in the self-same month.

ARNHOLM: And it didn't?

WANGEL: Not in any way. Traces and signs of it could be detected long before. It's true that, quite by chance, just three years ago in March, she suffered a particularly violent attack—

ARNHOLM: Well, then—!

WANGEL: But there's a quite simple explanation for that—the condition she was in at the time.

ARNHOLM: So—signs against signs.

WANGEL: *(Clenching his hands.)* And then not to be able to help her! Not knowing what advice to offer! Or find the right cure—!

ARNHOLM: What if you decided to change where you live—to move somewhere else? So she could live in surroundings where she felt more at home?

WANGEL: Ah, my friend, don't you think I've suggested that? I proposed we should move out to Skjoldvik, but she won't do it.

ARNHOLM: Not that, either?

WANGEL: No, because she thinks there'd be no point in it. And no doubt she's right.

ARNHOLM: Hm— Is that what you think?

WANGEL: Yes. Then there's another thing, when I go into it more deeply. I really don't know how I could go through with it, because, for the girls' sakes, I can't see how I could justify moving to such an out-of-the-way place. They need to live somewhere where there's *some* prospect of being provided for.

ARNHOLM: Provided for? Are you thinking about that already?

WANGEL: Good lord, yes—I need to think about that, too. But then, on the other hand, I need to consider my poor Ellida—! Oh my dear Arnholm, in many ways I find myself caught between fire and water!

ARNHOLM: Maybe you needn't be so concerned on Boletta'a account— *(Breaking off.)* Where has she—where have they gone, I wonder? *(He goes up to the open door and looks out.)*

WANGEL: *(Over by the piano.)* I'd gladly make any sacrifice for all three of them. If only I knew what.

(ELLIDA enters through the door on the left.)

ELLIDA: *(Quickly, to WANGEL.)* You won't be going out this morning?

WANGEL: No, no, rest assured. I'll stay home with you. *(Pointing to ARNHOLM who approaches.)* But won't you say good morning to our friend?

ELLIDA: *(Turning.)* Oh, there you are, Mr. Arnholm. *(Giving him her hand.)* Good morning!

ARNHOLM: Good morning, Mrs. Wangel. No bathing today, for a change?

ELLIDA: No, no, no! I can't even think of it today. But won't you sit down for a moment.

ARNHOLM: Not just now, thank you. *(Looking at WANGEL.)* I promised the girls I'd join them in the garden.

ELLIDA: Heaven knows if you'll meet them in the garden. I can never fathom where they get to.

WANGEL: They're almost sure to be down by the pond.

ARNHOLM: Well, no doubt I'll pick up their trail. *(He nods and goes across the veranda out into the garden on the right.)*

ELLIDA: What time is it, Wangel?

WANGEL: *(Looks at his watch.)* It's just after eleven.

ELLIDA: Just after eleven. And tonight at eleven o'clock—or half past—the steamer will be here. Oh, if only I was through with it all!

WANGEL: *(Coming closer to her.)* Ellida, dear—there's something I need to ask you.

ELLIDA: What is it?

WANGEL: The night before last—up at Prospect Park—you said that during these last three years you'd often seen him in your mind as clear as day.[1]

ELLIDA: Yes, so I have. You must believe me.

WANGEL: Well, how did you see him?

ELLIDA: How did I see him?

WANGEL: I mean, what did he look like when you imagined you saw him?

ELLIDA: But, dear, you know yourself what he looks like.

WANGEL: And that's the way he looked in your imagination?

ELLIDA: Yes, like that.

WANGEL: Exactly the way he looked in reality last night?

ELLIDA: Yes, exactly the same.

WANGEL: Well, how is it then that you didn't recognize him at first?

ELLIDA: *(Startled.)* I didn't?

WANGEL: No. Afterwards, you said yourself you'd no idea at first who the stranger was.

ELLIDA: *(Struck by this.)* Yes, I really think you're right! Isn't that extraordinary, Wangel? That I didn't recognize him straight away!

WANGEL: It was only the eyes, you said.

ELLIDA: Ah yes, the eyes, the eyes!

WANGEL: But at Prospect Park you said he always appeared to you just as he looked when you parted—out there ten years ago.

ELLIDA: Did I say that?

WANGEL: Yes.

ELLIDA: Then he must have looked then as he does now.

WANGEL: No. The night before last, on the way home, you gave a completely different description of him. Ten years ago he had no beard, so you said. He was dressed quite differently, too. Then there's the tie-pin with the pearl in it—the man yesterday had nothing like that.

ELLIDA: No—so he didn't.

WANGEL: *(Looking searchingly at her.)* Ellida dear, think a little more. Or—maybe you no longer remember what he looked like when you stood together at Bratthammer?

ELLIDA: *(Reflecting, closing her eyes for a while.)* Not very clearly. No—today I really can't. Isn't that strange?

WANGEL: Not so strange after all. A new image of reality has entered your mind, and it's eclipsed the old one—so you can't see it any longer.

ELLIDA: Do you think so, Wangel?

WANGEL: Yes. And it's eclipsed all your morbid imaginings, too. It's a good thing reality's taken over.

ELLIDA: Good! Do you call it good?

WANGEL: Yes, good that it arrived—it might be the cure you need.

ELLIDA: *(Sitting on the sofa.)* Wangel, come and sit with me here. I must tell you everything that's on my mind.

WANGEL: Yes, do that, Ellida dear. *(He sits on a chair the other side of the table.)*

ELLIDA: It was really a great misfortune—for both of us—that we two should have come together.

WANGEL: *(Stunned.)* What are you saying?

ELLIDA: Yes, it was. And it couldn't be otherwise. It couldn't have led to anything but unhappiness—not after the way we came together.

WANGEL: What was wrong with the way—

ELLIDA: Listen, Wangel—it's no good our going on here lying to ourselves—and to each other.

WANGEL: Is that what we're doing? Lying, you say?

ELLIDA: Yes, we are. Or, at least, hiding from the truth. Because the truth—the pure, simple truth is—that you came out there and—and bought me.

WANGEL: Bought—! You say "bought"?

ELLIDA: Oh, I wasn't a hair's breadth better than you. I agreed. I went and sold myself to you.

WANGEL: *(With a pained expression.)* Ellida, you have the heart to call it that?

ELLIDA: What other name for it is there? You couldn't bear the emptiness of your house any longer, so you searched for a new wife—

WANGEL: And a new mother for the children, Ellida.

ELLIDA: Maybe that, too—along with the rest. Though you didn't know in the least if I was up to the job. You'd barely seen me and had spoken a little to me a couple of times. Then you took a fancy to me and so—

WANGEL: Well, call it whatever you like.

ELLIDA: And for my part—there I was, helpless and bewildered and so utterly alone. So it was only natural that I should accept—when you offered to provide for me for the rest of my life.

WANGEL: I didn't see it as providing for you, Ellida. I asked you frankly if you'd share what little I could call mine with me and the children.

ELLIDA: Yes, you did. But I shouldn't have accepted, just the same! Not for any price have accepted—and sold myself! The harshest work, the most miserable poverty would have been better—if it was from my own free will—from my own choice!

WANGEL: (Getting up.) Then have the five–six years we've lived together been worth nothing to you?

ELLIDA: No, don't ever think that, Wangel! It's been as good living with you as anyone could wish for. But I didn't come to you of my own free will. That's the point.

WANGEL: (Looking at her.) Not of your own free will!

ELLIDA: No, I didn't act with my free will when I went with you.

WANGEL: Ah—I remember—those words from yesterday.

ELLIDA: Everything became clear in those words. It makes me see it all, now, in a new light.

WANGEL: What do you see?

ELLIDA: I see that the life we two have been living together is in fact no marriage at all.

WANGEL: (Bitterly.) There you speak truly. The life we're living *now* is no marriage.

ELLIDA: Nor was it before, either. Not from the beginning. (Looking before her.) The first—*that* might have been a complete and true marriage.

WANGEL: The first? What first do you mean?

ELLIDA: Mine—with *him*.

WANGEL: (Looking at her, astonished.) I simply don't understand you.

ELLIDA: Ah, Wangel my dear, don't let's lie to each other. Or to ourselves, either.

WANGEL: Very well! Now what follows?

ELLIDA: You see—we can never get away from one fact—that a promise given freely is as completely binding as a wedding vow.

WANGEL: But what on earth—!

ELLIDA: (Getting up impetuously.) You must let me leave you, Wangel!

WANGEL: Ellida—! Ellida—!

ELLIDA: Yes, yes, just give me permission to leave you! Believe me, there's nothing else for it. Not after the way we were brought together.

WANGEL: *(With controlled anguish.)* How could the gulf between us become so wide?

ELLIDA: It had to be. It couldn't be otherwise.

WANGEL: *(Looking sadly at her.)* So the life we shared didn't win you for me. You've never, ever been mine.

ELLIDA: Oh, Wangel, if only I could love you the way I want to, as richly as you deserve. But I feel so deeply it can never happen.

WANGEL: A divorce, then. It's a complete and legal divorce you want?

ELLIDA: Dearest, how little you understand me. It isn't the formalities I care about. Because it seems to me such outward things don't really matter. What I want is that we two agree to release each other of our own free wills.

WANGEL: *(Bitterly, nodding slowly.)* Dissolve the contract—I see.

ELLIDA: *(Eagerly.)* Exactly! Dissolve the contract.

WANGEL: And afterwards, Ellida. The future? Have you thought about how it will be like for both of us—how things will turn out, for you and for me?

ELLIDA: They'll turn out as they will. What's to come will work out in its own way. What I'm begging and imploring you for, Wangel, *that's* the most important thing. Just set me free. Give me back my full freedom!

WANGEL: Ellida, it's a fearful thing you're asking me. At least give me time to collect myself before I decide. Let's go into this together more thoroughly. And give yourself time to think what you're doing!

ELLIDA: But I've no time to waste in that way. I must have my freedom again this very day!

WANGEL: And why, just now?

ELLIDA: Because it's tonight he's coming.

WANGEL: *(Starting.)* Coming? He? What's this stranger to do with this?

ELLIDA: I want to confront him in full freedom.

WANGEL: And what—what will you do afterwards?

ELLIDA: I'll not hide behind the excuse that I'm another man's wife. I'll not plead I've no choice. There'd be no decision in that.

WANGEL: You speak of choice! Choice, Ellida? Choice, in such a matter?

ELLIDA: Yes, it's choice I need. To choose on both sides. I must either let him go away alone—or follow where he goes.

WANGEL: Have you any idea what you're saying? Follow him? Put your whole life in his hands?

ELLIDA: Didn't I put my whole life in your hands? Unconditionally?

WANGEL: Maybe so. But with him! A total stranger! A man you know almost nothing about!

ELLIDA: I knew maybe even less about you. Yet I went with you, just the same.

WANGEL: At least at the time you'd some idea what kind of life to expect. But like this? This? Only think about it. What do you know in this case? Nothing of who he is—or what he is.

ELLIDA: *(Looking before her.)* That's true. And *that*, precisely, is the horror.

WANGEL: Yes, horrible is what it is.

ELLIDA: That's why I feel I must go through with it.

WANGEL: Because you feel it as something horrible?

ELLIDA: Yes, exactly.

WANGEL: *(Closer.)* Tell me, Ellida—what do you understand by the horror?

ELLIDA: *(Reflecting.)* The horror—it's something that terrifies yet attracts.

WANGEL: Attracts as well?

ELLIDA: Attracts most of all, I think.

WANGEL: *(Slowly.)* You belong with the sea.

ELLIDA: There's horror there, too.

WANGEL: And that horror is in you. You both terrify and attract.

ELLIDA: Do you feel that, Wangel?

WANGEL: At any rate, I've never really known you. Not right to the depths. It's beginning to dawn on me now.

ELLIDA: That's why you should set me free—free me from every tie to you and yours. I'm not the person you took me for—you can see that for yourself. Now we can part as friends—and of our own free will.

WANGEL: *(Sadly.)* Maybe it *is* best for us both—that we part. But I can't, all the same. Because, more than the horror, it's the attraction in you that's strongest, Ellida.

ELLIDA: Is that what you think?

WANGEL: Let's see if we can get through this day thoughtfully, in complete calm of mind. I *daren't* let you go today—I don't have the right to. Not for your own sake, Ellida. I claim my right and my duty to protect you.

ELLIDA: Protect? What is there here to protect me from? It's no outside power or force that threatens me. The horror lies deeper, Wangel. It's a horror within my own mind that I'm drawn toward. And what can you do against that?

WANGEL: I can give you the strength and support to fight against it.

ELLIDA: Yes—if I *want* to fight against it.

WANGEL: And you don't want to?

ELLIDA: Ah, *that's* just what I don't know myself.

WANGEL: It will all be settled tonight, Ellida dear—

ELLIDA: *(Breaking out.)* Yes, just think. The moment of decision so near! That will decide my whole life!

WANGEL: And then, tomorrow—

ELLIDA: Yes, tomorrow. When my true life could be thrown away.

WANGEL: Your true—?

ELLIDA: A whole lifetime of freedom wasted—for me and maybe for him, too.

WANGEL: *(Quietly, gripping her by the wrists.)* Ellida, are you in love with this stranger?

ELLIDA: Am I—? Oh, how can I know! I only know for me he's the horror that attracts and that—

WANGEL: And that—?

ELLIDA: *(Breaking free.)* And that I feel I belong with him.

WANGEL: *(Sinking his head.)* I'm beginning to understand most of this.

ELLIDA: Then what help can you offer against it? What advice do you have?

WANGEL: *(Looking sadly at her.)* Tomorrow—he'll have gone. Then the misery will be banished from your mind, and I'll consent to let you go free. We'll cancel the contract, Ellida.

ELLIDA: Oh, Wangel—tomorrow! That will be much too late.

WANGEL: *(Looking toward the garden.)* The children—let's spare the children— at least until later.

(ARNHOLM, BOLETTA, HILDA, and LYNGSTRAND enter from the garden. LYNGSTRAND takes leave and goes out to the left. The others come into the room.)

ARNHOLM: You ought to know we've been making plans—

HILDA: We're going out on the fjord tonight and—

BOLETTA: No, don't tell everything!

WANGEL: We've been making plans as well.

ARNHOLM: Ah, really?

WANGEL: Ellida will be going away to Skjoldvik—for a while.

BOLETTA: Going away—?

ARNHOLM: Well, that's a very good decision, Mrs. Wangel.

WANGEL: Ellida wants to go back home. Back to the sea.

HILDA: *(With a start toward ELLIDA.)* You're going away? Leaving us?

ELLIDA: *(Surprised.)* But Hilda, whatever's the matter?

HILDA: *(Controlling herself.)* Oh, it's nothing. *(Half audibly, turning away.)* Just go away!

BOLETTA: *(Anxiously.)* But Father—I can tell—you're going away, too. To Skjoldvik.

WANGEL: Definitely not, no! I'll look in there, now and then—

BOLETTA: And then look in here—?

WANGEL: Yes, I assure you—

BOLETTA: Now and then, yes!

WANGEL: It has to be that way, my dear. *(He crosses the room.)*

ARNHOLM: *(Whispering.)* We'll talk later, Boletta. *(He goes over to WANGEL. They talk quietly together by the door.)*

ELLIDA: *(Half audibly to BOLETTA.)* What's the matter with Hilda? She seemed so upset.

BOLETTA: Haven't you ever noticed what Hilda's been longing for, day after day?

ELLIDA: Longing for?

BOLETTA: Ever since you came into this house.

ELLIDA: No, no. What is it?

BOLETTA: A single word of affection from you.

ELLIDA: Ah—! Might there be a purpose for me *here*? *(She clasps her hands to her head and stares fixedly in front of her as if invaded by warring thoughts and feelings.)*

(WANGEL and ARNHOLM approach, whispering together as they cross the room. BOLETTA goes and looks into the side room to the right. Then she holds the door open.)

BOLETTA: Come, Father, lunch is now on the table, if you're ready—

WANGEL: *(With forced composure.)* Is it, dear? That's excellent. After you, Arnholm. Now we'll go in and drink a parting toast to—to the "lady from the sea."

(They go through the door to the right).

END OF ACT FOUR

ACT FIVE

The far side of DR. WANGEL'S house by the carp pond. The summer twilight gradually darkens. ARNHOLM, BOLETTA, LYNGSTRAND, and HILDA, in a boat, are poling themselves along the bank on the left.

HILDA: See? We can easily jump ashore here!

ARNHOLM: No, no, don't do it!

LYNGSTRAND: I can't jump, Miss Hilda.

HILDA: How about you, Mr. Arnholm, can't you jump either?

ARNHOLM: I'd prefer to pass that up.

BOLETTA: Then let's land at the steps of the bathing hut.
    (They punt off to the right. At the same time BALLESTED enters on the footpath to the right, carrying notebooks and a French horn. He greets those in the boat, turning and talking to them. Their answers can be heard increasingly further away.)

BALLESTED: What's that you say—? Yes, that's right—for the sake of the English steamer—it's the last time he comes here this year. But if you want to enjoy the music, don't go out too far. *(Calling.)* What? *(Shaking his head.)* Can't hear what you're saying.
    (ELLIDA, with a shawl over her head, enters from the left, followed by WANGEL.)

WANGEL: But Ellida, dear, I assure you, there's plenty of time yet.

ELLIDA: No, no, there isn't. He could appear any moment.

BALLESTED: *(Outside the garden fence.)* Hallo! Good evening, Dr. Wangel. Good evening, Mrs. Wangel!

WANGEL: *(Remains where he is.)* Ah, so it's you. There's going to be music tonight, too?

BALLESTED: Yes, our wind ensemble likes to make itself heard. There's no lack of festive occasions at this time of year. Tonight it's in honor of the Englander.[1]

ELLIDA: The Englander! He's[2] already been sighted?

BALLESTED: Not yet. But he slips in—between the islands. Before you can say it, he's right upon us.

ELLIDA: Yes, that's just how it is.

WANGEL: *(Half to ELLIDA.)* Tonight's the final voyage. He won't be back again.

BALLESTED: A sad thought, Doctor. But that's why, as I said, we're going to do him the honors. Ah well, ah well! Now the happy summer days are quickly drawing to a close. "Soon all sea lanes will be locked in ice" as it says in the tragedy.

ELLIDA: "All sea lanes locked,"—yes.

BALLESTED: A melancholy thought. We've been summer's happy children these weeks and months. It's hard to adapt to the days of darkness—at first, at least. For humans can always acli-a-cclimatise themselves, Mrs. Wangel. Yes, that's what they can do. *(He bows and exits to the left.)*

ELLIDA: *(Looking out over the fjord.)* Oh, this agonizing suspense! These unnerving final minutes before I must decide.

WANGEL: Are you still determined to talk to him yourself?

ELLIDA: I *must* talk to him myself. I shall make my choice of my own free will.

WANGEL: You don't have any choice, Ellida—you've no right to choose. I won't give you that right.

ELLIDA: You can't prevent me choosing—not you nor anyone else. You can forbid me to go away with him—to follow him—if that's what I choose. You can keep me here by force, against my will. You can do that. But as to my choosing—from my inmost heart—choosing him and not you—if I should want to—that's something you can't prevent.

WANGEL: No, you are right. I can't prevent that.

ELLIDA: And besides, I've nothing whatever to stand in my way. No earthly tie here at home to compel and hold me. I've no roots whatever in this house, Wangel. The children don't belong to me—not in their hearts, I mean. They've never belonged. When I go away—*if* I go away—either with him tonight or else out to Skjoldvik tomorrow, I won't even have a key to hand over—not an instruction to leave behind about anything at all. That's how completely rootless I've been in this house, how completely an outsider from the beginning.

WANGEL: You wanted it that way, yourself.

ELLIDA: No, I didn't. Neither one way nor the other. I simply let everything stay as I found it the day I came here. It was you—and no one else—who wanted it like that.

WANGEL: I thought I was doing what was best for you.

ELLIDA: Oh yes, Wangel, I know that very well. But that has its consequences. Now it's taking its revenge. Now there's no compelling reason, nothing to hold me, or help me stay—nothing pulling me back toward all that should have been our most precious, shared possession.

WANGEL: I see that well enough, Ellida. And that's why, from tomorrow on, you'll have your freedom again and live you own life.

ELLIDA: *That's* what you call my own life? Oh no, my own life—my true life—I lost track of that when I came to live with you. *(Clenching her hands in anxiety and distress.)* And now, tonight, in half an hour, he'll be here, the man I betrayed, the man I should have held to as faithfully as he's held to me. He'll come now and offer me this last chance to live my life again—my own true life—the life that appalls and attracts me—which I cannot let slip by. Not of my own free will.

WANGEL: Precisely the reason you need your husband—and your doctor—to take charge on your behalf.

ELLIDA: Yes, Wangel, I see that very well. Oh you mustn't think there aren't times when I long for the safety and peace of finding shelter in you—and trying to defy all the tempting and terrifying powers. But I can't do that, either. No, no, I can't!

WANGEL: Come, Ellida, let's walk a little together.

ELLIDA: I'd like to, but I daren't. He said I must wait for him here.

WANGEL: Come with me. You've plenty of time.

ELLIDA: Do you think so?

WANGEL: Ample time, I'm sure.

ELLIDA: Then just for a little.

(They go out in the foreground to the right. At the same time ARNHOLM and BOLETTA enter from the other side of the pond.)

BOLETTA: *(Noticing the pair leaving.)* Look there—!

ARNHOLM: Sh! Let them go.

BOLETTA: Can you imagine what's going on between those two these last few days?

ARNHOLM: Have you noticed anything?

BOLETTA: Have I!

ARNHOLM: Anything in particular?

BOLETTA: Oh yes, one thing and another. Haven't you?

ARNHOLM: Well, I don't quite know what to—

BOLETTA: Of course you have, but you won't come out with it.

ARNHOLM: I think it would be good for your stepmother to go away for a while.

BOLETTA: You think so?

ARNHOLM: Yes. I'm convinced it will be best for all concerned if she gets away from time to time.

BOLETTA: If she goes home to Skjoldvik tomorrow, she'll never come back to us again.

ARNHOLM: But my dear Boletta, whatever makes you think that?

BOLETTA: Yes, it's what I firmly believe, just wait and see! She'll not come back—at least as long as Hilda and I are in the house.

ARNHOLM: Hilda, too?

BOLETTA: Well, with Hilda it could work out, because she's still hardly more than a child. And then, under everything, she actually adores Ellida,

I believe. But with me it's different, you see—a stepmother not much older than oneself.

ARNHOLM: My dear Boletta, it might not be so very long before you get to leave home.

BOLETTA: *(Eagerly.)* You think so? Then you've talked to Father about it?

ARNHOLM: Yes, I've done that, too.

BOLETTA: Well—and what did he say?

ARNHOLM: Hm— Your father's so taken up with other problems these days—

BOLETTA: Yes, it's as I said before.

ARNHOLM: But I did get this much out of him—that you mustn't count on any help from him.

BOLETTA: I mustn't—?

ARNHOLM: He explained very clearly to me how he stood. It seems anything of the kind is completely impossible for him.

BOLETTA: *(Reproachfully.)* And you can have the heart to stand there and make fun of me.

ARNHOLM: I'm not doing that at all my dear Boletta. It's entirely up to you—whether you get away or not.

BOLETTA: You say it's up to me?

ARNHOLM: Whether or not you go out into the world. Learn all the things you want and take part in all you've been longing for here at home. Get to live your life in happier circumstances, Boletta. What do you say to that?

BOLETTA: *(Clasping her hands.)* Oh, dear God—! But all this is completely impossible. Not when Father won't or can't—because I've no one else in the world to turn to.

ARNHOLM: Couldn't you accept a helping hand from your old—from your former tutor?

BOLETTA: From you, Mr. Arnholm. Would you really be willing to—?

ARNHOLM: To stand by you? Yes, most gladly, in word and deed. You can depend on it. Do you accept? Well? Will you go along with it?

BOLETTA: Go along with it! To get away—get to see the world—really get to learn something! All the wonderful things that seemed to me so impossible—!

ARNHOLM: Yes, all of that can be a reality for you now—if you only want it.

BOLLETA: All this happiness beyond words? You'll really help me to it? Oh no—how can I accept such a gift from a stranger?

ARNHOLM: You can easily accept it from me, Boletta. Accept whatever you want.

BOLETTA: *(Grasping his hands.)* Yes, I really believe I could, too. I don't know why it is but— *(Breaking out.)* Oh, I could both laugh and cry from joy! From happiness! I'll really get to live after all. I was beginning to be so afraid that life would pass me by.

ARNHOLM: There's no need to be afraid on that account, dear Boletta. But now you must tell me quite frankly if there's anyone—anyone at all— binding you to this place.

BOLETTA: Binding me? No, there's no one.

ARNHOLM: No-one at all?

BOLETTA: None at all. Oh, in a way I'm bound to Father. And Hilda, too. But—

ARNHOLM: Well, you'd have to leave your father sooner or later. And Hilda will soon want to go her own way in life. All this is only a question of time, nothing more. But otherwise there's nothing binds you to here, no kind of hold on you whatever?

BOLETTA: No, none at all. I can go away as soon as the moment arises.

ARNHOLM: Well, in that case, Boletta dear, you shall come away with me.

BOLETTA: *(Clapping her hands.)* Oh, God in heaven, how marvellous to think of!

ARNHOLM: Because I trust you've complete faith in me.

BOLETTA: Oh yes, I have!

ARNHOLM: And you feel completely safe putting yourself and your future into my hands, Boletta? You feel, that, don't you?

BOLETTA: Yes, of course! Why shouldn't I? How can you think otherwise? You've been my old teacher—my teacher from the old days, I mean.

ARNHOLM: Not just because of that. I don't attach much importance to that aspect of the situation any more. But—well—since you're free, Boletta, and there are no ties to hold you—I'm asking if you would be willing to—willing to be joined to me—for life?

BOLETTA: *(Shrinking back in fear.)* Ah—what are you saying?

ARNHOLM: For our whole lives, Boletta. If you would be my wife.

BOLETTA: *(Half to herself.)* No, no, no. It's impossible. Quite impossible.

ARNHOLM: Would it really be so completely impossible for you to—?

BOLETTA: But how in the world can you mean what you say, Mr. Arnholm? *(Looking at him.)* Or— All the same— Was that what you meant—when you offered to do so much for me?

ARNHOLM: Please hear me out, Boletta. I've startled you quite a bit, it seems.

BOLETTA: How could something like this—from you—how could it not startle me?

ARNHOLM: Maybe you're right. You didn't know—you couldn't know—it was for your sake I took this trip here.

BOLETTA: You came here for my sake!

ARNHOLM: Yes I did, Boletta. Last spring I got a letter from your father. And in it I read something that led me to believe—hm—that you remembered your former tutor in—in a somewhat more than friendly manner.

BOLETTA: How could Father write such a thing?

ARNHOLM: It wasn't what he'd meant at all. But I entered into the illusion that here was a young girl longing for me to come back. No, you mustn't interrupt me, Boletta dear! And, you see, when a man in my situation—someone no longer in his days of youth—entertains such an idea—or illusion—it makes a powerful impression on him. So there began to grow in me a vivid—a grateful affection for you. I felt I must go to you, see you again, tell you I shared all the feelings I imagined you felt for me.

BOLETTA: But now that you know it isn't so   that you made a mistake—?

ARNHOLM: It doesn't help, Boletta. Your image I carry inside me will always be shaped and colored by the mood that created the illusion. You probably can't understand that, but it's the way it is.

BOLETTA: I never imagined anything like this could happen.

ARNHOLM: But now you know it can? What do you say, Boletta? Couldn't you bring yourself to—well—to be my wife?

BOLETTA: It seems so completely impossible, Mr. Arnholm. I see you as my tutor and can't imagine standing in any other relationship to you.

ARNHOLM: Very well, if you really don't think you can. But the situation still hasn't changed, my dear Boletta.

BOLETTA: What do you mean?

ARNHOLM: Naturally I stand by my promise, just the same. I'll make sure you get away and discover the world for yourself. Get to learn the things you really long to while living securely and independently. I'll take care of your later years too, Boletta. You'll find me a good, faithful, reliable friend—you can count on that.

BOLETTA: But good lord, Mr. Arnholm, all that's quite impossible now.

ARNHOLM: Is *that* impossible, too?

BOLETTA: Yes, you must see it is. After all you've said to me—and after the answer I gave you—oh, you must see yourself I couldn't possibly accept such an enormous gift from you! There's nothing in the world I could take from you—not after this!

ARNHOLM: You'd rather resign yourself to sitting here at home letting life pass you by?

BOLETTA: Oh, it's too horribly painful to bear thinking about!

ARNHOLM: And give up the opportunity of seeing the world out there? Of taking part in all those things you say you've dreamed of? Knowing there's so infinitely much—yet all the same never discovering any of it? Think carefully, Boletta.

BOLETTA: Yes, yes you are so right, Mr. Arnholm.

ARNHOLM: And then, one day when your father's no longer here, you may find yourself helpless and alone in the world. Or maybe have to marry some other man whom you—possibly—couldn't care very much for, either.

BOLETTA: Yes, I see how true it all is—all you are saying— But just the same—! And yet—

ARNHOLM: *(Quickly.)* Well?

BOLETTA: *(Doubtfully, looking at him.)* Perhaps it's not so completely impossible, after all—

ARNHOLM: What, Boletta?

BOLETTA: That I could let you—agree to—to what—to what you're suggesting.

ARNHOLM: Meaning you could bring yourself to—you'll grant me the happiness of helping you as a friend.

BOLETTA: No, oh no, never that! That would be completely impossible now. No, Mr. Arnholm, I'd rather you take me—as—

ARNHOLM: Boletta! Then you will, after all!

BOLETTA: Yes—I believe—I *will* do it.

ARNHOLM: That you'll definitely be my wife?

BOLETTA: Yes. If you still feel that—you want me.

ARNHOLM: If I feel—! *(Taking her hand.)* Oh thank you, thank you, Boletta! All the other things you said—your uncertainties earlier—they don't alarm me. If I don't yet possess your whole heart, I'm convinced I *shall* win it. Oh, Boletta, I'll take such good care of you.

BOLETTA: And I'll get to see the world—live my life in it? You promised me that.

ARNHOLM: And I stand by it.

BOLETTA: And be allowed to learn all that I want to?

ARNHOLM: I'll be your teacher myself. Just like before, Boletta. Do you remember our last school year—?

BOLETTA: *(Quiet and engrossed in herself.)* Imagine—to know I'm free—able to go out into the unknown. Not needing to worry about the future. No more worry over petty needs—

ARNHOLM: No, you'll never need waste another thought on such things. Don't you agree, my dear Boletta—*that's* a good thing, too?

BOLETTA: Yes, really—that's true for sure.

ARNHOLM: *(Placing his arm round her waist.)* You'll see how happily and cozily we'll arrange things for ourselves. How fine and safe and contented we'll be together, Boletta.

BOLETTA: Yes, I'm beginning to—I really think—that it might work out. *(Looking out to the right and quickly freeing herself.)* Ah! Be sure not to say anything!

ARNHOLM: What is it, dear?

BOLETTA: It's that poor— *(Pointing.)* Look over there.

ARNHOLM: Is it your father?

BOLETTA: No, it's that young sculptor, walking down there with Hilda.

ARNHOLM: Lyngstrand. What's the matter with him?

BOLETTA: Well, you know how weak and poorly he is.

ARNHOLM: Yes, if it isn't only imagination.

BOLETTA: Oh no, it's true enough. He can't last much longer. But maybe that's best for him.

ARNHOLM: My dear, how can that be for the best?

BOLETTA: Yes, because—because nothing will come of his art anyway. Let's go before they get here.

ARNHOLM: Gladly, my dear Boletta.

(HILDA and LYNGSTRAND enter from the pond side.)

HILDA: Hi! Hi there! Won't you fine folk wait for us?

ARNHOLM: Boletta and I want to take the lead for a bit. *(He and BOLETTA go out to the left.)*

LYNGSTRAND: *(Laughing quietly.)* Isn't it amusing how everyone goes around in couples these days, always two by two.

HILDA: *(Looking after them.)* I'd almost swear he's gone and proposed to her.

LYNGSTRAND: Really? Have you noticed anything?

HILDA: Oh yes—it's not so hard if you've a pair of eyes in your head.

LYNGSTRAND: But Miss Boletta won't have him—I'm sure of it.

HILDA: No, because she thinks he's horribly old looking. Besides, she thinks he's going bald.

LYNGSTRAND: Yes, but that's not the only reason. She wouldn't have him anyhow.

HILDA: How can you know that for sure?

LYNGSTRAND: Because there's someone else she's promised to think of.

HILDA: Only to think of?

LYNGSTRAND: While he's away, yes.

HILDA: Oh, so you're the one she's promised to think of?

LYNGSTRAND: It could just be.

HILDA: She's promised you that?

LYNGSTRAND: Yes, imagine—she promised me! But you mustn't tell her you know.

HILDA: May God guard my tongue—I'll be as silent as the grave.

LYNGSTRAND: I think it was really nice of her.

HILDA: And when you come back home again—will you get engaged to her? And marry her, too?

LYNGSTRAND: No, that wouldn't be such a good idea. I daren't think about anything like that for the first few years. And by the time I'm well enough off, I imagine she'll be too old for me.

HILDA: Yet just the same you want her to go around here thinking of you?

LYNGSTRAND: Yes, because it would be so helpful to me—as an artist, you understand. And it's so easy for her, as she's got no real vocation. Still, it's nice of her, all the same.

HILDA: You believe you can work better on your art if you know Boletta's going around here thinking of you?

LYNGSTRAND: Yes, I'm sure I will. You see, it's a matter of knowing somewhere in the world a lovely young, well-bred woman's quietly going about her life dreaming about me. I think that must be so—so— I really don't know the right word for it.

HILDA: You mean thrilling, maybe?

LYNGSTRAND: Thrilling? Oh yes—thrilling's just what I mean. Or something like that. *(Looking at her for a moment.)* You're so clever, Miss Hilda, really very clever. When I come home again, you'll be about the same age as your sister is now. Maybe you'll look just like she does now. Even think just like she thinks now, too. Then you'll be like both yourself and her at the same time—in one form [gestalt], as it's called.

HILDA: You'd really like that?

LYNGSTRAND: I'm not quite sure. Yes, I almost think so. But now, just for this summer, I'd prefer you to be just like yourself. Exactly as you are.

HILDA: You like me best this way?

LYNGSTRAND: Yes, very much that way.

HILDA: Hm. Tell me—as an artist—do you think it's a good thing I always wear these light summer clothes?

LYNGSTRAND: Yes, I like it very much.

HILDA: You think light colors suit me?

LYNGSTRAND: Yes, to my mind, you look splendid in light colors.

HILDA: But tell me—as an artist—how do you think I'd look if I decided to dress all in black.

LYNGSTRAND: In black, Miss Hilda?

HILDA: Yes, completely in black. Do you think *that* would suit me?

LYNSTRAND: Black isn't really the right thing for summer. Otherwise, I'd say you'd look very striking in black, too. Especially with your complexion.

HILDA: *(Staring ahead.)* All in black, right up to my neck. A black frill all around. Black gloves—and a long black veil hanging at the back.

LYNGSTRAND: If you dressed like that, Miss Hilda, I'd want to be a painter, and paint you as a young, beautiful, grieving widow.

HILDA: Or a young, grieving bride.

LYNGSTRAND: Yes, that would be even better. But you wouldn't want to dress like that, would you?

HILDA: I don't rightly know. But I think it would be thrilling

LYNGSTRAND: Thrilling?

HILDA: Thrilling to imagine, yes. *(Pointing suddenly to the left.)* No, but see over there!

LYNGSTRAND: *(Looking.)* The big English steamer! And right in at the pier! *(WANGEL and ELLIDA enter from the side of the pond.)*

WANGEL: No, I assure you, my dear Ellida—you're wrong! *(Sees the others.)* Ah—you both here? Isn't it true, Mr. Lyngstrand, he's not in sight yet?

LYNGSTRAND: The big English ship?

WANGEL: That's right!

LYNGSTRAND: *(Pointing.)* He's there already, Doctor.

ELLIDA: Ah—! I knew for certain!

WANGEL: He's come!

LYNGSTRAND: He comes like a thief in the night, you might say. Completely without warning, silently—

WANGEL: Why don't you take Hilda down to the pier. Hurry! She'll want to hear the music.

LYNGSTRAND: Yes, we were just going, Doctor.

WANGEL: We'll probably join you later—in a little while.

HILDA: *(Whispering to LYNGSTRAND.)* There goes another couple! *(She and LYNGSTRAND go out through the garden to the left. Music from the wind ensemble can be heard from far out on the fjord during the following.)*

ELLIDA: He's come! Yes, yes, he's here! I can feel it.

WANGEL: You should go indoors, Ellida. Let me speak with him alone.

ELLIDA: Ah—that's impossible! Impossible, I tell you. *(With a cry.)* Ah—do you see him, Wangel? *(The STRANGER enters from the left and stops on the footpath outside the fence.)*

STRANGER: *(Greeting.)* Good evening. You see I've come back, Ellida.

ELLIDA: Yes, yes, yes—the hour has come.

STRANGER: Are you ready to leave? Or not?

WANGEL: You can see yourself she's not.

STRANGER: I'm not asking about travelling clothes and suchlike. Nor packed suitcases, either. I've got everything she'll need for the voyage on board. And I've taken a cabin for her. *(To ELLIDA.)* I'm asking if you're ready to go with me—to go of your own free will.

ELLIDA: *(Pleadingly.)* Oh, don't ask me! Don't tempt me that way!

(A ship's bell is heard in the distance.)

STRANGER: That was the first bell to embark. Now you must say yes or no.

ELLIDA: *(Wringing her hands.)* To decide! Decide for my whole life. Never able to turn back!

STRANGER: Never. In half an hour it will be too late.

ELLIDA: *(Looks shyly and searchingly at him.)* Why do you hold so fast to me?

STRANGER: Don't you also feel we two belong together?

ELLIDA: Because of our vow, you mean?

STRANGER: Vows bind no one, neither man nor woman. I hold so fast to you because I can't do otherwise.

ELLIDA: *(Quietly, trembling.)* Why didn't you come before?

WANGEL: Ellida!

ELLIDA: *(Vehemently.)* Oh—all that's pulling at me, tempting and luring me into the unknown! The whole power of the sea is gathered in this man.

(The STRANGER climbs over the garden fence.)

ELLIDA: *(Shrinking behind WANGEL.)* What—what is it—what do you want?

STRANGER: I can see it—and hear it in your voice, Ellida. It's me you'll choose in the end.

WANGEL: *(Advancing toward him.)* My wife *has* no choice in this. I'll both decide for her and defend her. Yes, defend her! If you don't take yourself out of here—and out of the country too—and never come back—do you realize what's in store for you?

ELLIDA: No, no, Wangel. Don't do this!

STRANGER: What will you do to me?

WANGEL: I'll see you're arrested as a criminal. Right away, before you go back on board. I know all about the murder out at Skjoldvik.

ELLIDA: Oh, Wangel, how can you—?

STRANGER: I was prepared for that. And so—*(Takes a revolver from his breast pocket.)* I provided myself with this.

ELLIDA: *(Throwing herself before WANGEL.)* No, no, don't kill him. Kill me instead.

STRANGER: Neither you nor him—stay calm. This is for myself. I intend to live and die a free man.

ELLIDA: *(In mounting agitation.)* Wangel, listen to what I say, and let him hear, too. You can keep me here—you have the power and means to, and no doubt you'll do so. But my mind, all my thoughts, all the longings and desires pulling at me—*these* you can never control. They'll yearn and reach out—searching into the unknown that I was created for—that you've shut out from me.

WANGEL: *(In quiet pain.)* I see it only too well, Ellida. Little by little you're slipping away from me. Your craving for the boundless and the infinite—and for the unattainable—in the end will drive your mind into the darkness.

ELLIDA: Yes, yes, I can feel it—like black, soundless wings hovering over me.

WANGEL: It shan't come to that. There's no other rescue for you—at least none I can see. So therefore—therefore I—the contract's now cancelled. Now you can choose your path—in complete freedom.

ELLIDA: *(Staring speechlessly at him for a moment.)* Is that true—true—what you're saying? Do you really mean it—in your inmost heart?

WANGEL: Yes, from the depths of my heart's anguish—I mean it.

ELLIDA: And you *can* do this? You can let this *happen?*

WANGEL: Yes, I can—I can because I love you so much.

ELLIDA: Have I come to be so close, so deep a part of you?

WANGEL: The years, and our life together, brought that about.

ELLIDA: *(Clasping her hands.)* And I saw so little of this!

WANGEL: Your thoughts went elsewhere. But now—now you're completely free from me and all that's mine. Now your life—your innermost self—can take its true path again. Because now you can choose freely—with full responsibility, Ellida.

ELLIDA: *(Her hands to her head, looking directly at WANGEL.)* In freedom, with full responsibility! With full responsibility as well? But then with this, everything's transformed!

(The ship's bell rings again.)

STRANGER: You hear that, Ellida? Now it rings for the last time. Follow me!

ELLIDA: *(Turning and looking resolutely at him and saying in a firm voice.)* I can never go with you after this.

STRANGER: You're not going?

ELLIDA: *(Clinging to WANGEL.)* Oh, I can never leave you after this!

WANGEL: Ellida, Ellida!

STRANGER: It's all over, then?

ELLIDA: Yes, it's over—for ever.

STRANGER: So I see. There's something here stronger than my will.

ELLIDA: Your will hasn't the least power over me now. To me you are a dead man—who's come home from the sea. And who'll go back to it again. I no longer dread you—nor am I drawn to you.

STRANGER: Goodbye, then![3] *(He vaults over the garden fence.)* From now on you're no more—than a shipwreck I've survived. *(He goes out to the left.)*

WANGEL: *(Looking at her a moment.)* Ellida—your mind's like the sea. It ebbs and flows. What brought the change?

ELLIDA: Don't you understand the change came—*had* to come—when I could choose freely.

WANGEL: And the unknown—it no longer attracts you?

ELLIDA: Neither attracts nor terrifies. I could have faced it—entered it—if I'd wanted to. But because I could choose to, so I could reject it.

WANGEL: I'm beginning to understand you. You think and experience in images—in visual forms. Your longings, your yearning for the sea—your attraction toward him—toward this stranger—all these have been expressions of an awakening and growing urge for freedom. No more.

ELLIDA: Oh, I don't know what to say to that. But you've proved a good doctor to me. You found and dared use the right remedy—the only one that could help me.

WANGEL: Yes, in the direst need and danger we doctors will dare to risk much. But now you'll come back to me, Ellida?

ELLIDA: Yes, my dear, faithful Wangel—now I'll come back to you. I can, now, because I come to you freely—of my free will—and on my own responsibility.

WANGEL: *(Looking tenderly at her.)* Ellida! Ellida! To think we now can live entirely for each other—

ELLIDA: —and with shared memories. Yours—as well as mine.

WANGEL: Yes, that's so, isn't it, my dear?

ELLIDA: —and for our two children, Wangel.

WANGEL: *Ours,* you called them?

ELLIDA: Who are not mine, yet. But I shall win them.

WANGEL: Ours! *(Quickly and joyfully kissing her hands.)* I can't tell you how grateful I am for that word.

(HILDA, BALLESTAD, LYNGSTRAND, ARNHOLM, and BOLETTA enter the garden from the left. At the same time many of the town's young people and summer visitors pass along the footpath.)

HILDA: *(Half aloud to LYNGSTRAND.)* Do you see that! She and Father look like they've just got engaged.

BALLESTAD: *(Overhearing.)* It's summertime, young Miss!

ARNHOLM: *(Looking at WANGEL and ELLIDA.)* The Englander's sailing now.

BOLETTA: *(Going to the fence.)* You can see him best from here.

LYNGSTRAND: Last voyage of the year.

BALLESTAD: "Soon all the sea lanes will be closed," as the poet says. It's sad, Mrs. Wangel. And now we're going to lose *you* for a while, too. Tomorrow you're moving out to Skioldvik, I hear.

WANGEL: No, that won't happen. Because, just this evening, we changed our minds.

ARNHOLM: *(Looking at each alternately.)* Ah—really?

BOLETTA: *(Coming forward.)* Father, is this true?

HILDA: *(Going to ELLIDA.)* So you're staying with us after all!

ELLIDA: Yes, Hilda dear—if you'll have me.

HILDA: *(Struggling between tears and joy.)* Oh—if I'll have you!

ARNHOLM: *(To ELLIDA.)* Well, this truly comes as a surprise.

ELLIDA: *(Smiling gravely.)* Well, you see, Mr. Arnholm—you remember how we talked of this yesterday. Once you've become a land creature, there's no finding your way back to the sea again. Nor back to the life of the sea, either.

BALLESTAD: But that's exactly the case with my mermaid.

ELLIDA: About the same, yes.

BALLESTAD: Except with this difference—the mermaid dies because of it. Human beings, on the other hand, you understand, Mrs. Wangel, can accla—acclimatize themselves. Ah, yes.

ELLIDA: Yes, if they're free they can, Mr. Ballestad.

WANGEL: And have full responsibility, Ellida dear.

ELLIDA: *(Quickly, taking his hand.)* Yes, that's exactly it.

(The great steamer glides silently over the fjord. The music can be heard closer to the land.)

END OF PLAY

NOTES

ACT ONE

[1] Ballestad uses the word *fremmede*—which also means "strangers" — thus sounding the theme of the approaching Stranger (*den fremmede*) in the opening lines of the play.

[2] *Prestegården*. The priest's house, in opposition to Ellida's "pagan" identity.

[3] *Fyrtårnet*. Lit. "fire tower."

ACT TWO

[1] *Kven*, Quain. This little exchange can be omitted.

ACT THREE

[1] The Stranger uses the familiar *du* form not permitted to strangers.

ACT FOUR

[1] *Lys levende*. Alive as light: this little phrase, with its "light" motif, is used frequently by Ibsen.

ACT FIVE

[1] Englander, the English one. This can refer to the ship or to the Stranger, and the ambiguity is important in this Act.

[2] The masculine pronoun *han* used for a ship in Norwegian, maintains the ambiguity as to whether the ship or the Stranger is the object of the dialogue.

[3] The Stranger utters the untranslatable and dismissive phrase *Farvel frue* — "Goodbye, woman."

LITTLE EYOLF

+⊨ 1894 ⊨+

CHARACTERS

ALFRED ALLMERS, a man of property, man of letters, former part-time teacher
MRS. RITA ALLMERS, his wife
EYOLF, their child, nine years old
MISS ASTA ALLMERS, Alfred's younger half-sister
BORGHEJM, an engineer
THE RAT-WOMAN*

*Usually translated as Rat-Wife, although *Rottejomfruen* is, literally, the Rat-Virgin or Rat-Maid.

TIME AND PLACE

The action takes place on Allmer's estate beside the fjord, a few miles outside the town. All scene directions are from the audience's point of view.

ACT ONE

A prosperously elegant garden room with a profusion of furniture, flowers, and plants. Glass doors in the background open onto a veranda with a wide prospect over the fjord. Wooded mountain ranges in the distance. There is a door on each of the side walls, that to the right being a double door set upstage. Downstage right is a sofa with loose cushions and rugs. Chairs and a small table beside the sofa. Downstage left is a larger table with armchairs around it. On this table stands an open travelling bag. It is an early summer morning in warm sunshine.

RITA ALLMERS is standing by the table facing left, unpacking the bag. She is a handsome blonde woman, well-built and full of vitality, about thirty years old. She is dressed in a light-colored housecoat.

Soon after, ASTA ALLMERS enters through the door to the right. She is dressed in a light-brown summer outfit with hat, jacket, and a parasol. Under one arm she is carrying a large portfolio. She is slim, of middle height, with dark hair and deep, serious eyes. She is about twenty-five.

ASTA: *(In the doorway.)* Good morning, Rita dear.

RITA: *(Turning her head and nodding to her.)* No, is it really you, Asta! Coming from town so early? All the way out here?

ASTA: *(Setting her things on a chair by the door.)* Yes, I just couldn't feel easy or calm until I came and looked in on little Eyolf today. And on you, too. *(Places the portfolio on the table by the sofa).* So I took the steamer here.

RITA :*(Smiling at her.)* And you didn't by any chance happen to meet one of your friends on board? Completely by accident, I mean.

ASTA: *(Calmly.)* No, no one I knew at all. *(Sees the travelling bag.)* But, Rita, whatever's that?

RITA: *(Continues unpacking.)* Alfred's travelling bag. Don't you recognize it?

ASTA: *(Joyfully, coming closer.)* What! Has Alfred come home?

RITA: Yes, just imagine—he came quite unexpectedly by the night train.

ASTA: Ah, so that was what I was feeling! That's what drew me out here! And he didn't write you in advance? Not even a postcard?

RITA: Not a single word.

ASTA: No telegram, either?

RITA: Oh yes, just one hour before he arrived. A few words and no fuss. *(Laughs.)* That's just like him, don't you agree, Asta?

ASTA: Yes. He takes everything so calmly.

RITA: Which makes it all the more delightful to get him back again.

ASTA: Yes, I can well imagine.

RITA: A whole two weeks earlier than I expected him!

ASTA: And he's in good spirits? Not depressed?

RITA: *(Claps the bag shut, smiling at her.)* He looked completely transformed when he came through the door.

ASTA: Not the least bit tired, either?

RITA: Oh, I think he was tired all right. Hugely tired. After all, the poor thing had done almost the whole trip on foot.

ASTA: And no doubt the mountain air was hard on him.

RITA: No, I don't think so at all. I've not heard him cough even once.

ASTA: There then—you see! So it was the best thing after all, the doctor persuading him to take that trip.

RITA: Yes, now it's over and done with. But, you can imagine what a terrible time it's been for me, Asta. I've never liked to talk about it—and you hardly ever came out to see me—

ASTA: Yes, that wasn't very thoughtful of me. But—

RITA: No, no, no—you had the school there in town. *(Smiling.)* And our road builder—he was away too—

ASTA: Oh, stop it, Rita!

RITA: Very well, then. We'll let the road builder go his way. But how I longed for Alfred! How empty it seemed here. How desolate. It felt just like a tomb.

ASTA: Good Lord, Rita! It's only been six, seven weeks!

RITA: Yes, but you must remember, Alfred's never been away from me before. Not even for as long as a day. Not once in these ten years—

ASTA: Well, that's why I think it was time he got away for a while this year. He ought to have gone on a mountain trip every summer. That's what he should have done.

RITA: *(Smiling slightly.)* Oh yes, it's easy for you to talk. If I were as—as cool headed as you, I might have let him slip away before now. Maybe. But that's something I couldn't do, Asta! For me, it was as if I'd never get him back again. You can understand that, can't you?

ASTA: No, but that's because I've no one to lose.

RITA *(With a teasing smile.)* You've really no one at all—?

ASTA: None I'm aware of. *(Changing the subject.)* But, tell me Rita, where *is* Alfred? Is he still sleeping?

RITA: Far from it. He was up today as early as usual.

ASTA: So he couldn't have been so very tired, after all.

RITA: Yes, he was last night—when he got back. But now he's had Eyolf in with him for over an hour.

ASTA: That poor, pale little boy! Is he going to be doing nothing but studying again?

RITA: *(Shrugging her shoulders.)* Well, you know that's how Alfred wants it.

ASTA: Yes, but I think you should put a stop to it, Rita.

RITA: *(Somewhat impatiently.)* No—I really can't get involved—you understand? Besides, Alfred's sure to know about these things much better than I. And what should Eyolf be doing? He can't run around and play—like other children.

ASTA: *(Firmly.)* I'll have to speak to Alfred about this.

RITA: Yes, dear, you do that. But, here they are—

(ALFRED ALLMERS in a summer suit enters through the door, left, leading EYOLF by the hand. He is a slim, delicately built man about thirty-six or thirty-seven years old, with gentle eyes, and thin brown hair and beard. He has a serious and thoughtful expression. EYOLF is wearing a suit cut like a uniform with gold braid and buttons with lions on them. He is lame and walks with a crutch under his left arm. His leg is paralyzed. He is undersized, and looks frail but has beautiful intelligent eyes.)

ALLMERS: *(Releasing EYOLF and going joyfully over to ASTA extending both his hands.)* Asta! Dearest Asta! So you've come out here! How good to see you so soon!

ASTA: I felt I had to —Welcome home again.

ALLMERS: *(Shaking her hands.)* Thanks!

RITA: Isn't he looking splendid?

ASTA: *(Looking intently at him.)* Wonderful! Simply wonderful! How lively his eyes are! You must have written a great deal while you were away. *(Joyfully exclaiming.)* Maybe you've even finished the book, Alfred?

ALLMERS: *(Shrugs his shoulders.)* The book—? Oh, *that*—

ASTA: Yes, I imagined it would be so easy for you to write if you could just get away.

ALLMERS: That's what I imagined, too. But, you see, it turned out quite otherwise. I haven't written a single line of the book.

ASTA: You've haven't written—!

RITA: So that's it! I couldn't understand why there was all that blank paper in your bag.

ASTA: But, Alfred dear, what were you doing in all that time?

ALLMERS *(Smiling.)* Just walking and thinking and thinking—and thinking.

RITA: *(Placing her arm round his shoulders.)* Thinking a little of those who stayed here at home?

ALLMERS: Yes, you can be sure of that. Very much. Every single day.

RITA: *(Letting go of him.)* So, then everything's well and good.

ASTA: But nothing at all written on the book? And yet you can still seem so happy and contented? That's not your usual way. When your work's not going well, I mean.

ALLMERS: Yes, you're right. Because before, I was so stupid, you see. Thinking's the best part of us. What gets put down onto paper's not worth all that much.

ASTA: *(Crying out.)* Not worth much!

RITA: *(Laughing.)* Have you gone mad, Alfred?

EYOLF: *(Looks trustfully at him.)* Oh, but Papa, what you write *is* important.

ALLMERS: *(Smiling and stroking his hair.)* Well, well, if *you* say so, then— But take my word for it, someone who'll come after me will do it better.

EYOLF: Who will that be? Oh, tell me!

ALLMERS: Give him time. He will arrive and announce himself.

EYOLF: What will you do then?

ALLMERS: *(Gravely.)* I'll go back up to the mountains—

RITA: Shame on you, Alfred!

ALLMERS: Up to the heights and the great open spaces.

EYOLF: Papa, do you think I'll soon be well enough to come along with you?

ALLMERS: *(Painfully touched.)* Ah yes, perhaps so—my little boy.

EYOLF: Because I think it would be great fun if I could climb the mountains, too.

ASTA: *(Changing the subject.)* My, how fine and smart you're looking today, Eyolf!

EYOLF: Yes, don't you think so, Auntie?

ASTA: I do. Did you put on these new clothes for Papa's sake?

EYOLF: Yes, I asked Mama to let me. Because I wanted Papa to see me in them.

ALLMERS: *(Softly, to RITA.)* You shouldn't have got him that kind of suit.

RITA: *(Quietly.)* Oh, but he plagued me so long for it. Begged me incessantly. He wouldn't leave me in peace.

EYOLF: Just think, Papa—Borgheim's bought me a bow. And he's taught me how to shoot with it, as well.

ALLMERS: Well, that's really just the thing for you, Eyolf.

EYOLF: And next time he comes, I'm going to ask him if he'll teach me to swim, too.

ALLMERS: To swim! Why do you want to do that?

EYOLF: Because all the boys down at the shore—they can swim. I'm the only one who can't.

ALLMERS: *(Moved, putting his arms around him.)* You shall be allowed to learn whatever you want! Anything you like.

EYOLF: Do you know what I'd like most of all, Papa?

ALLMERS: No. Tell me.

EYOLF: Most of all I want to learn to be a soldier.

ALLMERS: Ah, little Eyolf, there are so many other things better than that.

EYOLF: Yes, but when I'm big, I've got to be a soldier. You know that.

ALLMERS: *(Clenching his fists.)* Yes, yes, yes—we'll see—

ASTA: *(Sitting by the table, left.)* Eyolf! Come over here to me. I've something to tell you.

EYOLF: *(Goes over to her.)* What is it, Auntie?

ASTA: Just think, Eyolf—I've seen the Rat-Wife.

EYOLF: What! You've seen the Rat-Wife! Aw, you're just teasing me.

ASTA: No, it's true. I saw her yesterday.

EYOLF: Where did you see her?

ASTA: I saw her on the road, outside town.

ALLMERS: I saw her too, somewhere out in the countryside.

RITA: *(Sitting on the sofa.)* Maybe we'll get to see her too, Eyolf.

EYOLF: Auntie, isn't it strange she's called the Rat-Wife?

ASTA: People just call her that because she goes around the country and drives away all the rats.

ALLMERS: Actually, I gather her real name is Varg.

EYOLF: Varg? That means 'wolf', doesn't it?

ALLMERS: *(Patting him on the head.)* You know that too, do you Eyolf?

EYOLF: *(Thoughtfully.)* So maybe it's true after all, that she turns into a werewolf at night. Do you think so, Papa?

ALLMERS: Oh no, I don't believe that. But now you should go and play a little in the garden.

EYOLF: Don't you think I'd better take some books with me.

ALLMERS: No, no more books from now on. Instead, go down to the shore with the other boys.

EYOLF: *(Embarrassed).* No, Papa, I don't want to go down and play with the other boys today.

ALLMERS: Why ever not?

EYOLF: No, because I'm wearing these clothes.

ALLMERS: *(Frowning.)* Do they make fun of—of your fine clothes?

EYOLF: *(Evasively.)* No, they wouldn't dare. For then I'd hit them.

ALLMERS: Well then—why not—

EYOLF: But they're so mean, those boys. And then they say I can never be a soldier.

ALLMERS: *(Restraining his anger.)* Why do they say that, do you think?

EYOLF: I think they envy me. Because, you see Papa, they're so poor that they have to go barefoot.

ALLMERS: *(Softly, his voice shaking.)* Ah, Rita, how it gnaws at my heart, all of this.

RITA: *(Soothingly.)* There, there, there.

ALLMERS: *(Threateningly.)* But those boys—one day they'll find out who's master, down at the shore!

ASTA: *(Listening.)* There's someone knocking.

EYOLF: It must be Borgheim!

RITA: Come in!

(RAT-WIFE enters, quietly and unassumingly, through the door on the right. She is a little, thin, shrivelled old woman, gray haired, with sharp, piercing eyes. She is dressed in an old-fashioned, flowered dress with a black bonnet and cape. She carries a large red umbrella and from her arm a black bag hangs on a string.)

EYOLF: *(Softly, gripping ASTA by her dress.)* Auntie! That must be her!

RAT-WIFE: *(Curtseys by the door.)* My deepest apologies—but have the master and mistress anything that's gnawing away, here in the house?

ALLMERS: We? No, not that I know of.

RAT-WIFE: Because otherwise I'd be only too glad to help them get rid of it.

RITA: Yes, yes, we understand. But we've nothing of that kind here.

RAT-WIFE: That's really a pity, that is. For I'm just making my rounds now. And there's no knowing when I'll be back in these parts again. Oh, how tired I am!

ALLMERS: *(Offering her a chair.)* Yes, you look tired.

RAT-WIFE: One should never be tired doing good for all those poor little creatures, so hated—and hunted down so cruelly. But it takes all the strength out of you.

RITA: Maybe you'd like to sit and rest for a while?

RAT-WIFE: Many, many thanks. *(Sits on a chair between the door and the sofa.)* Because all night I've been out working away.

ALLMERS: You have?

RAT-WIFE: Yes, over on the islands. *(Chuckling.)* The folks there had to send for me in the end. They did it with ill-grace all right, but there was nothing else for it. They had to put a brave face on it and bite the sour apple. *(Looking at EYOLF and nodding.)* Sour apple, little master, sour apple.

EYOLF: *(Involuntarily, a little fearfully.)* Why did they have to—

RAT-WIFE: What?

EYOLF: To bite it?

RAT-WIFE: Why, you see, they could no longer feed themselves. Because of the rats and all the little rat babies, you understand, young master.

RITA: Ugh! The poor people—were there so many of them?

RAT-WIFE: Oh yes, it swarmed with them. How they crept and they crawled. *(Laughs with quiet amusement.)* Up in the beds clambering and clawing the whole night long. Down into the milk pails they plopped. Over the floorboards, scrambling and scuttling this way and that.

EYOLF: *(Softly, to ASTA.)* I'll never go out there, Auntie.

RAT-WIFE: But then I came—and one other. And we took them with us, all of them. The sweet little creatures! We did away with every one of them.

EYOLF: *(With a shriek.)* Papa—look, look!

RITA: Good heavens, Eyolf!

ALLMERS: Whatever's the matter?

EYOLF: *(Pointing.)* Something's wriggling in her bag.

RITA: *(Moving left, with a scream.)* Ugh! Get rid of her, Alfred!

RAT-WIFE: *(Laughing.)* Ah, sweetest lady, there's nothing to be afraid of with this poor little rascal.

ALLMERS: But what is it you've got there?

RAT-WIFE: It's only Mopsemand[1] *(Untying the bag.)* Come up from the dark, you dear little fellow.

(A little dog with a broad, black snout sticks his head out of the bag. The RAT-WIFE nods and beckons to EYOLF.)

RAT-WIFE: Don't be afraid, my little wounded soldier. He won't bite you. Come on! Come on!

EYOLF: *(Clinging to ASTA.)* No, I'm scared to.

RAT-WIFE: Don't you agree, young master, he has a gentle, loving countenance?

EYOLF: *(Astonished, pointing.)* That there?

RAT-WIFE: Yes, that's right, him.

EYOLF: *(Half whispering, staring fixedly at the dog.)* I think he's got the most horrible—countenance I've ever seen.

RAT-WIFE: *(Closing the bag.)* Oh, it will come. It will come.

EYOLF: *(Involuntarily coming closer to her, then lightly strokes the bag.)* But beautiful—he's beautiful, just the same.

RAT-WIFE: *(Gently.)* But just now he's so tired and weary, poor fellow. So dreadfully tired, he is. *(Looking at ALLMERS.)* Because it drains all your strength—this kind of game, you ought to know.

ALLMERS: What kind of game, do you mean?

RAT-WIFE: The luring game.

ALLMERS: Ah, I take it the dog lures the rats, is that right?

RAT-WIFE *(Nodding.)* Mopsemand and I. We two between us. Then it all goes so smoothly. If you could just see it. All he needs is a string through his collar. Then I lead him three times round the house. And play on my mouth harp. And when they hear *that* they can't help but come up from the cellars and down from the lofts and out from their holes—all the blessed little creatures.

EYOLF: Then does he bite and kill them?

RAT-WIFE: Oh, not in the least! No, we go down to the boat, he and I. And then they follow after us. Both the grown ones and all their little ones, too.

EYOLF: *(Excitedly.)* And then what—? Tell me!

RAT-WIFE: Then we pull away from land. And I scull with one oar and play on my mouth harp. And Mopsemand—he swims after me. *(Her eyes glistening.)* And then all of them—all who crept and crawled, they come following and following us out into the deep waters. Ah, yes, because they *have* to.

EYOLF: Why do they have to?

RAT-WIFE: Just because they don't want to. Because they are so deathly afraid of the water—that's why they have to go out in it.

EYOLF: Then do they drown?

RAT-WIFE: Every last one of them. *(More softly.)* And then it's as quiet and lovely and dark as they ever could wish for, the little darlings. Sleeping down there, so sweet and so long a sleep. All of those whom people hate and persecute. *(Getting up.)* Once upon a time I had no need for Mopsemand. I did the luring myself. I alone.

EYOLF: What was it you lured?

RAT-WIFE: Men. One, most of all.

EYOLF: *(Excitedly.)* Who was that? Tell me!

RAT-WIFE: *(Laughing.)* It was my dearest true love, little heart-breaker!

EYOLF: And where is he now?

RAT-WIFE: *(Harshly.)* Down there with all the rats. *(Gently, once more.)* But now I must be off on my rounds again. Always on the move. *(To RITA.)* Has the lady absolutely nothing for me to take care of today? Because I could deal with it right away.

RITA: No, thank you. We don't need anything like that.

RAT-WIFE: Well, well, dearest lady—you never can tell— If you should happen to notice anything here that nibbles and that gnaws and creeps and crawls—all you need do is send for me and Mopsemand. Farewell, farewell, a thousand times farewell.

(She goes out through the door on the right.)

EYOLF: *(Quietly triumphant, to ASTA.)* Auntie, just think—I've seen the Rat-Wife, too!

(RITA goes out to the veranda and fans herself with her pocket handkerchief. A little while later, EYOLF steals out unnoticed through the door, right.)

ALLMERS: *(Takes the portfolio from the table by the sofa.)* Is this your portfolio, Asta?

ASTA: Yes. I've got some of those old letters in it.

ALLMERS: Ah, family letters—

ASTA: Because you asked me to go through them, while you were away.

ALLMERS: *(Pats her head.)* So you found time to do so, then!

ASTA: Yes. I did it partly out here and partly at home in town.

ALLMERS: Thanks, dear. Did you find anything interesting in them?

ASTA: *(Casually.)* Oh, you know one always finds something or other in old papers like those. *(More quietly and gravely.)* Those in the portfolio are letters to Mother.

ALLMERS: Well, naturally you must keep those.

ASTA: *(With an effort.)* No. I want you to go through them as well, Alfred. Sometime—at a later time. I don't have the key to the portfolio with me today.

ALLMERS: There's no need for it, Asta. I'd never read your mother's letters in any case.

ASTA: *(Fixes her eyes on him.)* Well then, at some time—maybe one quiet evening—I'll tell you something of what's in them.

ALLMERS: Yes, that would be the best thing to do. Only keep hold of your mother's letters. You don't have so many things to remind you of her.
(He gives ASTA the portfolio. She takes it and sets it down on the chair under her overcoat. RITA comes into the room again.)

RITA: Ugh, I believe that horrible old woman brought the stench of corpses in with her.

ALLMERS: Yes, she was rather horrible, in fact.

RITA: I almost felt ill all the time she was in the room.

ALLMERS: However, I can really understand that power of compelling and attracting she spoke of. The solitude up in the mountains, among those vast open spaces, has a similar effect.

ASTA: *(Looking intently at him.)* What is this that's happened to you, Alfred?

ALLMERS: *(Smiling.)* To me?

ASTA: Yes. Something has. Almost like a transformation. Rita's noticed it, too.

RITA: Yes, I saw it immediately you got back. But it's only for the good, isn't it, Alfred?

ALLMERS: It should be for the good. And it must—it has to be for the good.

RITA: *(Exclaiming.)* You've been through some experience on that trip. Don't deny it, because I can see it in you.

ALLMERS: *(Shaking his head.)* Not an earthly thing—outwardly. But—

RITA: *(Tensely.)* But—?

ALLMERS: Inwardly—what's happened is some sort of—revolution.

RITA: Oh, God—!

ALLMERS: *(Reassuringly, patting her hand.)* Only for the good, Rita dear. It will all be all right.

RITA: *(Sits on the sofa.)* Then you must tell us all about it right away. Everything!

ALLMERS: *(Turning toward ASTA.)* Very well. So let's sit down, too. I'll try to tell you. As best I can.

(He sits on the sofa beside RITA. ASTA pulls up a chair and sits close beside him. A short pause.)

RITA: *(Looks at him impatiently.)* Well, then—?

ALLMERS: *(Gazing straight ahead.)* When I think back on my life—on the shape it's taken—these last ten-eleven years, it appears to me almost like a fairy tale or a dream. Don't you think so too, Asta?

ASTA: Yes, in many ways I do think so.

ALLMERS *(Continuing.)* When I consider what we two were before, Asta. Without parents—without a penny.

RITA: *(Impatiently.)* Yes, yes—that was all so long ago.

ALLMERS: *(Not listening to her.)* And now we're sitting here, in comfort and splendor. I'm able to follow my calling, to work and study any way I please. *(Reaching out his hand.)* And all this great, this incredible good fortune—we owe to you, my dearest Rita.

RITA: *(Half jokingly, half involuntarily, slaps his hand.)* Now will you please put a stop to such talk.

ALLMERS: I mention it only as a kind of introduction—

RITA: Well, leave out the introduction!

ALLMERS: Rita, you mustn't think it was the doctor's advice that drove me up into the mountains.

ASTA: It wasn't, Alfred?

RITA: What, then, drove you?

ALLMERS: It was because I could no longer find peace continuing to write.

RITA: Not find peace! Dearest, who disturbed you?

ALLMERS *(Shaking his head.)* No one or nothing outside me. But I had the feeling that I was in effect misusing—or—no, neglecting my best abilities. That I was wasting my time.

ASTA: *(Her eyes wide.)* While you sat writing your book?

ALLMERS: *(Nodding.)* Because I must have abilities for more than just that. I ought to be able to accomplish other things, too.

RITA: And that's what you sat brooding over.

ALLMERS: Yes, that most of all.

RITA: So that's why you'd become so discontented with yourself lately. And with us, as well. Oh, yes, because you were, Alfred!

ALLMERS: *(Gazing straight ahead.)* There I'd sit, bent over the table, writing day after day. Many times half the night, too. Writing and writing in that huge, thick book, *Human Responsibility.* Hm!

ASTA: *(Placing her hand on his arm.)* But, dear—that book is to be your life's work.

RITA: You've said so often enough.

ALLMERS: And I believed so. From the time I grew up. *(With a warm expression in his eyes.)* Then you, Rita dear, set me up so that I could go ahead with it.

RITA: Don't be absurd!

ALLMERS: *(Smiling at her.)* You with your gold and your green forests—

RITA: *(Half laughing, half vexed.)* If you go on with that nonsense I shall slap you.

ASTA: *(Looking anxiously at him.)* But the book, Alfred?

ALLMERS: It seemed to become more and more distant. And step by step my thoughts were being led upwards, to the claims of higher duties.

RITA: *(Beaming, gripping his hand.)* Alfred!

ALLMERS: Thoughts of Eyolf, Rita dear.

RITA: *(Letting go his hand.)* Oh—of Eyolf.

ALLMERS: Deeper and deeper poor little Eyolf has entered into my thoughts. After that tragic fall from the table—and most of all since we learned he can never be cured—

RITA: *(Insistently.)* But you do everything you can for him, Alfred.

ALLMERS: As a schoolmaster, yes. But not as a father. And I intend being a father to Eyolf from now on.

RITA: *(Looking at him and shaking her head.)* I don't understand you at all.

ALLMERS: I mean I'll do all in my power to make what can't be cured as easy to bear as it's possible to imagine.

RITA: But dear—thank God—I don't believe he feels it so deeply.

ASTA: *(With emotion.)* Oh yes, Rita, he does.

ALLMERS: Yes, you can be sure he feels it deeply.

RITA: *(Impatiently.)* But, dear—what more can you do for him?

ALLMERS: I will try to bring to light all the rich possibilities now dawning in that child's soul. All the stirrings of nobility in him—these I want to bring to full growth so they blossom and bear fruit. *(More and more warmly, getting up.)* And I want to do more than that! I want to help him bring his dreams in harmony with goals that are possible for him. As he is now, all his yearnings are toward what for the rest of his life he can never attain. I want to guide his mind toward happiness.

RITA: You should take all this more calmly, Alfred!

ALLMERS: *(Stands by the table, left, and looks at them.)* Eyolf shall take up my whole life's work. If that's what he wants. Or he can choose something that's completely his own. Maybe that's better. Well, at any rate, I will set mine aside.

RITA: *(Getting up.)* But, Alfred dearest—can't you work both for yourself and for Eyolf?

ALLMERS: No, that I can't do. Impossible! I can't divide myself in this. Therefore, I must yield to him. Eyolf shall be the one fulfilled in our family. And I want to make it my new life's work to guide him to that fulfillment.

ASTA: *(Has risen and gone over to him.)* This has cost you a fearfully hard struggle, Alfred.

ALLMERS: Yes, it has. Here at home I'd never have won my way to that resolve. Never have forced myself to make that renunciation. Never here, in this house.

RITA: Was that, then, why you went away this summer?

ALLMERS: *(His eyes shining.)* Yes! And then I went up into the infinite solitude. Watched the sun rise, flaring over the mountain peaks. Felt myself closer to the stars. Almost as if in an understanding and fellowship with them. It was then I could do it.

ASTA: *(Looking at him sadly.)* But you'll never write any more on the book about human responsibility?

ALLMERS: No, never, Asta. I can't split myself between two callings, I tell you. But I'll follow through with human responsibility—in my own life.

RITA: *(Smiling.)* And you believe you can keep up such high principles here at home?

ALLMERS: *(Taking her hand.)* With you beside me, I can. *(Reaching out his other hand.)* And with you beside me, too, Asta.

RITA: *(Drawing back her hand.)* With two, then. So you *can* divide yourself.

ALLMERS: But, my dearest Rita—

(RITA leaves him and stands in the garden doorway. There is a rapid, light knocking on the door to the right. BORGHEJM, the engineer, briskly enters. He is a young man, about thirty with a cheerful, confident expression and upright bearing.)

BORGHEJM: Good morning, good morning, Mrs. Allmers! *(Stops, happy at seeing ALLMERS.)* But what do I see! Home again already, Mr. Allmers?

ALLMERS: *(Shaking his hand.)* Yes, I got back last night.

RITA: *(Gaily.)* He wasn't allowed to stay away longer, Mr. Borghejm.

ALLMERS: Well, that's not exactly true, Rita—

RITA: *(Approaching closer.)* It certainly is true. His leave had run out.

BORGHEJM: So you hold your husband on a tight leash, Mrs. Allmers?

RITA: I hold onto my rights. All things must come to an end.

BORGHEJM: Not all things, I hope. Good morning, Miss Allmers.

ASTA: *(Evasively.)* Good morning.

RITA: *(Looking at BORGHEJM.)* Not all things, you say?

BORGHEJM: Yes, I believe with all my heart there are at least *some* things in this world that won't come to an end.

RITA: You're thinking now about love—and suchlike.

BORGHEJM: *(Ardently.)* I'm thinking of everything that's lovely!

RITA: And which will never end. Yes, let's think so. And hope so—all of us.

ALLMERS: *(Crossing over to them.)* Are you just about finished with building your road out here?

BORGHEJM: I'm completely finished. Since yesterday. It's taken long enough. But, thank God, *that* came to an end.

RITA: And so that's why you're so full of high spirits?

BORGHEJM: Yes, that's why.

RITA: Well, I must say—

BORGHEJM: What, Mrs. Allmers?

RITA: It isn't terribly nice of you, Mr. Borghejm.

BORGHEJM: Really? Why not?

RITA: Because you'll not be coming around these parts often from now on.

BORGHEJM: You're right, that's true. I hadn't thought of that.

RITA: Well, now and again you must come out to see us, at least.

BORGHEIM: No, that's going to be completely impossible for some time.

ALLMERS: Oh? Why is that?

BORGHEJM: You see, I've just been given a huge new project which I must start on straight away.

ALLMERS: No, have you really? *(Shakes his hand.)* I'm delighted to hear it.

RITA: Congratulations, congratulations, Mr. Borghejm.

BORGHEJM: Ssh! I'm really not supposed to mention it just yet! But I just can't keep it bottled up. It's a huge road job—up in the north. With mountains to be tackled and with the most incredible obstacles to overcome! *(Ardently.)* What a great and beautiful world—and how incredibly lucky to be a road builder!

RITA: *(Smiling at him teasingly.)* And is it just for the sake of road building that you arrive here today simply bursting with wild enthusiasm?

BORGHEJM: No, not just for that. For all the bright and hopeful prospects that are opening up for me.

RITA: *(As before.)* Aha! Then maybe there's something even lovelier still to come!

BORGHEJM: *(Shooting a glance toward ASTA.)* Who knows! When good luck comes it rushes in like the spring floods. *(Turning to ASTA.)* Miss Allmers, shouldn't we two take a little walk together? Like we used to?

ASTA *(Quickly.)* No, no thanks. Not just now. Not today.

BORGHEJM: Please do! Just for a short walk! I feel I have so much to say to you before I go away.

RITA: Something else you're not supposed to mention just yet?

BORGHEJM: Hm, it all depends on—

RITA: Well, you can always whisper it. *(Half audibly.)* Asta, you really ought to go with him.

ASTA: But, Rita dear—

BORGHEJM: *(Pleading.)* Miss Asta—remember this will be a farewell walk, our last for a long, long time.

ASTA: *(Taking her hat and parasol.)* Very well, let's walk a little around the garden.

BORGHEJM: Ah, thanks, thanks for that!

ALLMERS: And look out for little Eyolf, while you're there.

BORGHEJM: Yes, Eyolf. That's right! Where is Eyolf today? I've got something for him.

ALLMERS: He's out playing somewhere down there.

BORGHEJM: Is he really? So he's started to play now? Usually he just sits indoors reading.

ALLMERS: All that's going to come to an end. He's going to become a real outdoors boy.

BORGHEJM: That's the right thing. Let him get out into the fresh air, poor fellow. Good lord, there's nothing better in this blessed world than to be playing. I think the whole of life is a game of sorts. Come then, Miss Asta! *(BORGHEJM and ASTA go out by the veranda and down into the garden.)*

ALLMERS: *(Stands, looking after them.)* What do you think, Rita? Is there something between those two?

RITA: I don't quite know what to say. At one time I thought there was. But Asta's become so unfathomable—almost a stranger to me lately.

ALLMERS: Really, has she? While I've been away?

RITA: Yes, in the last couple of weeks, I'd say.

ALLMERS: You think she's no longer really interested in him?

RITA: Not seriously. Not heart and soul—zealously. I don't think so. *(Looking searchingly at him.)* Would you be set against it if she was?

ALLMERS: Not set against it. But I can't deny it would make me uneasy.

RITA: Uneasy?

ALLMERS: Yes, because you mustn't forget I'm responsible for Asta. For her happiness in life.

RITA: You're responsible! Asta's a grown-up now. She knows enough to choose for herself in such matters, I'd have thought.

ALLMERS: Yes, let's hope so, Rita.

RITA: For my part, I know nothing at all to hold against Borghejm.

ALLMERS: No, dear—I don't either. Quite the reverse. Just the same—

RITA: *(Continuing.)* And I'd be most happy to see the pair of them settled.

ALLMERS *(Displeased.)* Oh? Why in particular?

RITA: *(In increasing emotion.)* Because then she'd have to go far away with him! And then she'd never be able to come visiting us again!

ALLMERS: *(Staring astonished at her.)* What! You could wish to be rid of Asta!

RITA: Yes, yes, Alfred!

ALLMERS: But why in all the world—?

RITA: *(Throws her arms passionately around his neck.)* Yes, because then I would have you always to myself alone! Although—not even *then* either! Not all to myself! *(Bursts into choking sobs.)* Oh, Alfred, Alfred—I can't let you go!

ALLMERS: *(Gently freeing himself.)* But Rita, dearest, be reasonable!

RITA: I can't care in the least about being reasonable! I care only about you! About you alone in the whole world! *(Throws her arms round his neck again.)* About you—you—you alone.

ALLMERS: Please—let go—you're strangling me—!

RITA: *(Releasing him.)* If only I could! *(Looking at him, her eyes flashing.)* Ah, if only you knew how I've hated you—!

ALLMERS: Hated me—!

RITA: Yes—when you'd sit in there all by yourself. Brooding so long over your work till late, late into the night. *(Wailing.)* So long, and so late, Alfred. Oh, how I hated your work.

ALLMERS: But now that's all finished with.

RITA: *(Laughing bitterly.)* Oh yes! Because now you're taken up with something even worse

ALLMERS: *(Horrified.)* Worse! You say our child is even worse?

RITA: *(Heatedly.)* Yes, I do. Where our relationship's concerned, I call him worse. Because the child, above all else, is a living human being. *(With rising anger.)* But I won't stand for it, Alfred! I won't stand for it—I'm warning you!

ALLMERS: *(Looking fixedly at her and speaking in a low voice.)* There are times I'm almost afraid of you, Rita.

RITA: *(Darkly.)* I'm often afraid of myself. And just for that reason, you mustn't rouse the evil in me.

ALLMERS: But in God's name—do I do that?

RITA: Yes, you do, when you tear to pieces what is holiest between us.

ALLMERS: *(Meaningfully.)* Think what you're saying, Rita. It's your own child, our own child, we're talking about.

RITA: The child is only half mine. *(Again crying out.)* But *you* must be mine alone. You *shall* be mine alone! I have the right to demand that of you!

ALLMERS: *(Shrugging his shoulders.)* Ah, Rita dear, it's no use demanding such things. Everything must be freely given.

RITA: *(Looking intently at him.)* And from now on you can't do that?

ALLMERS: No, I can't. I have to share myself between Eyolf and you.

RITA: But what if Eyolf had never been born? What then?

ALLMERS: *(Evasively.)* Well, that would be another matter. Then I'd only have you to consider.

RITA: *(Quietly, her voice trembling.)* Then I could wish I had never borne him.

ALLMERS: *(Flaring up.)* Rita! You don't know what you're saying!

RITA: *(Agitatedly.)* I brought him into the world in unspeakable pain. Yet I endured all that joyfully for your sake.

ALLMERS: *(Warmly.)* Yes, yes, I know that.

RITA: *(Firmly.)* But that's now over with. I want to live my own life. Together with you. Only with you. I can't go on here just being Eyolf's mother and nothing more. I won't do that, I tell you. I *can't* do it! I want to be everything to you, Alfred!

ALLMERS: But you *are* that, Rita. Through our child—

RITA: Oh! Feeble, lukewarm phrases— Nothing more! And that's not enough for me. I was made to *become* the child's mother. But not to go on *being* it's mother. You must take me as I am, Alfred.

ALLMERS: Yet you were so fond of Eyolf before.

RITA: I was so sorry for him. Because you gave him no love or attention. Just set him to reading and cramming. You hardly even noticed him.

ALLMERS: *(Nodding slowly.)* No, I was blind. The moment hadn't yet arrived for me—

RITA: *(Regarding him.)* But now it *has* arrived?

ALLMERS: Yes, now it has. Now I see that the highest duty I can perform in this world is to be a true father to Eyolf.

RITA: And to *me?* What will you be to *me?*

ALLMERS: *(Gently.)* I will go on loving you. With calm, heartfelt emotion. *(He tries to take her hand.)*

RITA: *(Avoiding him.)* I'm not interested in your calm, heartfelt emotion. I must have you—all of you—to myself—alone! The way I had you in those first, overwhelmingly sweet years— *(Fiercely and harshly.)* I'll never let myself be fobbed off with mere scraps and leftovers, Alfred!

ALLMERS: *(Mildly.)* Surely there's enough happiness here for all three of us, Rita.

RITA: *(Scornfully.)* Then you can't want much. *(Sits by the table to the left.)* Listen now.

ALLMERS: What is it?

RITA: *(Looks up at him with a slight gleam in her eye.)* When I got your telegram last night—

ALLMERS: Yes. What then?

RITA: I dressed myself in white—

ALLMERS: Yes, I noticed you were wearing white when I came in.

RITA: I let down my hair—

ALLMERS: Your rich, fragrant hair—

RITA: So that it flowed down over my shoulders and back—

ALLMERS: I saw it. I saw it. Oh, you were beautiful, Rita!

RITA: There were rose-red shades over both lamps. And we were alone, just the two of us. The only ones awake in the whole house. And there was champagne on the table.

ALLMERS: Which I didn't drink.

RITA: *(Looking at him bitterly.)* No, how true. *(Laughs sharply.)* "You were offered champagne, but you would not touch it" as the poem goes. *(She gets up from the armchair and goes somewhat wearily to sit, half-reclining, on the sofa.)*

ALLMERS: *(Goes across and stands over her.)* I was so taken up with serious thoughts. I'd made up my mind to speak with you about our future. And above all, about Eyolf.

RITA: *(Smiling.)* Which you certainly did, my dear—.

ALLMERS: No, I didn't get to. Because you began to undress.

RITA: Yes, and all the time you talked about Eyolf. Don't you remember? You asked how everything was with little Eyolf's stomach.

ALLMERS: *(Looking reproachfully at her.)* Rita!

RITA: And then you lay down in your bed. And had a wonderful sleep.

ALLMERS: *(Shaking his head.)* Rita!

RITA: *(Lying down full length and gazing up at him.)* Well? Alfred?

ALLMERS: Yes?

RITA: "You were offered champagne, but you would not touch it."

ALLMERS: *(Almost harshly.)* No, I didn't touch it.

> *(He goes away from her and stands in the doorway to the garden. RITA lies for a moment motionless, her eyes closed.)*

RITA: *(Springing up.)* But I will tell you one thing, Alfred.

ALLMERS: *(Turning in the doorway.)* Yes?

RITA: You shouldn't be too sure of yourself.

ALLMERS: Too sure?

RITA: No. You shouldn't take things for granted. Don't be so sure you *have* me!

ALLMERS: *(Coming closer.)* What do you mean by that?

RITA: *(With trembling lips.)* Not once have I thought of being unfaithful to you, Alfred! Not for an instant.

ALLMERS: No, Rita, I know that. I know you so well.

RITA: *(With flashing eyes.)* But if you should turn away from me—

ALLMERS: Turn away—! I don't know what you mean.

RITA: You've no idea of all that could be roused in me if—

ALLMERS: If—?

RITA: If at any time I discovered you no longer cared for me—loved me the way you once did.

ALLMERS: But, my dearest Rita, people change through the years. That's bound to happen with our relationship, too. Just as with everyone else.

RITA: Not with me! And I don't want to see any change in you, either. I couldn't endure that. I want to keep you all to myself.

ALLMERS: *(Looking uneasily at her.)* How fearfully jealous your mind is—

RITA: I can't make myself different from what I am. *(Threateningly.)* If you divide yourself between me and anyone else—

ALLMERS: Then what—?

RITA: I will have my revenge on you, Alfred.

ALLMERS: In what way revenge?

RITA: I don't know— Oh, yes, I know well enough!

ALLMERS: How?

RITA: I'll go from here and throw myself away—

ALLMERS: Throw yourself away?

RITA: Yes, that's what I'd do. Throw myself into the arms of the first man to come along.

ALLMERS: *(Looking warmly at her, shaking his head.)* You could never do that—my proud, honorable, faithful Rita!

RITA: *(Laying her arms around his neck.)* Ah, you don't know what I could become if you—if you lost interest in me.

ALLMERS: Lost interest in you, Rita? How can you say such a thing?

RITA: *(Half-laughing, releases him.)* I could set my snare for him—our road builder walking in the garden.

ALLMERS: *(Relieved.)* Ah, thank God, you're just joking.

RITA: In no way. Why not him as well as the next man?

ALLMERS: Well, for one thing he seems already somewhat attached.

RITA: So much the better! Because then I'd be taking him from someone else. That's exactly what Eyolf has done to me.

ALLMERS: You say our little Eyolf's done *that?*

RITA: *(Pointing her finger at him.)* There, see! See! The instant you mention Eyolf's name, your voice becomes soft and trembles. *(Threateningly, clenching her fists.)* Oh, I could almost bring myself to wish— Ah!

ALLMERS: *(Looking anxiously at her.)* What could you wish, Rita—?

RITA: *(Violently, moves away from him.)* No, no, no—I won't tell you! Never!

ALLMERS: *(Coming closer to her.)* Rita, I implore you, for your sake and mine, don't be tempted into anything evil.

(BORGHEJM and ASTA come in from the garden. Both are controlling their agitation. They look downcast and somber. ASTA remains outside on the veranda. BORGHEJM comes into the room.)

BORGHEJM: So—Miss Allmers and I have taken our last walk together.

RITA: *(Looks at him in surprise.)* Ah! There won't be a long journey to follow that walk?

BORGHEJM: Yes, for me.

RITA: For you alone?

BORGHEJM: Yes, for me alone.

RITA: *(Glances darkly at ALLMERS.)* You hear that, Alfred? *(Turning to BORGHEJM.)* I wouldn't mind betting it's the evil eye that's played a trick on you here.

BORGHEJM: *(Staring at her.)* The evil eye?

RITA: *(Nods.)* Yes, the evil eye.

BORGHEJM: Do you believe in the evil eye, Mrs. Allmers?

RITA: Yes, now I'm beginning to believe in the evil eye. Mostly a child's evil eye.

ALLMERS: *(In a shocked whisper.)* Rita—how can you—!

RITA: *(Half audibly.)* It's you who are making me vile and evil, Alfred.

(Confused shouts and cries are heard far off in the distance, down by the water.)

BORGHEJM: *(Going to the French windows.)* What's all that noise—?

ASTA: *(In the doorway.)* Look at all those people running out on the pier!

ALLMERS: What can it be? *(Looking out for a moment.)* Those street urchins are up to something again.

BORGHEJM: *(Calling over the railings.)* Hi, you boys down there! What's going on?

(Several voices can be heard indistinctly replying, reaching up to the veranda.)

RITA: What are they saying?

BORGHEJM: They say a child's been drowned.

ALLMERS: A child drowned?

ASTA: *(Uneasily.)* A little boy, they're saying.

ALLMERS: Oh, they can swim, every one of them.

RITA: *(Crying out in fear.)* Where's Eyolf?

ALLMERS: Keep calm. Calm. Eyolf's playing in the garden.

ASTA: No, he's not in the garden.

RITA: *(Raising her arms.)* Oh, if only it isn't *him!*

BORGHEJM: *(Listening, then calling down.)* Whose child did you say?
       *(Indistinct voices are heard. BORGHEJM and ASTA let out stifled cries and
       rush down through the garden)*

ALLMERS: *(In utter dread.)* It isn't Eyolf! It isn't Eyolf, Rita!

RITA: *(On the veranda, listening.)* Hush! Be quiet! Let me hear what they're
       saying! *(With a dreadful shriek she flees back into the room.)*

ALLMERS: *(Following her.)* What did they say?

RITA: *(Sinking down into an armchair to the left.)* They said, the crutch is
       floating!

ALLMERS: *(Almost paralyzed.)* No! No! No!

RITA: *(Hoarsely.)* Eyolf! Eyolf! They *must* save him!

ALLMERS: *(Almost delirious.)* It can't be! It can't be! So precious a life! So
       precious a life!

       (He runs down through the garden)

END OF ACT ONE

ACT TWO

A little narrow valley in the forest on ALLMERS's estate. Tall, ancient trees lean out over the scene. Down the slope in the background a stream foams, losing itself among stones on the edge of the wood. A path winds alongside the stream. To the right stand scattered trees through which the fjord can be seen. In the foreground, the corner of the boathouse is visible, with a boat beached beside it. Beneath the old trees to the left stands a table with a bench and a few chairs, all made of slender birchwood. It is a heavily overcast day with drifting clouds.

ALFRED ALLMERS, dressed as previously, is sitting on the bench, his arms resting on the table. His hat lies in front of him. He is staring, motionlessly and abstractedly out over the water. Soon after, ASTA ALLMERS comes down the path. She is carrying an open umbrella.

ASTA: *(Goes quietly and cautiously to him.)* You shouldn't be sitting down here in this damp weather, Alfred.

(ALLMERS nods slowly without answering.)

ASTA: *(Closing the umbrella.)* I've been looking for you such a long time.

ALLMERS: *(Tonelessly.)* Thanks.

ASTA: *(Pulls up a chair and sits beside him.)* Have you been sitting down here long? The whole time?

ALLMERS: *(Not answering. After a little he speaks.)* No, I can't fathom it. It seems so completely impossible—all this.

ASTA: *(Lays her hand comfortingly on his arm.)* Poor Alfred.

ALLMERS: *(Staring at her.)* Is it all really true, Asta? Or have I gone mad? Or am I just dreaming? Oh, if only it were a dream! Think, how beautiful if I woke up now!

ASTA: And if I were only able to wake you!

ALLMERS: *(Staring across the water.)* How pitiless the fjord looks today. Lying so heavy—and sluggish. Blue-gray—with flecks of gold—reflecting the rain clouds.

ASTA: *(Pleading.)* Alfred, don't sit there staring at the fjord!

ALLMERS: *(Not listening.)* On the surface, yes. But deep down—*there* the undertow's pulling—

ASTA: *(Fearfully.)* For God's sake, don't brood on what's below.

ALLMERS: *(Looking gently at her.)* I expect you think he is lying just out there, don't you? But he isn't, don't believe that. Because you have to remember how strong the current runs here. Right to the sea.

ASTA: *(Throws herself sobbing over the table, her hands covering her face.)* Oh God—oh God!

ALLMERS: *(Dully.)* Which means little Eyolf's gone so far, far away from all of us by now.

ASTA: *(Imploring.)* Oh, Alfred, don't talk like that!

ALLMERS: Well, you can work it out for yourself—you, who are so clever! In twenty-eight, twenty-nine hours— Let me see—! Let me see—!

ASTA: *(Screams, her hand over her ears.)* Alfred—!

ALLMERS: *(His clenched fists pressed hard against the table.)* Well, can you find any meaning in such a thing?

ASTA: *(Looking at him.)* In what?

ALLMERS: In what has happened to me and Rita.

ASTA: The meaning of it?

ALFRED: *(Impatiently.)* Yes, meaning I said. For there must *be* a meaning in it. Life, existence—fate—can't be so totally meaningless.

ASTA: Oh, Alfred, who can speak with complete certainty on these things?

ALLMERS: *(Laughing bitterly.)* No, no, you're probably right about that. Perhaps it's the play of mere chance—everything. It all continues like a wrecked ship, drifting, without a rudder. It really must be like that—at least that's how it seems.

ASTA: *(Quietly.)*. And what if it only seems?

ALLMERS: *(Heatedly.)* Then can *you* make any sense of it for me? Because I can't. *(More gently.)* Here is Eyolf, on the verge of a spiritually awakened life. The bearer of such endless possibilities—the richest possibilities, perhaps. Who would fill my existence with pride and joy. And all that's needed is for a crazy old woman to come along—and reveal a dog in a bag—

ASTA: But we don't know for sure what actually happened.

ALLMERS: Yes, we know. The boys saw her row out over the fjord. They saw Eyolf standing alone at the far end of the pier. Saw him staring after her—and seem to become dizzy. *(Tremblingly.)* And then he fell forward—and was gone.

ASTA: Just the same—

ALLMERS: She dragged him into the depths. Have no doubt about it.

ASTA: But dear—why should she?

ALLMERS: Yes, you see—that's the whole point! Why should she? There's no retribution behind it—nothing to atone for, I mean. Eyolf had never harmed her in any way. Never shouted abuse at her. Or thrown stones at her dog. He'd never set eyes on her or her dog before yesterday. So it can't be retribution. It's baseless, all of it. So completely meaningless, Asta. And yet it served the need of the order of things.

ASTA: Have you talked about this to Rita?

ALLMERS: *(Shaking his head.)* I feel I can talk about it more easily to you. And about everything else, as well.

(ASTA takes her sewing things and a little packet wrapped in paper from her pocket. ALLMERS sits watching her vacantly)

ALLMERS: What's that you have there, Asta?

ASTA: *(Taking his hat.)* Some black crepe.

ALLMERS: What will you do with that?

ASTA: Rita's asked me to. May I?

ALLMERS: Oh, yes; by all means.

(She sews the crepe on his hat.)

ALLMERS: .*(Sits looking at her.)* Where *is* Rita just now?

ASTA: Walking in the garden, I think. Borghejm's with her.

ALLMERS: *(A little surprised.)* Really? Borghejm's out here again today?

ASTA: He arrived with the mid-day train.

ALLMERS: I hadn't expected that.

ASTA: *(Sewing.)* He thought the world of Eyolf.

ALLMERS: Borghejm's a loyal soul, Asta.

ASTA: *(With quiet warmth.)* Yes, he's truly loyal, that's a fact.

ALLMERS: *(Fixing her eyes on her.)* You care for him, don't you.

ASTA: Yes, I do.

ALLMERS: But, just the same, you can't bring yourself to—

ASTA: *(Breaking in.)* Oh, Alfred—dearest, let's not talk about *that!*

ALLMERS: Very well. Only, just tell me why you can't—

ASTA: No, no, please, I beg you! You mustn't ask—ever. It's too distressing for me. There you are, the hat's done.

ALLMERS: Thanks.

ASTA: And now there's the left arm.

ALLMERS: That, too?

ASTA: Yes, it's the custom.

ALLMERS: Very well, just as you wish.

(She moves closer to him and begins to sew.)

ASTA: Keep your arm still. So I won't prick you.

ALLMERS: *(With a half smile.)* This is like old times.

ASTA: Yes, isn't it?

ALLMERS: When you were a little girl, you'd sit just like this mending my clothes.

ASTA: As best I could, anyway.

ALLMERS: The first thing you sewed for me was black crepe, too.

ASTA: Oh?

ALLMERS: On my student cap. When Father died.

ASTA: Did I really? Strange, I don't remember.

ALLMERS: You wouldn't. You were so small at the time.

ASTA: Yes, I was at that time.

ALLMERS: And then, just two years later—when we lost your mother—you sewed a black band on *my* arm, too.

ASTA: I thought it the right thing to do.

ALLMERS: *(Patting her hand.)* Yes, yes, that was just as it should have been, Asta. And then, when we found ourselves alone in the world, we two— Are you done already?

ASTA: Yes. *(Gathers up her sewing things.)* That was a beautiful time for us, all the same, Alfred. Just the two of us.

ALLMERS: Yes, it really was. Despite all the hard work.

ASTA: It was you who worked hard.

ALLMERS: *(Livelier.)* Oh no, you worked hard too, in your own way. *(Smiles.)* My dear—faithful—Eyolf.

ASTA: Oh, now—don't remind me of that foolish business with the name.

ALLMERS: All the same, if you'd been a boy, you'd have been called Eyolf.

ASTA: Yes, *if!* But then, when you became a student— *(Smiling involuntarily.)* Imagine, you being so childish.

ALLMERS: *I* was being childish?

ASTA: Yes, I think so, when I look back on it. Because you were so embarrassed you didn't have a brother. Only a sister.

ALLMERS: No, you were the one. You were embarrassed.

ASTA: Oh, yes, I too a little, maybe. I think I felt somehow sorry for you—

ASTA: Yes, you must have done. So you found those old clothes I wore as a boy—

ASTA: Your nice Sunday clothes, yes. Do you remember the blue blouse and the knee breeches?

ALLMERS: *(His eyes dwelling on her.)* I remember so well you going around wearing them.

ASTA. Yes, but I only did it when we were at home alone.

ALLMERS: How seriously we took ourselves. So self-important. And I would always call you Eyolf.

ASTA: But, Alfred, you've never said anything about this to Rita?

ALLMERS: I believe I did mention it once to her.

ASTA: But Alfred, how could you have done!

ALLMERS: Well, you see, a man tells his wife everything—just about.

ASTA: Yes, I can see that.

ALLMERS: *(As if awakening, clasps his forehead and springs up.)* Ah! That I can sit here and—

ASTA: *(Getting up and looking anxiously at him.)* What's the matter?

ALLMERS: He'd slipped away from me. Left me completely

ASTA: Eyolf!

ALLMERS: Here I sat, living in memories. And he wasn't there.

ASTA: Oh, yes, Alfred—little Eyolf was behind everything we said.

ALLMERS: He was *not*! He slipped out of my mind. Out of my thoughts. He wasn't there for an instant while we talking together. I'd completely forgotten him the whole time.

ASTA: But you must find some rest from your grief.

ALLMERS: No, no, no—that's just what I musn't do. I don't have the right to—nor the heart for it, either. *(Walks in agitation to the right.)* I should be only where he lies drifting—out there, deep, deep down.

ASTA: *(Goes after him, holding him fast.)* Alfred—Alfred! Don't go to the fjord!

ALLMERS: I *must* go out to him! Let go of me, Asta! I'm taking the boat.

ASTA: *(Crying out in terror.)* Not near the fjord, I tell you!

ALLMERS: *(Complying.)* No, no, I won't. Just leave me alone.

ASTA *(Leading him to the table.)* You must find some rest from these thoughts, Alfred. Come and sit here.

ALFRED: *(About to sit down on the bench.)* Yes, yes, just as you wish.

ASTA: No, you're not to sit there.

ALLMERS: Yes, let me.

ASTA: No, not there. Because you'll only be looking out over the— *(Forces him down on a chair with its back to the right.)* There, that's better. *(She sits on the bench.)* So, let's talk again for a bit.

ALLMERS: *(Sighing audibly.)* It was good finding relief from the pain and sorrow for a moment.

ASTA: You have to, Alfred.

ALLMERS: But don't you think me crass and unfeeling—being *able* to do so?

ASTA: Oh no! Because it's simply impossible to keep circling for ever round the same thought.

ALLMERS: For me it's impossible. Before you came down to me I was sitting here agonizing over this unceasing, gnawing grief—

ASTA: Yes?

ALLMERS: And would you believe it, Asta—? Hm—

ASTA: Well?

ALLMERS: In the middle of all this agony I found myself wondering what we'd be having for dinner today.

ASTA: *(Soothingly.)* Well, as long as there was some relief in that—

ALLMERS: Yes, imagine—I believe it did offer some relief. *(Reaching his hand to her across the table.)* How good it is that I have you, Asta. It brings me such happiness—happiness even in sorrow.

ASTA: *(Looking seriously at him.)* You should feel happy above all that you have Rita.

ALLMERS: Yes, that goes without saying. But Rita and I aren't family. It isn't like having a sister.

ASTA: *(Tensely.)* Is that what you feel, Alfred?

ALLMERS: Yes, *our* family is somehow set apart. *(Half jokingly.)* Our names have always begun with vowels. You remember how we used to speak about it before? And all our relatives—they're all equally poor. And we all have the same kind of eyes.

ASTA: You think I also—

ALLMERS: No, you take after your mother, completely. You're not at all like the rest of us. Not like Father, even. But, just the same—

ASTA: Just the same—?

ALLMERS: Yes, I feel that just the same our life together has somehow shaped us two in each other's image. In our minds, I mean.

ASTA: *(Warmly, moved.)* No, never say that, Alfred. It's I alone who've been shaped by you. You, to whom I owe everything—everything of value in this world.

ALLMERS: *(Shaking his head.)* You owe me nothing, Asta. On the contrary—

ASTA: I owe everything to you. You must realize that, yourself. No sacrifice has been too great—

ALLMERS: *(Breaking in.)* Oh, honestly—sacrifice! You musn't talk like that. I've simply loved you, Asta—ever since you were a little girl. *(After a short pause.)* And I always felt there were so many wrongs I had to make up for.

ASTA: Wrongs! *You?*

ALLMERS: Not so much on my part. But—

ASTA: *(Tensely.)* But—?

ALLMERS: On Father's.

ASTA: *(Half rising from the bench.)* On Father's! *(Sits again.)* What do you mean by that, Alfred?

ALLMERS: Father was never very kind to you.

ASTA: *(Impetuously.)* You mustn't say that!

ALLMERS: Yes, because it's true. He didn't love you—not as he should have done.

ASTA: *(Evasively.)* No, maybe not the way he loved you. But that's only understandable.

ALLMERS: *(Continuing.)* And he was often so hard on your mother, too. At least during their last years.

ASTA: *(Softly.)* Mother was so very much younger than him, don't forget.

ALLMERS: You think they didn't get along together?

ASTA: Maybe they didn't.

ALLMERS: Well, but all the same—Father, who was otherwise so kind and warm-hearted—so friendly toward everyone—

ASTA: *(Quietly.)* Mother wasn't exactly all she should have been.

ALLMERS: Your mother wasn't?

ASTA: Perhaps not always.

ALLMERS: You mean, to Father?

ASTA: Yes.

ALLMERS: I never noticed anything of the sort.

ASTA: *(Rises, struggling against an impulse to cry.)* Oh, Alfred, dear—let them rest—those who are gone. *(She walks over to the right.)*

ALLMERS: *(Standing up.)* Yes, let them rest. *(Wringing his hands.)* But they—who've gone—they won't let us rest, Asta. Not day or night.

ASTA: *(Regarding him warmly.)* But time will make everything bearable, Alfred.

ALLMERS: *(Looking helplessly at her.)* Yes, you do believe that too, don't you? But how I'm going to get through these first, terrible days— *(Hoarsely.)* I just can't imagine.

ASTA: *(Pleading, putting her hands on his shoulders.)* Go up to Rita. Please, I'm begging you—

ALLMERS: *(Violently, drawing back.)* No, no, no—don't even suggest it. I can't—you understand! *(More calmly.)* Just let me stay here with you.

ASTA. All right, I won't leave you.

ALLMERS: *(Grasping her hands and holding them fast.)* Thanks for that! *(Looking out for a while over the fjord.)* Where's my little Eyolf now? *(Smiling sadly at her.)* Can you tell me *that*—you, my big, wise Eyolf. *(Shaking his head.)* No one in the whole world can tell me that. All I know is the one, horrible certainty—that I no longer have him.

ASTA: *(Looking up to the left and withdrawing her hand.)* Here they come. *(RITA and BORGHEJM are walking down the path through the woods, she leading, he following. She wears a dark dress with a black veil over her head. She carries an umbrella under her arm)*

ALLMERS: *(Going to meet her.)* How are you, Rita.

RITA: *(Walking past him.)* Oh, don't ask.

ALLMERS: What do you want, here?

RITA: Only to look for you. What have you been doing?

ALLMERS: Nothing. Asta came down to be with me.

RITA: Yes, but before Asta came. You've been away from me all morning.

ALLMERS: I've been sitting here, looking out over the water.

RITA: Ugh—how can you!

ALLMERS: *(Impatiently.)* I prefer being alone right now.

RITA: *(Walking restlessly about.)* And to sit here so still. Riveted to the same spot.

ALLMERS: There's no earthly reason for me to go anywhere.

RITA: *I* can't stay in any one place. Least of all here—with the fjord right at one's feet.

ALLMERS: It's just because the fjord's so close.

RITA: *(To BORGHEJM.)* Don't you think he should go up and join the rest of us?

BORGHEJM: *(To ALLMERS.)* I believe it *would* be better for you.

ALLMERS: No, no—let me stay where I am.

RITA: Then I'll stay here with you, Alfred.

ALLMERS: Very well then, stay. You stay too, Asta.

ASTA: *(Whispering to BORGHEJM.)* Let's leave them alone together.

BORGHEJM: *(With an understanding look.)* Miss Asta, shall we walk a little—along the shore? For the very last time?

ASTA: *(Taking her umbrella.)* Yes, come. Let's walk awhile.

(ASTA and BORGHEJM go out together behind the boathouse. ALLMERS wanders about for a little, then sits on a stone under the trees, downstage left. RITA approaches, standing in front of him, her clasped hands hanging down in front of her.)

RITA: Can you take in the idea, Alfred—that we've lost Eyolf?

ALLMERS: *(Looking downwards, despondently.)* We must bring ourselves to take it in.

RITA: I can't. I can't. And I'll carry that dreadful image with me as long as I live.

ALLMERS: *(Looking up.)* What image? What have you seen?

RITA: I didn't see it myself. Just heard them describing it. Oh—!

ALLMERS: Tell me about it at once.

RITA: I took Borghejm with me down to the pier—

ALLMERS: Why did you do that?

RITA: To question the boys about how it happened.

ALLMERS: We know how.

RITA: We got to know more.

ALLMERS: Well!

RITA: It isn't true that he was pulled away all at once.

ALLMERS: They're saying that *now*.

RITA: They say they saw him lying down there, on the bottom. Deep down in the clear water.

ALLMERS: *(His teeth clenched.)* And they didn't save him!

RITA: They probably couldn't.

ALLMERS: They could swim—all of them. Did they say how he was lying when they saw him?

RITA: Yes. They say he lay on his back with wide, open eyes.

ALLMERS: Open eyes? But completely still?

RITA: Yes, completely still. And then something came and dragged him away. They called it the undertow.

ALLMERS: *(Nodding slowly.)* And *that* was the last they saw of him.

ASTA: *(Tear choked.)* Yes.

ALLMERS: *(In a low voice.)* And never—never will anyone see him again.

RITA: *(Wailing.)* Day and night—there he'll be, facing me, just as he was, lying down there.

ALLMERS: With wide open eyes.

RITA: *(Shuddering.)* Yes, with wide open eyes. I see them! I see them now!

ALLMERS: *(Rises slowly and looks at her, quietly and menacingly.)* Were they evil, those eyes, Rita?

RITA: *(Turning pale.)* Evil—?

ALLMERS: *(Closing in on her.)* Were they evil eyes staring upward? From the depths?

RITA: *(Shrinking back.)* Alfred—!

ALLMERS: *(Following her.)* Answer me! Were they a child's evil eyes?

RITA: *(Screaming.)* Alfred! Alfred!

ALLMERS: Now its come about—just what you wished for, Rita.

RITA: *I?* What did I wish?

ALLMERS: That Eyolf wasn't here.

RITA: Never in the world did I wish that! That Eyolf wouldn't stand between us—*that's* what I wished.

ALLMERS: Well then, from now on, he won't any more.

RITA: *(Softly, gazing ahead.)* Maybe, from now on, more than ever. *(Shudders.)* Oh, that dreadful sight.

ALLMERS: *(Nodding.)* The child's evil eyes, yes.

RITA: *(Fearfully, drawing back.)* Keep away from me, Alfred. You frighten me. I've never seen you like this before.

ALLMERS: *(Looking at her, hard and cold.)* Grief makes one cruel and ugly.

RITA: *(Frightened, but still defiant.)* I feel that too, I too.

(ALLMERS walks over to the right and looks over the fjord. RITA sits by the table. Short pause.)

ALLMERS: *(Turning his head toward her.)* You've never really and truly loved him. Never!

RITA: *(Cold and controlled.)* Eyolf would never really and truly give himself to me.

ALLMERS: Because you never wanted him to.

RITA: Oh yes, I wanted it very much. But someone stood in the way. Right from the start.

ALLMERS: *(Turning completely.)* You mean *I* stood in the way.

RITA: Oh no. Not at the start.

ALLMERS: *(Coming closer.)* Who, then?

RITA: His aunt.

ALLMERS: Asta?

RITA: Yes. Asta stood barring my way.

ALLMERS: You mean that, Rita?

RITA: Yes, Asta. She'd taken him up as her own—right from when it happened—that unfortunate fall.

ALLMERS: If that's what she did, she did it from love.

RITA: *(Violently.)* Yes, exactly! And I can't stand sharing with anyone else. Not where love's concerned.

ALLMERS: We should have shared him together. In love.

RITA: *(Regarding him scornfully.)* We? At bottom you've never loved him, either.

ALLMERS: *(Staring astonished at her.)* I've never—

RITA: No, you haven't. From the beginning you were completely taken up with your book—on responsibility.

ALLMERS: *(Firmly.)* Yes, I was. But then it was the book, precisely, that I sacrificed for Eyolf's sake.

RITA: Not out of love for him.

ALLMERS: Then why, do you believe?

RITA: Because you went about here, eaten up with self-distrust. Because you began to doubt whether you had any great calling in the world to live for.

ALLMERS: *(Searchingly.)* You saw something like that in me?

RITA: Oh, yes. Little by little. So you felt a need for something else, something to fill your life. I suppose I just wasn't enough any longer.

ALLMERS: That's the law of change, Rita.

RITA: And therefore you wanted to make a child prodigy of poor little Eyolf.

ALLMERS: That isn't what I wanted. I wanted him to achieve happiness. That's all I wanted.

RITA: But not out of love for him. Look into yourself. *(Warily.)* And examine everything in you lying buried—and hidden away.

ALLMERS: *(Evading her eyes.)* There's something you want to avoid.

RITA: So do you.

ALLMERS: *(Looking thoughtfully at her.)* If what you're thinking is true, then our child never really belonged to us.

RITA: No. Not with wholehearted love.

ALLMERS: Yet just the same we go on grieving so bitterly for him.

RITA: *(Caustically.)* Yes, it's strange to think, isn't it? To go on grieving like this for a little boy who was a stranger to us.

ALLMERS: *(Crying out.)* Oh, don't call him a stranger!

RITA: *(Shaking her head.)* We never won the boy's love. Neither you nor I.

ALLMERS: *(Wringing his hands.)* And now it's too late! Too late!

RITA: And so totally desolating—all of it.

ALLMERS: *(Suddenly flaring.)* It's *you* who are guilty!

RITA: *(Rises.)* I!

ALLMERS: Yes, *you.* It's *your* fault he became—what he became. It's *your* fault he couldn't save himself in the water.

RITA: *(Warding him off.)* Alfred—you're not putting this on *me!*

ALLMERS: *(More and more beside himself.)* Yes, yes, I am! You're the one who left the helpless baby on the table to look after himself.

RITA: He was lying so comfortably among the pillows. Sleeping so soundly. And you'd promised to look after him.

ALLMERS: Yes, so I had. *(His voice dropping.)* But then you came—you—and lured me in to you.

RITA: *(Regarding him defiantly.)* Say rather you forgot the child and everything else.

ALLMERS: *(With suppressed rage.)* Yes, you're right. *(More quietly.)* I forgot the child. In your arms.

RITA: *(Shaken.)* Alfred! Alfred—that is vile of you!

ALLMERS: *(Quietly, clenching his fists.)* In that hour you condemned little Eyolf to death.

RITA: *(Wildly.)* You as well! You as well—if that's the case.

ALLMERS: All right, if you want. Hold me accountable, too. We're both guilty. And so there *was* retribution in Eyolf's death, after all.

RITA: Retribution?

ALLMERS: *(More controlled.)* Yes. A judgment over you and me. Now we've got what we deserved. Our secret, cowardly remorse frightened us away from him while he lived. We couldn't bear to face it—that thing he had to drag around—

RITA: *(Softly.)* The crutch.

ALLMERS: Yes, exactly. And what we now call our pain and sorrow, that's just the gnawing of conscience, Rita. No more than that.

RITA: *(Staring helplessly at him.)* I believe this can lead only to despair—to madness even, for both of us. Because we can never, never set this right again.

ALLMERS:*(His mood calmer.)* I dreamed of Eyolf last night. I thought I saw him coming up from the pier. He could run, just like other boys. It was as if nothing had happened to him. Nothing at all. The paralyzing truth was nothing more than a dream. Oh, how I thanked and blessed— *(Stops short.)* Hm—

RITA: *(Looking at him.)* Whom?

ALLMERS: *(Evasively.)* Whom—?

RITA: Yes. Whom did you thank and bless?

ALLMERS: *(Deprecating.)* I was only dreaming, I said.

RITA: One you don't believe in yourself .

ALLMERS: The feeling overwhelmed me just the same. I was asleep, I tell you.

RITA: *(Reproachfully.)* You shouldn't have brought me to doubt my faith, Alfred.

ALLMERS: Would it have been right of me letting you live your life in empty delusion?

RITA: It would have been better for me. Because then I'd have had something to find comfort in. Now I've nowhere to turn.

ALLMERS: *(Looking closely at her.)* And if you could choose now. If you could follow Eyolf to there—where he is now—?

RITA: Yes, yes, what then?

ALLMERS: And you had full assurance that you would find him again— know him—understand him—?

RITA: Yes, yes, what then?

ALLMERS: Would you, willingly, leap the abyss over to him—of your own free will leave everything here behind? Renounce all this earthly life? Would you, Rita?

RITA: Now? Right away?

ALLMERS: Yes, now, today. This very hour. Answer me. Would you?

RITA: *(Hesitantly.)* Oh, I don't know, Alfred. No, I think I'd want to stay here with you awhile.

ALLMERS: For my sake?

RITA: Yes, only for your sake.

ALLMERS: But then, afterwards? Would you? Tell me.

RITA: Oh, how can I say? No, I just *couldn't* leave you. Never! Never!

ALLMERS: But what if now I went over to Eyolf? And you were completely certain that you would meet both him and me there. Would you then come over to us?

RITA: I'd want to so much. So gladly! So gladly! But—

ALLMERS Well?

RITA: *(Moaning softly.)* I couldn't do it—I feel sure I couldn't. No, no, I just couldn't do it. Not for all the promise of heaven.

ALLMERS: Neither could I.

RITA: No, that isn't true, Alfred. You couldn't do it either!

ALLMERS: No. Because we, the living, belong here—with life on earth. This is our home.

RITA: Yes, here is the only happiness we can understand.

ALLMERS: *(Darkly.)* Oh, happiness—happiness—

RITA: You mean that happiness—that we'll never find it again. *(Looks inquiringly at him.)* But what if—? *(Violently.)* No, no, I daren't say it! Daren't even think it!

ALLMERS: Yes, say it. Just say it, Rita.

RITA: *(Hesitantly.)* Couldn't we try to—? Shouldn't it be possible for us—to forget him?

ALLMERS: Forget Eyolf.

RITA: Forget the remorse, the nagging guilt.

ALLMERS: You could wish that?

RITA: Yes, if it were possible. *(In an outburst.)* Because what we're going through here—I can't bear it any longer. Oh, can't we find some way to help us forget!

ALLMERS: *(Shaking his head.)* What could that be?

RITA: Couldn't we try travelling—far away from here?

ALLMERS: Leave home? You, who can't bear to be anywhere but here?

RITA: Well, we could invite people here. Keep open house. Throw ourselves into something to deaden and numb the pain.

ALLMERS: That's not a life I could live. No, I'd rather try taking up my work again.

RITA: *(Acidly.)* Your work? Which you built like a wall between us?

ALLMERS: *(Slowly, looking coldly at her.)* There'll always be a wall between us from now on.

RITA: Why must there—

ALLMERS: Who knows if the huge, open eyes of a child won't be staring at us day and night.

RITA: *(Softly, shuddering.)* Alfred, that is a dreadful thought.

ALLMERS: Our love has been like a consuming fire. Now it must die out.

RITA: *(Going to him.)* Die out!

ALLMERS: *(Harshly.)* It died out already—in *one* of us.

RITA: *(As if turned to stone.)* You dare say that to me!

ALLMERS: *(More gently.)* It's dead, Rita. But in what I feel for you now, in the shared guilt and remorse, I glimpse something like a rebirth.

RITA: *(Violently.)* I'm not interested in any rebirth!

ALLMERS: Rita!

RITA: I'm a warm-blooded human being. I can't go around as if half-asleep—with fish blood in my veins. *(Wringing her hands.)* And then to be locked up for a lifetime—in a prison of resentment and remorse. Locked up with one who's no longer mine, mine, mine!

ALLMERS: It had to end some time, Rita.

RITA: Had to end like *this!* What began for us in such mutual love!

ALLMERS: My first feelings for you weren't love.

RITA: What did you feel for me at first?

ALLMERS: Terror.

RITA: I can understand that. But then how did I manage to win you, in spite of that?

ALLMERS: *(Quietly.)* You were so overwhelmingly beautiful, Rita.

RITA: *(Looks probingly at him.)* And that was all. Answer me, Alfred! Was it only that?

ALLMERS: *(With a struggle.)* No, there was something else.

RITA: *(Crying out.)* I can guess what it was. It was my "gold, and my green forests" as you put it. Wasn't that it, Alfred?

ALLMERS: Yes.

RITA: *(Looking at him in deep reproach.)* How could you? How could you?

ALLMERS: I had Asta to think of.

RITA: *(Vehemently.)* Asta, yes! *(Bitterly.)* So, at bottom, it was Asta who brought us together.

ALLMERS: She knew nothing. She has no inkling of it even now.

RITA: *(Dismissively.)* It was Asta, just the same! *(Smiling, with a scornful sidelong glance.)* Or, rather, no—it was little Eyolf. Little Eyolf, yes?

ALLMERS: Eyolf—?

RITA: Yes. Didn't you once call her Eyolf? I seem to remember you telling me that once—in a secret moment. *(Comes closer.)* Do you remember it, Alfred—that overwhelmingly beautiful hour?

ALLMERS: *(Recoiling, as if in dread.)* I don't remember anything! I won't remember!

RITA: *(Pursuing him.)* It was during that hour—when your other little Eyolf became a cripple.

ALLMERS: *(Heavily, supporting himself against the table.)* Retribution.

RITA: *(Threateningly.)* Yes, retribution.

(ASTA and BORGHEJM re-enter by the boathouse. She is carrying water lilies in one hand.)

RITA: *(Controlled.)* Well, Asta. Have you and Mr. Borghejm said all you had to say to each other?

ASTA: Oh, yes—more or less. *(She sets down her umbrella and places the flowers on a chair.)*

BORGHEJM: Miss Allmers has been very quiet during our walk.

RITA: No, has she? Well, Alfred and I have said enough to each other to last—

ASTA: *(Looking tensely at them.)* What has happened—?

RITA: —the rest of our lives, I imagine. *(Breaking off.)* Come, let's go up to the house, the four of us. We're going to need company around us from now on. Alfred and I can't cope with this alone.

ALLMERS: Yes, go on ahead, you two. But first I want a word with you, Asta.

RITA: *(Looking at him.)* Oh, yes! Well then, you come with me, Mr. Borghejm.

(RITA and BORGHEJM go up the path through the woods.)

ASTA: *(Anxiously.)* Alfred, what's going on?

ALLMERS: *(Darkly.)* It's just that I can't stay on here any longer.

RITA: Here! With Rita, you mean?

ALLMERS: Yes. Rita and I cannot go on living together.

ASTA: *(Shaking his arm.)* Alfred—you musn't say such a terrible thing.

ALLMERS: It's true, what I'm saying. We're making each other ugly and cruel.

ASTA: *(Painfully moved.)* I've never, never even suspected such a thing.

ALLMERS: I never realized it until today.

ASTA: And so you want to—well, what do you actually want, Alfred?

ALLMERS: To get away from here completely. Far away from all of it.

ASTA: And be totally alone in the world?

ALLMERS: *(Nodding.)* Yes, just like before.

ASTA: But you're not made to stand alone.

ALLMERS: I managed to once, at any rate.

ASTA Once, yes. But that time you had me with you.

ALLMERS: *(Tries to take her hand)* Yes. And it's you, Asta, I want to come home to again.

ASTA: *(Avoiding him.)* To me! No, no, Alfred! That's absolutely impossible.

ALLMERS: *(Looking somberly at her.)* So Borghejm stands between us after all.

ASTA: *(Forcefully.)* No, no, he doesn't. You're wrong about that!

ALLMERS: Good. So I'll come to you—my dear, dear sister. I must come back to you, back home to be cleansed and raised up from living with—

ASTA: *(Shocked.)* Alfred—this is sinning against Rita!

ALLMERS: I've already sinned against her—but not in this. Only remember, Asta—what it used to be, the life we once shared. Wasn't it like one high holy time from beginning to end?

ASTA: Yes, it was. But we can never live that past again.

ALLMERS: *(Bitterly.)* Meaning marriage has spoiled me for such a life?

ASTA: *(Calmly.)* No, I don't mean that.

ALLMERS: Well then, we'll both live our former life again.

ASTA: *(Firmly.)* We *can't,* Alfred.

ALLMERS: Yes, we can. Because a love between brother and sister—

ASTA: *(Tensely.)* Yes, what?

ALLMERS: Is the only relationship that isn't subject to the law of change.

ASTA: *(Softly, trembling.)* But what if that relationship isn't—

ALLMERS: Isn't?

ASTA: Isn't *our* relationship?

ALLMERS: *(Staring at her, amazed.)* Not ours? Asta, dear, what do you mean?

ASTA: It's best I tell you straight out, Alfred.

ALLMERS: Yes, yes, just tell me.

ASTA: Those letters from Mother. Those in the portfolio—

ALLMERS: Yes, well?

ASTA: You must take them and read them—when I've gone.

ALLMERS: Why should I do that?

ASTA: *(Struggling with herself.)* Because then you'll see that—

ALLMERS: Well!

ASTA: That I've no right to bear your father's name.

ALLMERS: *(Staggering.)* Asta! What's this you're saying!

ASTA: Read the letters. Then you'll see. And understand. And maybe find forgiveness—for what Mother did.

ALLMERS: *(His hand to his forehead.)* I can hardly grasp what you're saying! Can't conceive—Then, Asta, you're not my—

ASTA: You are not my brother, Alfred.

ALLMERS: *(Hurriedly, half defiantly, looking at her.)* Well, but how does this affect anything in our relationship. Basically, nothing at all.

ASTA: *(Shaking her head.)* It affects everything. Our relationship isn't that of brother and sister.

ALLMERS: No, but it's just as sacred for all that. It will always be sacred.

ASTA: Don't forget—it's now subject to the law of change—as you said just now.

ALLMERS: *(Looking inquiringly at her.)* Do you mean by that—

ASTA: *(Quietly, with warmth.)* Don't say anything more—my dear, dear Alfred. *(Takes the flowers from the chair.)* Do you see these water lilies?

ALLMERS: *(Nodding slowly)* They're the kind that shoot up—from the depths, far down below.

ASTA: I gathered them from the lake. Where it flows out into the fjord. *(Holding them out.)* Will you take them, Alfred?

ALLMERS: *(Taking them.)* Thank you.

ASTA: *(Her eyes filling with tears.)* They're a last greeting to you—from little Eyolf.

ALLMERS: *(Looking at her)* From Eyolf out there? Or from you?

ASTA: *(Softly.)* From us both. *(Taking her umbrella.)* Come. Let's go up to Rita. *(She goes up the path through the woods.)*

ALLMERS: *(Taking his hat from the table, whispering sadly.)* Asta. Eyolf. Little Eyolf—! *(He follows her up the path.)*

END OF ACT TWO

ACT THREE

A shrub-covered height in the ALLMERS's garden. In the background, a steep cliff, with a railing running across it, and a flight of steps descending on the left side. A broad view over the fjord, that lies far below. A flagstaff with lines but no flag stands close by the railing. In the foreground to the right is a summer house covered in creepers and wild vine. A bench stands outside it. It is a late summer evening with a clear sky and gathering dusk.

ASTA is seated on the bench, her hands in her lap. She is wearing outdoor clothes and a hat. Her parasol is by her side and a small travelling bag is on a strap over her shoulder.

BORGHEJM climbs up from the background, left. He also carries a travelling bag over his shoulder. He carries a rolled-up flag over his arm.

BORGHEJM: *(Catches sight of ASTA.)* Ah, so this is where you took yourself.

ASTA: I'm looking over the fjord for the last time.

BORGHEJM: So it's a good thing I came looking up here, too.

ASTA: Have you been looking for me?

BORGHEJM: Yes, I have. I wanted very much to say goodbye, for now. Not for the last time, I hope.

ASTA: *(Smiles faintly.)* You're very tenacious, aren't you?

BORGHEJM: A road builder needs to be.

ASTA: Did you see anything of Alfred? Or Rita?

BORGHEJM Yes, I saw them both.

ASTA: Together?

BORGHEJM: No. They were apart.

ASTA: What will you do with that flag?

BORGHEJM: Mrs. Allmers asked me to come and raise it.

ASTA: Raise it—now?

BORGHEJM: To half-mast. It will hang there day and night, she said.

ASTA: *(Sighing.)* Poor Rita. And poor Alfred.

BORGHEJM: *(Involved with the flag.)* Can you have the heart to leave them? I ask, because I see you're dressed for travelling.

ASTA: *(In a low voice.)* I *have* to leave.

BORGHEJM: Well, if you *must* then—

ASTA: And *you're* going tonight, too.

BORGHEJM: Yes, I have to, as well. I'm taking the train. You also?

ASTA: No. I'm going by the steamer.

BORGHEJM: *(With a glance at her.)* Two separate ways, then?

ASTA: Yes.

(She sits watching him while he raises the flag to half-mast. When he is finished he goes over to her.)

BORGHEJM: Miss Asta, you can't imagine how I've grieved over little Eyolf.

ASTA: *(Looking up at him.)* Yes, I know how you have.

BORGHEJM: And it feels so painful. Because basically, it's not in my nature to grieve.

ASTA: *(Her eyes raised to the flag.)* But in time it will pass away, altogether. All the sorrows.

BORGHEJM: All? Do you believe that?

ASTA: Just like summer showers. When you're far away from here, then—

BORGHEJM: It will have to be very far away, in that case.

ASTA: And then you have that huge new road project.

BORGHEJM: But no one to help me with it.

ASTA: Oh, you certainly will have.

BORGHEJM: *(Shaking his head.)* No one. No one to share the joy of it. For it's sharing the joy that matters most.

ASTA: Not the challenge and difficulty?

BORGHEJM: Huh—you can always overcome that kind of thing alone.

ASTA: But the joy—that has to be shared with someone, you mean?

BORGHEJM: Yes, for how else is there joy in the achievement?

ASTA: Yes, maybe there's something in that.

BORGHEJM: Of course, naturally you go on for a time being happy inside yourself. But that won't last long. No, joy—it needs two for that.

ASTA: Always just two? Never more than two? Not many?

BORGHEJM: Well, you see—that's a different situation. Miss Allmers, can you really not bring yourself to share happiness and joy—and the challenge and difficulty with one—with only one special person?

ASTA: I've tried that—once.

BORGHEJM: You *have?*

ASTA: Yes, all the time my brother—that Alfred and I lived together.

BORGHEJM: Yes, with your brother, true. That's something quite different. I'd say that's rather more like peace than like joy.

ASTA: It was beautiful, all the same.

BORGHEJM: There, see—already, you felt even just *that* was beautiful. But imagine—if he'd not been your brother!

ASTA: *(Wants to get up, but remains sitting.)* Then we'd never have lived together. Because I was a child at the time. And he not much more.

BORGHEJM: *(Shortly after.)* Was it so beautiful, that time?

ASTA: Oh yes, believe me, it was.

BORGHEJM: It was a time of true joy and happiness?

ASTA: Oh, so much so. Unbelievably so.

BORGHEJM: Tell me a little about it, Miss Asta.

ASTA: They were only little things, essentially.

BORGHEJM: Such as—? Well?

ASTA: Such as the time Alfred passed his exams—and was ranked so high. And when he advanced little by little from one school post to another. Or when he was writing his thesis and would read it out to me. And then afterwards got it published in a journal.

BORGHEJM: Yes, I can see how that must have been a beautiful, peaceful life. Brother and sister, sharing their joys. *(Shaking his head.)* It's beyond me how your brother could let you go, Asta!

ASTA: *(Repressing a movement.)* Alfred got married.

BORGHEJM: Wasn't that hard on you?

ASTA: Yes, in the beginning. I felt I'd completely lost him at the same time.

BORGHEJM: Well, fortunately you hadn't.

ASTA: No.

BORGHEJM: But all the same, how could he? Get married, I mean. When he could have had you all to himself!

ASTA: *(Looking ahead of her.)* He was acting under the law of change, I imagine.

BORGHEJM: Law of change?

ASTA: That's what Alfred calls it.

BORGHEJM: Huh—what a stupid law that must be! I don't believe in it for a minute.

ASTA: *(Getting up.)* In time you might come to believe in it.

BORGHEIM: Never in this world! *(Earnestly.)* But listen to me, Miss Asta! Be reasonable—for *once* at least. About this situation, I mean—

ASTA: *(Breaking in.)* Oh no, no—don't let's start on *that* again!

BORGHEJM: *(Continuing, as before.)* Yes, Asta—I can't possibly just let you slip away so easily. Now your brother has everything the way he could possibly want it. He's living his life contentedly without you. He doesn't need you at all. And then this happens—this that in one day changes your whole position out here—

ASTA: *(Starts.)* What do you mean?

BORGHEJM: Losing the child. What else?

ASTA: *(Recovering.)* Losing little Eyolf, yes.

BORGHEJM: So what more is there for you, actually, to do here? You've no longer got that poor little boy to take care of. No duties—no responsibilities in this place at all—

ASTA: Oh, please, Mr. Borghejm, don't make it so hard for me!

BORGHEJM: I'd have to be mad if I didn't try my utmost. One of these days

I'll be leaving town. I might not get to meet you before that. Maybe not see you for a long, long time. And who knows what might happen in the meantime?

ASTA: *(Smiling gravely.)* Are you afraid of the law of change, after all?

BORGHEJM: No, not in the least. *(Laughs bitterly.)* And there's really nothing here to be changed, anyway. Not where you're concerned, I mean. Because you don't care all that much for me, I can see.

ASTA: You know very well I do.

BORGHEJM: Yes, but nowhere near enough. Not the way I want you to. *(More vehemently.)* Good lord, Asta—Miss Asta—you're being as wrong about this as one could imagine! Just beyond today and tomorrow our whole life lies waiting for us. And we just let it lie there! Won't we come to regret *that* Asta?

ASTA *(Quietly.)* I don't know. But we must let all those bright prospects lie there, just the same.

BORGHEJM: *(Looking at her restrainedly.)* Then I must build my roads alone?

ASTA *(Warmly.)* Oh, if only I could be with you doing that. Help you with the challenge. Share the joy of it with you—

BORGHEJM: Would you really? If you could?

ASTA: Yes, I would.

BORGHEJM: But you can't?

ASTA: *(Looking down before her.)* Would you be content with only *half* of me?

BORGHEJM: No. I want you entirely and undivided.

ASTA: *(Looking at him, saying quietly.)* Then I can't.

BORGHEJM: Then goodbye, Miss Asta.

(He is about to go. ALLMERS climbs up from the back, left. BORGHEJM stops.)

ALLMERS: *(Reaches the top of the steps, pointing and saying quietly)* Is Rita there, in the summer house?.

BORGHEJM: No. No one's here but Miss Asta.

(ALLMERS approaches.)

ASTA: *(Going toward him.)* Shall I go down and look for her? Perhaps bring her up here?

ALLMERS *(Stopping her.)* No, no, no—don't bother. *(To BORGHEJM.)* Was it you who raised the flag?

BORGHEJM: Yes. Mrs. Allmers asked me to. That's why I came up here.

ALLMERS: And tonight you're leaving?

BORGHEJM: Yes, tonight I really am leaving.

ALLMERS: *(With a glance at ASTA.)* And you've made sure of a good travelling companion, I trust.

BORGHEJM: *(Shaking his head.)* I'm travelling alone.

ALLMERS: *(Astonished.)* Alone!

BORGHEJM: Completely alone.

ALLMERS *(Abstractedly.)* I see.

BORGHEJM: And remaining alone, too.

ALLMERS: There's something dreadful about being alone. The idea sends a chill through me.

ASTA: Oh, but Alfred, you're not alone at all.

ALLMERS: There can be something dreadful about that, too.

ASTA: *(Uneasily.)* Don't say such a thing! Don't think it!

ALLMERS: *(Not hearing her.)* But now you're not going with—? Now nothing's holding you—? Why not stay out here with me—and with Rita?

ASTA: *(Troubled.)* No, I can't do that. I need to go back to town now.

ALLMERS: But only to town, Asta. You hear!

ASTA: Yes.

ALLMERS: And promise me you'll be back here very soon.

ASTA: *(Quickly.)* No, no. I daren't promise that for a while.

ALLMERS: Very well. As you wish. But we'll meet each other in town, then.

ASTA: *(Pleading.)* But, Alfred, you *must* stay home with Rita just now.

ALLMERS: *(Not answering, turning to BORGHEJM.)* Maybe it's best for you to be travelling alone.

BORGHEJM: *(Grudgingly.)* How can you say such a thing!

ALLMERS: Yes, because you never know whom you might happen to meet. On the journey.

ASTA: *(Involuntarily.)* Alfred!

ALLMERS: The right travelling companion. When it's too late. Too late.

ASTA: *(Softly, trembling.)* Alfred! Alfred!

BORGHEJM:*(Looking from one to the other.)* What do you mean? I don't understand—

(RITA climbs up from the back, left)

RITA: *(Wailing.)* Oh, don't keep avoiding me, all of you!

ASTA: *(Going to meet her.)* You said you wanted to be alone—

RITA: I know. But I daren't. It's getting so horribly dark. I feel there are great open eyes staring at me.

ASTA: *(Gently, concerned.)* What if there are, Rita? You shouldn't be frightened of those eyes.

RITA: How you can say that! Not frightened!

ALLMERS: *(Urgently.)* Asta, I beg you—stay here—for all the world stay here—with Rita.

RITA: Yes! And with Alfred, too! Do that! Do that, Asta!

ASTA: *(Struggling.)* Oh, I can't say how much I want to—

RITA: Well, then do it! Because Alfred and I can't go through our pain and grief alone.

ALLMERS: *(Darkly.)* Say, rather through the gnawing of our consciences.

RITA: Whatever you call it—we two can't bear it alone. Oh, Asta, I implore you, beg you, stay here and help us! Take Eyolf's place for us—

ASTA: *(Trembles.)* Eyolf's—

RITA: Yes. She must stay with us, yes Alfred?

ALLMERS: If she can and wants to.

RITA: You called her your little Eyolf, once. *(Grasps her hand.)* From now on you shall be *our* Eyolf, Asta! Eyolf, as you once used to be!

ALLMERS: *(Controlling his emotion.)* Stay, and share life with us, Asta. With Rita. With me. Me—your brother.

ASTA: *(Resolved, pulling back her hand)* No. I can't. *(Turns.)* When does the steamer leave, Borgheim.

BORGHEJM: Any moment now.

ASTA: Then I must go on board. Will you come with me?

BORGHEJM: *(Controlling his exultation.)* Will I! Yes, yes, yes.

ASTA: Then let's go.

RITA: *(Slowly.)* Ah, so that's it. Yes, then of course you *can't* stay with us.

ASTA: *(Throwing her arms round RITA's neck.)* Thank you for everything, Rita. *(Goes over and grasps ALLMER's hand.)* Alfred—goodbye! A thousand, thousand goodbyes.

ALLMERS *(Quietly, intently.)* What is this, Asta? It looks like you're running away.

ASTA: *(In quiet anguish.)* Yes, Alfred—I *am* running away.

ALLMERS: Running away—from *me!*

ASTA: *(Whispering.)* From you—and from myself.

ALLMERS: *(Drawing back.)* Ah—!

ASTA *hurries to go down the steps in the background. BORGHEJM, waving his hat, follows her. RITA leans against the entrance to the summer house. ALLMERS, in great inward agitation, goes over to the railing and stands there and stares downward. Pause.*

ALLMERS: *(Turning and saying with forced composure.)* Here comes the steamer. Look, Rita—there!

RITA: I daren't look at it.

ALLMERS: You daren't?

RITA: No. For it has eyes. One red. And one green. Great, glowing eyes.

ALLMERS: You know they are only lanterns.

RITA: From now on they are eyes. For me. Staring and staring out from the darkness. And into the darkness, too.

ALLMERS: Now it's putting in to dock.

RITA: Where is it mooring tonight?

ALLMERS: *(Approaching her.)* At the pier, as usual.

RITA: *(Draws herself up.)* How *can* they moor her there!

ALLMERS: They've no choice.

RITA: But it's *there* that Eyolf— How can those people moor it there?

ALLMERS: Yes, life is merciless, Rita.

RITA: Humans are heartless. They show no consideration. Not to the living, nor to the dead.

ALLMERS: You're right. Life goes its own way, just as if nothing at all had happened.

RITA: *(Staring in front of her.)* Nothing, really, *has* happened. Not to the others. Only to you and me.

ALLMERS: *(His pain reviving.)* Yes, Rita—how pointless it was, your bearing him in pain and anguish. For now he's gone again—with no trace remaining.

RITA: Only the crutch was saved.

ALLMERS: *(Vehemently.)* Be quiet! I won't hear that word!

RITA: *(Sorrowfully.)* Oh, I can't bear to think he's no longer with us.

ALLMERS: *(Cold and bitter.)* You managed to do without him well enough while we had him. You could go most of the day without setting eyes on him.

RITA: That's because I knew I could see him any time I wanted.

ALLMERS: Yes, in that way we wasted the short time we had together with little Eyolf.

RITA: *(Listening fearfully.)* Do you hear, Alfred? It's tolling again!

ALLMERS: That's the bell of the steamer ringing. It's about to leave.

RITA: No, it isn't *that* bell I mean. All day I've been hearing it ringing in my ears. Now it's ringing again!

ALLMERS: *(Going to her.)* You're mistaken, Rita

RITA: No, I hear it so distinctly. It sounds like a funeral bell. Slowly, slowly. And always the same words.

ALLMERS: Words? What words?

RITA: *(Nodding the rhythm.)* "The-crutch-is-float-ing. The-crutch-is-float-ing." I'm sure you must be hearing it, too.

ALLMERS: *(Shaking his head.)* I hear nothing. There's nothing to hear.

RITA: Well, well, say what you like. I can hear it so clearly.

ALLMERS: *(Looking over the railing.)* They're on board now, Rita. Now the ship is making for town.

RITA: How extraordinary you can't hear it! "The-crutch-is-float-ing. The-crutch-is-float-ing. The-crutch—"

ALLMERS: *(Going to her.)* Don't stand there listening to something that doesn't exist. I tell you, Asta and Borghejm are on board. On their way already. Asta's gone.

RITA: *(Looking warily at him.)* So you'll be going away soon, too, Alfred?

ALLMERS: *(Quickly.)* What do you mean by *that?*

RITA: That you'll be following your sister.

ALLMERS: Has Asta said anything?

RITA: No. But you said yourself it was for Asta's sake that—that we two were brought together.

ALLMERS: Yes. But you have bound me to you. Through the life we've shared.

RITA: Though in your mind I'm no longer so overwhelmingly beautiful.

ALLMERS: The law of change might still hold us together, just the same.

RITA: *(Nodding slowly.)* Something is changing in me, now. I feel the pain of it.

ALLMERS: The pain?

RITA: Yes. Because this, too, is some kind of birth.

ALLMERS: That's what it is. Or a resurrection. A passage to a higher life.

RITA: *(Staring disconsolately ahead.)* Yes, with the loss of all life's happiness.

ALLMERS: That loss—it's no less than our victory.

RITA: *(Vehemently.)* Oh—just words! Good Lord, we humans are earthbound, after all.

ALLMERS: We're part kin with the sea and sky also, Rita.

RITA: You, perhaps. Not I.

ALLMERS: Oh, yes. *You* more than you're aware.

RITA: *(Takes a step closer to him.)* Listen, Alfred, couldn't you think of taking up your work again?

ALLMERS: That work you hated so much?

RITA: I'm more moderate, now. I'm willing to share you with the book.

ALLMERS: Why?

RITA: Only to keep you with me here. Close by.

ALLMERS: Oh, I can be of so little help to you, Rita.

RITA: But maybe I can help you.

ALLMERS: To continue my work, you mean?

RITA: No. To live your life.

ALLMERS: *(Shaking his head.)* I don't think I have any life to live for.

RITA: Well, to endure life, then.

ALLMERS: *(Darkly, almost to himself.)* I believe it would be best for us both if we separated.

RITA: *(Looks at him searchingly.)* Where would you go to? To Asta, after all?

ALLMERS: No. Never to Asta.

RITA: Where, then?

ALLMERS: Up into the solitude.

RITA: To the mountains?

ALLMERS: Yes.

RITA: But all this is mere fantasy, Alfred. You couldn't live up there!

ALLMERS: It's where I'm drawn to now, just the same.

RITA: Why? Answer me!

ALLMERS: Sit down. I want to tell you something.

RITA: Something that happened to you, up there?

ALLMERS: Yes.

RITA: Something you kept from Asta and me?

ALLMERS: Yes.

RITA: You're so secretive about everything. You shouldn't be.

ALLMERS: Sit down and I'll tell you about it.

RITA: Yes, yes, let me hear! *(She sits on the bench by the summer house.)*

ALLMERS: I was alone up there. In the middle of the high mountains. I came to an immense, desolate mountain lake. And I had to cross that lake. But I couldn't, because there was neither a boat nor a single human being in sight.

RITA: Well? And then?

ALLMERS: So I set off on my own into a side valley. Because *that* way I thought I would be able to climb over the heights and between the peaks. And then make my way down again to the other side of the lake.

RITA: Ah, and then you surely lost your way.

ALLMERS: Yes, I lost all sense of direction. Because there was no road or path there. And I walked the whole day. And the whole night, too. Until at last I believed I should never get back to the human world.

RITA: Not back to us at home? Ah, I know how much your thoughts must have been with us.

ALLMERS: No, they weren't.

RITA: No?

ALLMERS: No. It was so strange. Both you and Eyolf drifted so far, far away from my thoughts. And Asta, too.

RITA: What were you thinking about?

ALLMERS: I wasn't thinking at all. I dragged my way along the precipices— finding in the nearness of death, a new serenity and peace.

RITA: How can you talk like that about something so dreadful!

ALLMERS: It's how I felt. Completely without fear. It seemed as if death and I walked side by side like two good travelling companions. It all seemed so natural—so reasonable, at the time. In my family, people do not live to be old—

RITA: Don't talk like that, Alfred! You came out of it safe and sound, after all.

ALLMERS: Yes, suddenly I'd come through. On the other side of the lake.

RITA: It must have been a night of terror for you, Alfred. But now it's past, you won't admit it to yourself.

ALLMERS: That night I came to a decision. And so I turned back and came straight home. To Eyolf.

RITA: *(Quietly.)* Too late.

ALLMERS: Yes. And then, when my—companion came and took him—it was *then* there was horror in him. And in everything. In all of *this*—that we dare not relinquish. So earthbound as we are, you and I, Rita.

RITA: *(With a flash of joy.)* Yes, it's true! You as well! *(Comes closer.)* Oh, let's just live out our lives together as long as we can!

ALLMERS: *(Shrugging his shoulders.)* Live our lives, yes! While having nothing to fill them with. Desolate and empty as they are. Whichever way I look.

RITA: *(Anxiously.)* Oh, sooner or later you will leave me, Alfred! I can feel it! I can see it in you, too! You're going to leave me!

ALLMERS: With my travelling companion, you mean?

RITA: No. I mean something worse. You'll leave me of your own free will. Because you believe it's only here, with me, that you've nothing to live for. Answer me! Isn't that what you're thinking?

ALLMERS *(Looking fixedly at her.)* And what if I was—?
(The clamour of angry, heated voices can be heard rising from far below. ALLMERS goes to the railing.)

RITA: What's happening? *(Cries out.)* Oh, you'll see—they've found him!

ALLMERS: He'll never be found.

RITA: Then what *is* going on?

ALLMERS: *(Coming forward.)* They're just fighting—as usual.

RITA: Down by the shore?

ALLMERS: Yes. All those houses by the shore ought to be got rid of. Now the men are returning home—drunk, of course. Beating their children—you can hear the boys screaming. And the women howling for someone to save them—

RITA: Shouldn't we send someone down to help them?

ALLMERS: *(Hard and angry.)* Help them? Who wouldn't help Eyolf? No, let them perish—as they let Eyolf perish.

RITA: You mustn't talk like that, Alfred! Or think like it!

ALLMERS: I can't think any other way. All those old hovels should be torn down.

RITA: And what would become of all those poor people?

ALLMERS: They'd go somewhere else.

RITA: And the children?

ALLMERS: Can it matter that much where they end up?

RITA: *(Quietly reproachful.)* You're forcing yourself to be callous, Alfred.

ALLMERS: *(Vehemently.)* It's my *right* to be callous, from now on. And my duty.

RITA: Your duty!

ALLMERS: My duty to Eyolf. He mustn't lie unavenged. Yes, that's the way, Rita. Like I say. Think it over. Have the whole area levelled to the ground— when I'm gone.

RITA: *(Looks searchingly at him.)* When you're gone?

ALLMERS: Yes, for then you'll have something to fill your life with. And you'll need that.

RITA: *(Firm, decisive.)* You're right. I *will* need it. But can you guess what I'm going to do—after you're gone.

ALLMERS: No, what's that?

RITA: *(Slowly and firmly.)* As soon as you've left me, I'll go down to the shore and bring all those poor, neglected boys up here to the house. All those rowdy children—

ALLMERS: What will you do with them?

RITA: I want to make them mine.

ALLMERS: *You?*

RITA: Yes. On the day you leave, they'll stay here, all of them—as if they were my own.

ALLMERS: *(Shocked.)* In our little Eyolf's place!

RITA: Yes, in our little Eyolf's place. They'll live in Eyolf's room. They'll read his books. Play with his toys. Take turns sitting on his chair at the table.

ALLMERS: This is the most insane suggestion I've ever heard! I know of no one in the whole world less capable of such a thing than you.

RITA: Then I'll have to teach myself. Train and educate myself.

ALLMERS: If you're completely serious about this—in everything you say— then you must have undergone a great change.

RITA: Yes, that's it, Alfred. You've seen to that. You've created an empty place inside me. And I must try to fill it with something. Something that might resemble love.

ALLMERS: *(Looking thoughtfully at her for a moment.)* In fact, we haven't done much for those poor people down there.

RITA: We've done nothing for them.

ALLMERS: Hardly even given them a thought.

RITA: Not a compassionate thought, anyway.

ALLMERS: We, who had the "gold and the green forests."

RITA: Our hands were closed to them. And our hearts, as well.

ALLMERS: *(Nodding.)* So maybe it's only understandable they wouldn't risk their lives to save little Eyolf.

RITA: *(Quietly.)* If you think about it, Alfred—are you so sure *we'd* have dared risk our own?

ALLMERS: *(Uneasily dismissive.)* We must never doubt *that*, Rita!

RITA: Oh, but we are so earthbound, you and I.

ALLMERS: What do you imagine you'll be doing for all those neglected children?

RITA: To begin with, see if I can bring some gentleness—some finer feelings into their lives.

ALLMERS: If you can do *that*, Rita, then Eyolf wasn't born in vain.

RITA: Nor taken from us in vain, either.

ALLMERS *(Looking closely at her.)* Be clear about one thing, Rita—it isn't love that's moving you to do this.

RITA: No, it isn't love. At least, not yet.

ALLMERS: So, what is it, then?

RITA:*(Somewhat evasively.)* So many times you would talk to Asta about human responsibility—

ALLMERS: About the book you hated.

RITA: I still hate it. But I would sit listening to you talking. And I want to try carrying on from there—in my own way.

ALLMERS: *(Shaking his head.)* It's not for the sake of that unfinished book—

RITA: No, I have another reason.

ALLMERS: What is that?

RITA: *(Quietly, smiling sadly.)* I want to make my peace with those huge, staring eyes.

ALLMERS: *(Moved, glancing at her.)* Maybe I could join you. And help you, Rita?

RITA: Do you want to?

ALLMERS: Yes—if I was only certain I could.

RITA: *(Hesitantly.)* But then, of course, you'd have to stay here.

ALLMERS: *(Softly.)* Let's see if we can't make it work.

RITA: *(Just audible.)* Yes, let's try, Alfred.
(Both are silent. ALLMERS then walks over to the flagstaff and hoists it to the top. RITA stands by the summer house silently watching him)

ALLMERS: *(Crosses over to her.)* There'll be a hard day's work ahead of us, Rita.

RITA: You will see. A Sabbath calm will fall on us now and then.

ALLMERS: *(Quietly, moved.)* Then maybe we'll sense the spirits, visiting.

RITA: *(Whispering.)* Spirits?

ALLMERS: *(As before.)* Yes. Maybe then they'll be around us—those we've lost.

RITA: *(Nodding slowly.)* Our little Eyolf. And your big Eyolf, too.

ALLMERS: *(Staring ahead.)* It could happen that every now and then—on our way through life—we'll catch a glimpse of them.

RITA: Where shall we look, Alfred—?

ALLMERS: *(Fastens his eyes on her.)* Upward.

RITA: *(Nodding.)* Yes, yes—upward.

ALLMERS: Upward—toward the mountain peaks. Toward the stars. And toward that great silence.

RITA: *(Stretching her hand toward him.)* Thanks!

END OF PLAY

NOTE

ACT ONE

[1] Mopsemand. *Mopse* means "pug-faced."

JOHN GABRIEL BORKMAN

⚏ 1896 ⚏

translated with Rick Davis

ORIGINAL PRODUCTION

John Gabriel Borkman was originally produced at the Theater of the First Amendment, Fairfax, Virginia, Sept. 13–Oct. 1, 1995. It was directed by Rick Davis with the following cast, in order of appearance:

Mrs. Gunhild Borkman . . . . Pamela Ritchard Brown
Malene, a maid . . . . Deborah Hazlett
Ella Rentheim . . . . Mary Starnes
Fanny Wilton . . . . Naomi Jacobsen
Erhart Borkman . . . . Kyle Prue
John Gabriel Borkman . . . . Ralph Cosham
Frida Foldal. . . . . Madeleine Mager
Vilhelm Foldal . . . . Harry Winter

set design. . . . . Jason Rubin
costume design. . . . . Howard Vincent Kurtz
lighting design. . . . . David Zemmels
sound design . . . . Mark Anduss
dramaturg. . . . . Kristin Johnsen-Neshati

CHARACTERS

JOHN GABRIEL BORKMAN, formerly a bank president
GUNHILD BORKMAN, his wife
ERHART BORKMAN, their son, a student
MISS ELLA RENTHEIM, Mrs. Borkman's twin sister
MRS. FANNY WILTON
VILHELM FOLDAL, part-time clerk in a government office
FRIDA FILDAL, his daughter
MRS. BORKMAN'S MAID

TIME AND PLACE

The action takes place during a winter evening on the Rentheim family estate outside the capital city. All scene directions are from the audience's point of view.

ACT ONE

Mrs. Borkman's living room, furnished with old-fashioned, faded splendor. , In the background, an open sliding door leads into a garden room with windows and a glass door. Through these a view into the garden, where a snowstorm is swirling in the dusk. On the right is a door entering into a hall. Farther downstage a large iron stove, a fire burning in it. On the left, toward the back, a single, smaller door. Downstage, on the same side, a window hung with thick curtains. Between the window and the door, a sofa covered in horsehair and with a table in front of it covered with a thick cloth. On the table, a lighted lamp with a shade. By the stove, a high-backed armchair.

MRS. GUNHILD BORKMAN is seated on the sofa with her crochet-work. She is an elderly lady with a cold, distinguished appearance, a stiff bearing and inflexible features. Her abundant hair is completely gray. She has fine, transparent hands. She is dressed in a thick, dark silk dress that once was elegant but now is somewhat worn and shabby. A woolen shawl is across her shoulders.

She sits awhile, upright and unmoving, while crocheting. Then the sound of bells from outside is heard.

MRS. BORKMAN: *(Listening: then a gleam of joy in her eyes as she involuntarily whispers.)* Erhart! Finally!
(She gets up and looks out through the curtains. She seems disappointed, and once again sits down on the sofa with her work. Soon after, the MAID enters from the hallway with a visiting card on a small tray.)
MRS. BORKMAN: *(Quickly.)* So Erhart's come after all?
MAID: No, Ma'am. But there's a lady outside—
MRS. BORKMAN: *(Putting aside the crochet-work.)* Oh? So it's Mrs. Wilton—
MAID: *(Coming closer.)* No, it's a stranger—
MRS. BORKMAN: *(Taking the card.)* Let me see— *(Reads it, rises sharply, and looks hard at the MAID.)* You're sure this is for me?
MAID: That's what I understood, ma'am—for you.
MRS. BORKMAN: She really asked to speak with Mrs. Borkman?
MAID: Yes, she did.
MRS. BORKMAN: *(Curt, resolute.)* All right. Tell her I am at home.
(The MAID opens the door for the visitor and goes out. MISS ELLA RENTHEIM enters the room. She resembles her sister in appearance; but her face wears an expression more of suffering than hardness. She still carries traces of a former distinctive beauty. Her thick hair is gathered up in natural

waves from her forehead and is silvery white. She is dressed in black velvet with a hat and fur-lined coat of the same material.

Both sisters stand in silence for a while and look probingly at each other. Each apparently waits for the other to speak first.)

ELLA: *(Who has remained near the door.)* So, Gunhild—you seem surprised to see me.

MRS. BORKMAN: *(Stands upright, unyielding, between the sofa and the table, resting her fingertips on the tablecloth.)* Haven't you made a mistake? The estate manager lives over in the north wing—you know that.

ELLA: I'm not here to speak to the manager today.

MRS. BORKMAN: You want me?

ELLA: Yes. I have a few words to say to you.

MRS. BORKMAN: *(Coming forward.)* Well then—sit down.

ELLA: Thanks, but I'd rather stand.

MRS. BORKMAN: As you wish. At least unbutton your coat.

ELLA: *(Does so.)* Yes, it's very warm in here.

MRS. BORKMAN: I'm always freezing.

ELLA: *(Stands for a while looking around, with her arms resting on the back of an armchair.)* So, Gunhild—it's been eight years since we saw each other.

MRS. BORKMAN: *(Coldly.)* Or spoke to each other, anyway.

ELLA: Yes, that's more accurate—since we spoke to each other. I'm sure you've seen me now and then—when I make my annual visit to the manager.

MRS. BORKMAN: Once or twice, I think.

ELLA: And once or twice I've caught a glimpse of you—in the window there.

MRS. BORKMAN: Behind the curtains, then. You must have good eyes. *(Hard and cutting.)* But the last time we spoke to each other—you were here in this room with me.

ELLA: *(Apprehensively.)* Yes, yes, I know that, Gunhild!

MRS. BORKMAN: The week before he—before the President of the Bank was set free again.

ELLA: *(Crossing the floor.)* Yes, yes, yes—I haven't forgotten, not for one minute. But it crushes me completely just to think about it—even for a single instant—ah!

MRS. BORKMAN: *(In a dull tone.)* And yet—my mind revolves around nothing else! *(In an outburst, striking her hands together.)* No, I can't understand it! Never in this world! I can't grasp it, that such a thing—something so terrible—can overwhelm one family! And to think—our family! A family as prominent as ours. That it could just strike like that!

ELLA: Oh, Gunhild—that blow struck many others besides our family.

MRS. BORKMAN: Maybe so. But those others are of no great concern to me. They lost some money, or some papers—nothing more—but for us—for me! And for Erhart! Just a child then— *(With rising emotion.)* A cloud of shame over two innocent people. Dishonor! Terrible dishonor! And completely ruined—

ELLA: *(Cautiously.)* Tell me, Gunhild—how is he bearing it?

MRS. BORKMAN: Erhart?

ELLA: No—he himself. How does he bear it?

MRS. BORKMAN: *(Scornfully surprised.)* Do you think I inquire into that?

ELLA: Surely you don't need to inquire—

MRS. BORKMAN: *(Looks at her, astonished.)* I hope you don't think I have anything to do with him? Meet with him? Even see him?

ELLA: Not even see him—?

MRS. BORKMAN: *(As before.)* Him—who sat under lock and key for five years! *(Buries her face in her hands.)* A shame that crushed us all! *(Flaring up.)* Remember what the name John Gabriel Borkman once meant! No, no, no—I'll never see him again—never!

ELLA: *(Looking at her for a moment.)* You're hard, Gunhild.

MRS. BORKMAN: Yes—toward him.

ELLA: He's still your husband.

MRS. BORKMAN: He told the court that I was the one who began his ruin—that I spent so much money—

ELLA: *(Cautiously.)* Wasn't there some truth in that?

MRS. BORKMAN: He wanted it that way—he himself! Everything had to be so absurdly extravagant!

ELLA: I know. But that's why you should have resisted—and you never did.

MRS. BORKMAN: How was I to know the money he gave me to spend as I pleased—and that he spent as well—didn't belong to him?

ELLA: *(Quietly.)* Well—his position required it, I imagine—to a great extent, at least.

MRS. BORKMAN: *(Scornfully.)* Yes—we always had to show our style, he said—and he showed it, all right— Drove a four-horse carriage as if he were a king. Let people bow and scrape to him like a king. *(Laughing.)* And all over the country, people called him by his first name—like the king himself. "John Gabriel," "John Gabriel." They all knew what a great man "John Gabriel" was!

ELLA: *(Quickly, warmly.)* But he *was* a great man then!

MRS. BORKMAN: So it seemed. But he never said a word to me about his real situation. Never told me where the money came from.

ELLA: No, no—no one else knew, either.

MRS. BORKMAN: The others don't matter—but he owed the truth to me. And all he did was lie, lie to me continually—

ELLA: *(Interrupting.)* He certainly did not! He may have concealed some things, but he certainly didn't lie.

MRS. BORKMAN: Well, call it whatever you want. It comes to the same thing. Because it all collapsed. Everything. All that glory, gone.

ELLA: *(To herself.)* Yes, everything collapsed. For him, and for others.

MRS. BORKMAN: *(Menacing.)* But I tell you this, Ella—I'll never give up! I'll find a way to redeem my life, you can be sure of that!

ELLA: *(Tense.)* Redeem? What do you mean by that?

MRS. BORKMAN: Redemption—of name and honor and fortune. Redemption of an entire way of life, lying in ruins. That's what I mean. Someone is coming behind me—someone who will cleanse the stain from everything that he—that the President of the Bank has corrupted.

ELLA: Gunhild! Gunhild!

MRS. BORKMAN: *(Crescendo.)* An avenger lives! One who will erase every wrong his father committed against me!

ELLA: Erhart.

MRS. BORKMAN: Yes. My glorious boy. He'll bring about the redemption— of family, house, and name. Everything that can be redeemed—perhaps even more.

ELLA: And how do you think this will happen?

MRS. BORKMAN: It will happen as it happens. I don't know how. But I know that it will and that it finally must. *(Looks inquiringly at her.)* Yes, Ella—haven't you been thinking the same thing, more or less, since he was a child?

ELLA: No, I really can't say that I have.

MRS. BORKMAN: No? So why did you take charge of him then? When the storm hit—hit this house.

ELLA: Gunhild—you weren't able to, at the time.

MRS. BORKMAN: No—I wasn't able to. And his father—legally isolated— sitting there comfortably in his cell.

ELLA: *(Outraged.)* How can you say things like that?

MRS. BORKMAN: *(With a poisonous expression.)* And that you could bring yourself to take in a—a child of John Gabriel! Exactly as if he were your own—take him from me, to your home, and keep him with you, year after year. Till he was almost grown! *(Looking suspiciously at her.)* Why did you really do it, Ella? Why did you keep him?

ELLA: I came to care for him so deeply.

MRS. BORKMAN: More than his mother?

ELLA: *(Evasively.)* That I don't know. But then Erhart was a little delicate as a boy—

MRS. BORKMAN: Erhart—delicate!

ELLA: Yes, I thought so—at the time, anyway. And the air out there on the west coast is so much softer—you know that.

MRS. BORKMAN: *(Smiling bitterly.)* Hm. Is it really? *(Abruptly.)* Well—you've certainly done a lot for him. *(Changing tone.)* And it's understandable — you had the means to do it. *(Smiles.)* You were very lucky, Ella. Somehow you saved everything of yours.

ELLA: *(Offended.)* I had nothing to do with that, I assure you. I had no idea— at least, not until long after the fact—that my securities—the ones I had on deposit with the bank—had been spared.

MRS. BORKMAN: Well, well—I really don't understand these things. I'm only saying you were lucky. *(Looks inquiringly at her.)* But when you took it on yourself to raise Erhart for me—what was your motive in that?

ELLA: *(Looking at her.)* My motive?

MRS. BORKMAN: Yes—you must have had a motive. What did you want to make him into? Make of him, I mean?

ELLA: *(Slowly.)* I wanted to pave the way for him—so Erhart could live in the world as a happy man.

MRS. BORKMAN: *(Snorts.)* Ach! People in our condition have plenty to do without thinking about happiness.

ELLA: Such as what?

MRS. BORKMAN: *(Looks at her meaningfully and solemnly.)* Erhart must be sure—above all else—that his life will burn so brightly, shine its light so widely, that no one in this land will ever see the shadow his father has cast over me—and over my son.

ELLA: *(Probingly.)* Tell me, Gunhild—is that the goal Erhart has set for his life?

MRS. BORKMAN: *(Surprised.)* Yes, we dare to hope!

ELLA: Isn't it a goal you've set for him instead?

MRS. BORKMAN: *(Curtly.)* Erhart and I always set the same goals for ourselves.

ELLA: *(Slowly and sadly.)* You're that sure of your son, Gunhild.

MRS. BORKMAN: *(Secretly exultant.)* Yes, praise God, I am. Absolutely.

ELLA: Then it seems to me that you must feel fortunate—deep down—in spite of all the rest.

MRS. BORKMAN: Yes I do. As far as that goes. But then, you see, every minute or two, all the rest of it sweeps over me like a storm.

ELLA: *(With a change of tone.)* Tell me—it might as well be now—because this is why I've really come out here to see you—

MRS. BORKMAN: What?

ELLA: There's something I have to talk to you about. Tell me—Erhart doesn't live out here with—all of you?

MRS. BORKMAN: *(Stiffly.)* Erhart cannot live here with me. He has to live in town—

ELLA: That's what he wrote me.

MRS. BORKMAN: For the sake of his studies. He comes out here to me for a while every evening.

ELLA: Could I see him then, perhaps? Speak to him?

MRS. BORKMAN: He hasn't come yet. But I'm expecting him any moment.

ELLA: But, Gunhild—he must have come—I can hear him walking back and forth upstairs.

MRS. BORKMAN: *(Glancing upward.)* Up there, in the salon?

ELLA: Yes, I've heard him walking around up there ever since I got here.

MRS. BORKMAN: *(Averting her eyes.)* That isn't him, Ella.

ELLA: *(Puzzled.)* Isn't Erhart? *(Understanding.)* Who is it, then?

MRS. BORKMAN: The President of the Bank.

ELLA: *(Softly, in suppressed grief.)* Borkman. John Gabriel Borkman!

MRS. BORKMAN: He walks up and down like that. Back and forth. Morning till night. Day after day.

ELLA: Of course I've heard talk about something like that—

MRS. BORKMAN: I can believe it. There must be plenty of talk about us out here.

ELLA: Erhart talked about it a little, in his letters. About how his father keeps to himself, up there—and you, to yourself, down here.

MRS. BORKMAN; Yes, Ella, that's how it has been. Ever since they let him out. And sent him home to me. Through every one of these eight long years.

ELLA: But I never thought it could really be true. That it was possible—

MRS. BORKMAN: *(Nodding.)* Oh, it's true. And it can never be otherwise.

ELLA: *(Looking at her.)* This must be a horrible life, Gunhild.

MRS. BORKMAN: More than horrible. It won't be possible to hold on much longer.

ELLA: I can understand that very well.

MRS. BORKMAN: Always hearing his footsteps up there. From early morning till late into the night. And so loud—just as if he were here, right here.

ELLA: Yes, it's extraordinary how clear it sounds in here.

MRS. BORKMAN: It often seems to me I have a sick wolf up there in the salon, pacing back and forth in his cage. Right over my head. *(Listens and whispers.)* Just listen, Ella! Back and forth, back and forth goes the wolf.

ELLA: *(Cautiously.)* Can't it be any other way, Gunhild?

MRS. BORKMAN: *(Dismissively.)* He's made no move in that direction.

ELLA: Couldn't you make the first move?

MRS. BORKMAN: *(Flaring up.)* I? After everything he's done to me? No thank you! Let the wolf go on padding around up there.

ELLA: It's getting to be too warm for me now— I'd like to take my coat off after all.

MRS. BORKMAN: Yes, I already asked you to—

(ELLA removes her coat and hat, puts them on a chair by the hall door.)

ELLA: So you never see him away from the house?

MRS. BORKMAN: *(With a sarcastic laugh.)* In society, you mean?

ELLA: I mean when he goes out for some air. In the woods, or—

MRS. BORKMAN: The President of the Bank never goes out.

ELLA: Not even at night?

MRS. BORKMAN: Never.

ELLA: *(Moved.)* He can't bring himself to do it?

MRS. BORKMAN: Apparently not. He keeps his cloak and hat hanging in the closet—you know, in the hall—

ELLA: *(To herself.)* The one we played in when we were small—

MRS. BORKMAN: *(Nodding.)* And every now and then—late in the evening—I hear him coming down the stairs—to put on his things and go out. But then he stops—usually halfway down—and turns around. And then he goes back up to the salon.

ELLA: *(Softly.)* Don't any of his old friends ever go up there to see him?

MRS. BORKMAN: He has no old friends.

ELLA: He used to have so many.

MRS. BORKMAN: Hm! He certainly found the way to get rid of them. Yes, John Gabriel turned out to be quite a dear friend to all his old friends.

ELLA: You're probably right about that.

MRS. BORKMAN: *(Vehemently.)* Still, I must say that it's despicable—it's mean, petty, and small-minded to focus so heavily on whatever little losses he might have caused them. All they lost was money—nothing more than that.

ELLA: *(Without answering.)* And so he lives completely alone up there. Entirely by himself.

MRS. BORKMAN: Yes he does. Although I've heard that an old copy-clerk—something like that—goes up to see him now and then.

ELLA: That must be Foldal. They were friends when they were young.

MRS. BORKMAN: I believe that's right. But that's all I know about him. He wasn't part of our social circle. When we had one—

ELLA: And he visits Borkman now?

MRS. BORKMAN: Yes, I imagine he's not too particular. But even so, you know, he only comes around after dark.

ELLA: This Foldal—he suffered a loss when the bank collapsed.

MRS. BORKMAN: *(Indifferently.)* Yes, I remember now—I believe—that he lost some money. But it couldn't have been that significant.

ELLA: *(With slight emphasis.)* It was everything he had.

MRS. BORKMAN: *(Smiling.)* Good lord—everything he had must have been practically nothing. Not even worth mentioning.

ELLA: Foldal didn't mention it at the trial, did he?

MRS. BORKMAN: Well, anyway, I assure you that Erhart has more than made up to him for the little bit he lost.

ELLA: *(Surprised.)* Erhart has? How did Erhart manage that?

MRS. BORKMAN: He's taken on Foldal's youngest daughter—tutored her— so that she can become something, and provide for herself some day. And that, you see, is a great deal more than her father could ever have done for her.

ELLA: Yes, I imagine her father's fallen on rather hard times.

MRS. BORKMAN: So Erhart has arranged for her to study music. She's good enough now to go up and—play for him in the salon.

ELLA: So he still enjoys music?

MRS. BORKMAN: It would seem so. He has that piano you sent out here— during that time—while he was waiting—

ELLA: And she plays it for him?

MRS. BORKMAN: Yes, every so often. In the evenings. Erhart's also responsible for that.

ELLA: So the poor girl has to come all the way out here—and then back home to town again?

MRS. BORKMAN: No, because Erhart has arranged for her to stay with a woman who lives close by—a Mrs. Wilton.

ELLA: *(Her interest aroused.)* Mrs. Wilton!

MRS. BORKMAN: A very wealthy lady. No one you know.

ELLA: I've heard the name. Mrs. Fanny Wilton, I believe—

MRS. BORKMAN: That's right.

ELLA: Erhart has written to me about her often. Does she live out here now?

MRS. BORKMAN: Yes, she's rented a villa here. She moved out from town some time ago.

ELLA: *(Somewhat hesitant .)* People say that she's divorced.

MRS. BORKMAN: The husband has been dead for many years.

ELLA: Yes, but they were divorced. He divorced her.

MRS. BORKMAN: He left her. It was certainly not her fault.

ELLA: How well do you know her, Gunhild?

MRS. BORKMAN: Fairly well. She lives close by, and calls on me from time to time.

ELLA: And you like her?

MRS. BORKMAN: She's exceptionally understanding. Very clearheaded in her judgments.

ELLA: Of people, you mean?

MRS. BORKMAN: Yes, especially of people. For example, she's come to understand Erhart right to the depths of his soul. And so she idolizes him—which is understandable.

ELLA: *(Leading her.)* So perhaps she knows Erhart even better than she knows you.

MRS. BORKMAN: Yes, Erhart used to meet her in town, before she moved out here.

ELLA: *(Involuntarily.)* But even so, she moved out here.

MRS. BORKMAN: *(Startled, looks sharply at her.)* Even so! What do you mean by that?

ELLA: *(Evasive.)* Good Lord—I mean—

MRS. BORKMAN: You said it so strangely. You meant something by it, Ella.

ELLA: *(Looking straight at her.)* Yes, Gunhild. I meant something by it.

MRS. BORKMAN: Then just say it!

ELLA: I have to tell you *this*, first: I believe that *I*, also, have a kind of claim on Erhart. Maybe you don't agree.

MRS. BORKMAN: *(Looking around the room.)* Well, good lord, after all the money you spent on him—

ELLA: Oh, not because of that, Gunhild—but because I love him.

MRS. BORKMAN: *(Smiling scornfully.)* You love my son? Can you? In spite of everything?

ELLA: Yes I can. In spite of everything. And I do. I love Erhart. As much as I *can* love anyone now. At my age.

MRS. BORKMAN: Yes, yes, all right then. But—

ELLA: And so, you see, it upsets me when I see something threatening him.

MRS. BORKMAN: Threatening Erhart? *What* threatens him? Or rather, *who* threatens him?

ELLA: Well, to begin with—*you*—in your way—

MRS. BORKMAN: *(Agitated.)* I?

ELLA: And there's this Mrs. Wilton. I'm afraid of her.

MRS. BORKMAN: *(Stares speechlessly at her for a moment.)* You can think that about Erhart? About my son? My son, with his great mission to carry out?

ELLA: *(Scornfully.)* His mission—really—

MRS. BORKMAN: *(Furiously.)* You dare to speak that way?

ELLA: Do you really believe that a young man, Erhart's age—healthy and full of joy—do you believe he'll sacrifice himself for something like a "mission?"

MRS. BORKMAN: *(Firmly.)* Erhart will! I know that absolutely!

ELLA: *(Shaking her head.)* You don't know it—or believe it, either.

MRS. BORKMAN: Not believe it!

ELLA: It's just something you've dreamed up—because without that to cling to, you know you'd fall into total despair.

MRS. BORKMAN: Yes, that *would* mean total despair for me. *(Fiercely.)* And maybe that's what you'd like to see, Ella, yes?

ELLA: *(Head erect.)* Yes, I would—if the only way you can free yourself is by making Erhart suffer.

MRS. BORKMAN: *(Threatening.)* You want to come between us! Between mother and son! *You!*

ELLA: I want to free him from your power—your control—your domination.

MRS. BORKMAN: *(Triumphantly.)* You can't do that anymore! You had him in your net until he was fifteen. But now, you see, I've won him back.

ELLA: Then I'll win him from you a second time. *(In a hoarse half-whisper.)* The two of us—we've fought a life-and-death battle over a man before— isn't that right, Gunhild?

MRS. BORKMAN: *(Looks gloatingly at her.)* Yes. And I won.

ELLA: *(A mocking smile.)* Do you still feel as if you won anything?

MRS. BORKMAN: *(Darkly.)* No, that's the brutal truth of it.

ELLA: And you'll win nothing this time, either.

MRS. BORKMAN: Win nothing—in keeping a mother's power over Erhart!

ELLA: No—because *power* over him is all you want.

MRS. BORKMAN: And what about you?

ELLA: *(Warmly.)* I want his loving self—his soul—his whole heart!

MRS. BORKMAN: *(Fiercely.)* You'll never get them back—not in this world.

ELLA *(Looking at her.)* You've taken care of that, I suppose?

MRS. BORKMAN: *(Smiling.)* Yes, I've taken advantage of my opportunities. Couldn't you see it in his letters?

ELLA: *(Nodding slowly.)* Yes. At the end, it was all you in his letters.

MRS. BORKMAN: *(Provocatively.)* I've used these last eight years—while I've had my eyes on him.

ELLA: *(Restrained.)* What have you been saying about me to Erhart? If you can bring yourself to tell me.

MRS. BORKMAN: Yes, I can tell you.

ELLA: Go ahead.

MRS. BORKMAN: I have simply told him the truth.

ELLA: Oh?

MRS. BORKMAN: I've continually reminded him—day after day—that we have you to thank for living as well as we do. Or even that we can live at all.

ELLA: That's all?

MRS. BORKMAN: Oh, that kind of thought gnaws away at you— I feel it in myself.

ELLA: But it's nothing more than Erhart already knew.

MRS. BORKMAN: When he came home to me, he carried an image inside him—that you'd done all this out of a kind heart. *(Looks maliciously at her.)* He no longer believes that, Ella.

ELLA: What does he believe now?

MRS. BORKMAN: The truth. I asked him to explain why aunt Ella never came to visit us out here—

ELLA: *(Interrupting.)* He already knew why!

MRS. BORKMAN: And now he knows even better. You'd planted an image in his mind—that it was to spare me and—him—the one who's pacing back and forth up there—

ELLA: And so it was.

MRS. BORKMAN: Erhart doesn't believe that for a second any more.

ELLA: What have you made him believe about me now?

MRS. BORKMAN: The truth—that you're ashamed of us, you despise us. Can you say you don't? Didn't you want to tear him away from me completely? Think, Ella. You must remember.

ELLA: *(Dismissively.)* That was at the height of the scandal—when the case was in court. I don't want that any more.

MRS. BORKMAN: It wouldn't do you any good, anyway—because what would become of his mission then? No, thank you! Erhart needs *me* now, not you. And so he might as well be dead to you, and you to him!

ELLA: *(Cold, determined.)* We shall see. I'm staying out here now, you know.

MRS. BORKMAN: *(Staring at her.)* Here, on the estate?

ELLA: Yes, here.

MRS. BORKMAN: Here, with us? Overnight?

ELLA: I'll stay out here for the rest of my life, if need be.

MRS. BORKMAN: *(Composing herself.)* Yes, yes, Ella, of course, it's your estate.

ELLA: Oh, come!

MRS. BORKMAN: Everything here is yours. I sit on your chair. I lie, tossing and turning sleeplessly, in your bed. We even eat your food.

ELLA: It's the only possible arrangement. Borkman isn't allowed to own anything—they'd take it away from him immediately.

MRS. BORKMAN: I'm well aware of that. So we have to resign ourselves to living off of your charity, at your pleasure.

ELLA: *(Cold.)* I can't stop you from seeing it that way, Gunhild.

MRS. BORKMAN: No, you can't. When would you like us to move out?

ELLA: *(Looks at her.)* Move out?

MRS. BORKMAN: *(Very excitedly.)* Yes—you can't for a moment imagine that I could live under the same roof with you—! No, better the poorhouse, or the open road!

ELLA: Very well—then give me Erhart.

MRS. BORKMAN: Erhart! My own son! My child!

ELLA: Yes—and then I'll go straight home.

MRS. BORKMAN: *(After a short deliberation, determined.)* Erhart will choose between us.

ELLA: *(Looking at her, doubtful and uncertain.)* Erhart choose? You'd dare to risk that, Gunhild?

MRS. BORKMAN: *(With a hard laugh.)* Would I dare? To let my boy choose between you and his mother? I certainly do!

ELLA: *(Listening.)* Is someone coming? I think I hear—

MRS. BORKMAN: It must be Erhart.

(There is a quick knock on the hall door, which is opened immediately. MRS. WILTON enters, dressed for a party and wearing an outer coat. Behind her the MAID, who has not had time to announce her and is looking perplexed. MRS. WILTON is a strikingly pretty and voluptuous lady in her thirties. She has full, red, smiling lips. Playful eyes. Rich, dark hair.)

MRS. WILTON: Good evening, my dearest Mrs. Borkman.

MRS. BORKMAN: *(Somewhat dry.)* Good evening, Mrs. Wilton. *(To the maid, pointing to the garden room.)* Take the lamp in there and light it.[1]

(The MAID leaves with the lamp.)

MRS. WILTON: *(Seeing ELLA.)* Oh, I beg your pardon. You have company.

MRS. BORKMAN: Just my sister, who's visiting—

(ERHART BORKMAN comes storming through the half-opened door. He is a young man with bright, joyful eyes. Elegantly dressed. The beginnings of a moustache.)

ERHART: *(On the threshold, radiating happiness.)* What's this? Aunt Ella's here? *(Going to her, seizing her hands.)* Aunt, my dear Aunt! Is it really you?

ELLA: *(Flings her arms around his neck.)* Erhart! My dear, sweet boy. No, but look at how you've grown! Oh, it's so good to see you again!

MRS. BORKMAN: *(Sharply.)* What does this mean, Erhart—hiding out there in the hallway?

MRS. WILTON: *(Hurriedly.)* Erhart—Borkman arrived just when I did.

MRS. BORKMAN: *(Measuring him with her eyes.)* So, Erhart. You didn't call on your mother first?

ERHART: I had to stop at Mrs. Wilton's for a minute—to pick up little Frida.

MRS. BORKMAN: You have Miss Foldal with you too?

MRS. WILTON: Yes. We left her standing in the entryway.

ERHART: *(Speaking through the hall door.)* Go on upstairs now, Frida.

(A pause. ELLA observes ERHART. He seems embarrassed and somewhat impatient. His face takes on a colder, more tense expression. The MAID brings the burning lamp into the garden room and goes out again, closing the door after her.)

MRS. BORKMAN: *(With forced politeness.)* Well, Mrs. Wilton—if you'd like to spend the evening here as well—

MRS. WILTON: No, thank you very much, Mrs. Borkman, but I couldn't think of it. We have another invitation. We're going to a party at the lawyer's—at Mr. Hinkel's.

MRS. BORKMAN: *(Looking at her.)* We? What do you mean by "we"?

MRS. WILTON: *(Laughing.)* Well, actually only me. But I was assigned by the ladies of the house to bring young Mr. Borkman along if I happened to catch a glimpse of him.

MRS. BORKMAN: And you happened to, I see.

MRS. WILTON: Yes, fortunately. He was thoughtful enough to look in on me, on little Frida's account.

MRS. BORKMAN: *(Dryly.)* Well, Erhart—I had no idea you knew this family—the Hinkels.

ERHART: *(Irritated.)* No—well, I don't exactly know them. *(Goes on, a little impatiently.)* You know best, mother, who I know and don't know.

MRS. WILTON: Oh, fff. You get known pretty quickly in that house. Lively, cheerful people—quite hospitable—and cramful with young ladies.

MRS. BORKMAN: *(With emphasis.)* If I know my son at all, that's not his kind of company, Mrs. Wilton.

MRS. WILTON: But for heaven's sake, he's young himself!

MRS. BORKMAN: Yes, fortunately he's young. That's the only saving grace.

ERHART: *(Hiding his impatience.)* Yes yes yes, mother—obviously I won't be going down to the Hinkels' tonight. Of course I'll stay here with you and Aunt Ella.

MRS. BORKMAN: I was sure you would, my dear Erhart.

ELLA: No, Erhart, please don't stay on my account—

ERHART: Of course I will, Aunt. That's all there is to it. *(Looks uncertainly at*

MRS. WILTON.) How can we explain it, though? What will they think? You've already said "yes" for me.

MRS. WILTON: *(Vivaciously.)* Oh, nonsense! What are they supposed to think? When I alight—deserted and alone, remember—in those brilliant, festive rooms—I'll simply say "no" for you.

ERHART: *(Reluctantly.)* Well, then, as long as they won't think—

MRS. WILTON: *(Light, feisty.)* Oh, I've so often had occasion to say both "yes" and "no"—for myself. And how could you think of deserting your aunt, practically the moment she arrives? What kind of a son would you be?

MRS. BORKMAN: *(Much displeased.)* A son?

MRS. WILTON: Well then, a foster son, Mrs. Borkman.

MRS. BORKMAN: That's an important addition.

MRS. WILTON: And sometimes you have more to be thankful for from a good foster mother than from your own, real mother.

MRS. BORKMAN: Do you speak from experience?

MRS. WILTON: Oh, God knows—I barely knew my mother. But if I'd had such a good foster mother, maybe I wouldn't have turned out quite as— as wicked as people say I am. *(Turning to ERHART.)* So, young man— you stay cozy here at home, drinking tea with your mother and aunt! *(To the ladies.)* Goodbye, goodbye, dear Mrs. Borkman, and goodbye to you, Miss Rentheim.

(The LADIES silently return her salutation. She goes to the door.)

ERHART: *(Following MRS. WILTON.)* Should I go part of the way with you—?

MRS. WILTON: *(In the doorway, dismissing him.)* Not a step. I'm used to finding my way alone. *(Stands in the doorway, looking at him, and nodding.)* But watch out, young Mr. Borkman—I'm warning you.

ERHART: Why should I watch out?

MRS. WILTON: Because as I go down that road, deserted and alone, as I've told you before, I'm going to try casting a spell over you.

ERHART: *(Laughing.)* Oh, that! You're not going to try that again?

MRS. WILTON: *(Half serious.)* Yes—so watch out! As I make my way down there, I'll say to myself—right from the deepest center of my will—I'll say: Young Mr. Erhart Borkman—take your hat at once!

MRS. BORKMAN: And you think he'll take it?

MRS. WILTON: *(Laughing.)* Yes, he certainly will. Right then he'll go get his hat. And then I'll say: Put on your overcoat nice and snug, Erhart Borkman! And your galoshes—do not forget your galoshes! And follow me, right now. Do it, Erhart, do it!

ERHART: *(With constrained gaiety.)* Yes, you can be sure of it.

MRS. WILTON: *(With raised forefinger.)* Do it, do it! Good night! *(She laughs, nods to the ladies, and goes out closing the door behind her.)*

MRS. BORKMAN: Does she really practice those kinds of arts?

ERHART: No, not at all. How could you think that? It's just a sort of joke. *(Breaking off.)* But let's not talk about Mrs. Wilton now. *(He insists that ELLA sit in the armchair by the stove. Looks at her a moment.)* To think you've made the long journey here, Aunt Ella—and now, in the winter!

ELLA: It finally became necessary for me, Erhart.

ERHART: It did? Why?

ELLA: I had to come and see the doctors.

ERHART: Well, that's good!

ELLA: *(Smiling.)* You think so?

ERHART: That you decided to, I mean.

MRS. BORKMAN: *(On the sofa, coldly.)* Are you ill, Ella?

ELLA: *(Looking hard at her.)* You know very well I'm ill.

MRS. BORKMAN: Only that you've had a chronic sickness for many years now.

ERHART: When I was living with you, I was always telling you to see a doctor.

ELLA: Well, over in my corner of the world there was no one I really trusted. And besides, I wasn't feeling so bad then, either.

ERHART: Are you worse now, Aunt Ella?

ELLA: Oh yes, my dear boy, it's gotten quite a bit worse.

ERHART: But surely it's nothing serious?

ELLA: That depends on how you think about it.

ERHART: *(Warmly.)* Well, Aunt Ella—you know what, in that case?—we simply can't let you go home again right away.

ELLA: No, I definitely won't be doing that.

ERHART: You'll stay here in town. We have the very best doctors to choose from here.

ELLA: That's what I was thinking when I left home.

ERHART: And you can look for a really nice place to stay, a quiet, cozy guest house.

ELLA: This morning I checked in at the place where I've stayed before.

ERHART: Well, you'll certainly be comfortable there.

ELLA: Yes, but I won't be staying there after all.

ERHART: Really? Why not?

ELLA: No, I already decided that when I came out here.

ERHART: *(Surprised.)* What?—you decided—

MRS. BORKMAN: *(Crocheting, not looking up.)* Your aunt wants to live here, on her estate, Erhart.

ERHART: *(Looking from one to the other.)* Here! With us! With all of us!—
Aunt Ella, is it true?

ELLA: Yes, that's what I've decided to do now.

MRS. BORKMAN: *(As before.)* Everything belongs to your aunt, you know.

ELLA: And so I'm staying here, Erhart. At first, anyway. For the moment. I'll
make my own arrangements. Over in the manager's building.

ERHART: That's a good idea. You've always had a room ready for you there.
(Suddenly lively.) But Aunt Ella—aren't you exhausted from your trip?

ELLA: Yes, I suppose I'm a little tired.

ERHART: Well then—my suggestion is that you get yourself to bed nice and
early.

ELLA: *(Looking at him with a smile.)* I'll do that.

ERHART: *(Urging.)* And then we can have a real talk tomorrow—or some
other day. About everything. Free and open. You, mother, and me.
Wouldn't that be a lot better, Aunt Ella?

MRS. BORKMAN: *(Agitated, rising from the sofa.)* Erhart—I can see it in
your face—you want to leave me!

ERHART: *(Startled.)* What do you mean by that?

MRS. BORKMAN: You want to go down there—to that lawyer's house!

ERHART: *(Involuntarily.)* Oh yes, that's right! *(Collects himself.)* Do you really
think I should sit here keeping Aunt Ella up half the night? In her
condition? Remember that.

MRS. BORKMAN: You want to go down to the Hinkels', Erhart!

ERHART: *(Impatiently.)* Yes, but Mother, for God's sake—I really don't
think I can just leave it like this. What do you think, Aunt Ella?

ELLA: You should act in complete freedom, Erhart.

MRS. BORKMAN: *(Menacing.)* You want to tear him away from me!

ELLA: *(Rising.)* Oh yes—if I could really do that, Gunhild.
(Music is heard from above.)

ERHART: *(Writhing as in agony.)* Ah—I can't take this a minute more! *(Looking
around.)* Where's my hat? *(To ELLA.)* Do you know what they're playing
up there in the salon?

ELLA : No—what is it?

ERHART: *Danse macabre*, it's called. The Dance of Death. Don't you know
the Dance of Death, Aunt?

ELLA: *(Smiling sadly.)* Not yet, Erhart.

ERHART: Mother, please—I'm asking you nicely—please let me go.

MRS. BORKMAN: *(Looking hard at him.)* Away from your mother? That's
what you want?

ERHART: I'll come out here again—maybe tomorrow—

MRS. BORKMAN: *(Passionately agitated.)* You want to leave me! You want to be with those strangers! With—with—no, I can't even think about it!

ERHART: Down there, where all the lights are burning bright. And the faces are young and happy. And music, mother.

MRS. BORKMAN: *(Pointing upwards.)* Up there, there's also music, Erhart.

ERHART: Yes—and that music is what's driving me out of the house.

ELLA: Can't you allow your father a little escape from himself?

ERHART: Oh yes. A thousand times. As long as I don't have to listen to it.

MRS. BORKMAN: *(Looking at him reproachfully.)* Be strong, Erhart! Strong, my son! Never forget your great mission.

ERHART: Oh Mother—please don't talk that way. I'm not cut out to be a missionary. Good night, Aunt Ella. Good night, mother. *(He hurries out through the hall)*

MRS. BORKMAN: *(After a short silence.)* You got him back quickly enough, Ella.

ELLA: I wish I could truly believe that.

MRS. BORKMAN: But you won't get to keep him long. You'll see.

ELLA: Thanks to you, you mean?

MRS. BORKMAN: Thanks to me—or to her, that other one.

ELLA: Far better her than you.

MRS. BORKMAN: *(Nods slowly.)* I understand that. And I say the same. Better her than you.

ELLA: No matter what happens to him in the end—

MRS. BORKMAN: In the end, it all comes to the same thing, I think.

ELLA: *(Taking her coat over her arm.)* For the first time in our entire lives, we twin sisters agree. Good night, Gunhild *(She goes out through the hall. The music sounds louder up in the salon.)*

MRS. BORKMAN: *(Standing a moment, gives a start, shrinks, and whispers involuntarily.)* The wolf is howling again. The sick wolf. *(She stands still for a moment, then casts herself down on the carpets, writhing, moaning, whispering in anguish.)* Erhart! Erhart! Be faithful to me! Come back and help your mother! I can't bear this life another minute!

END OF ACT ONE

ACT TWO

The former grand salon in the Rentheim house. The walls are covered with old tapestries of hunting scenes, shepherds and shepherdesses, all in faded, bleached colors. In the wall on the left, a sliding door and farther downstage, a piano. In the corner of the rear wall, an unframed door covered in tapestry to blend with the background. In the middle of the wall on the right is a large carved oak desk with many books and papers. Farther downstage on the same side, a sofa with a table and chair. The furniture is in severe Empire style. On the desk and table are lighted lamps.

JOHN GABRIEL BORKMAN stands, his hands behind his back, listening to FRIDA FOLDAL, who sits playing the last notes of the Danse Macabre. *BORKMAN is a man in his sixties, of average height, compactly and strongly built. Distinguished appearance, finely cut profile, piercing eyes, and gray-white curly hair and beard. He is dressed in a black, not very modern suit and a white neck cloth. FRIDA FOLDAL is a pretty, pale, fifteen-year-old girl with a rather tired, strained expression. Cheaply dressed in light-colored clothes.*

The music is played to the end. Silence.

BORKMAN: Can you guess where I first heard those kinds of sounds?

FRIDA: *(Looking up at him.)* No, Mr. Borkman.

BORKMAN: Down in the mines.

FRIDA: *(Not understanding.)* Really? In the mines?

BORKMAN: I'm a miner's son, as you probably know. Or didn't you know that?

FRIDA : No, Mr. Borkman.

BORKMAN: A miner's son. Sometimes my father would take me down into the mines. Down there the metal sings.

FRIDA: Really? It sings?

BORKMAN: *(Nodding.)* When it's cut loose. The hammer blows that loosen it—they're a midnight bell—striking and setting it free. That's why the metal sings—for joy—in its way.

FRIDA: Why does it do that, Mr. Borkman?

BORKMAN: It wants to come up into the light of day and serve mankind.
(He continues walking up and down the room with his hands behind his back.)

FRIDA: *(Sits waiting for a while, looks at her watch and gets up.)* Please excuse me, Mr. Borkman. I really have to go now.

BORKMAN: *(Standing in front of her.)* You want to go right now?

FRIDA: *(Placing the music in a folder.)* I really have to. *(Clearly embarrassed.)* I've got an engagement somewhere else tonight.

BORKMAN: Somewhere else? Is there a party?

FRIDA: Yes.

BORKMAN: And you'll perform for the guests?

FRIDA: *(Biting her lip.)* No, I'll be playing the dance music.

BORKMAN: Only the dance music?

FRIDA: Yes, they want to have some dancing after supper.

BORKMAN: *(Stands looking at her.)* Do you like playing for people's dancing? In the houses around here?

FRIDA: *(Putting on her outdoor coat.)* Yes, when they ask me—I'm always looking for a chance to earn a little, you know.

BORKMAN: *(Interrogating.)* Is that what you think about most, while you sit there and play for the dancers?

FRIDA: No. Most of all I think how sad it is that I can't join in the dance.

BORKMAN: *(Nodding.)* That's precisely what I wanted to know. *(Walking uneasily across the room.)* Yes, yes, yes, that's it. Not to join in, that's the hardest thing of all. *(Stops.)* But there's one thing that evens it up for you, Frida.

FRIDA: *(Looks up inquiringly.)* What's that, Mr. Borkman?

BORKMAN: That you've got ten times more music in you than that whole pack of dancers put together.

FRIDA: *(Smiling evasively.)* Oh, I'm not so sure about that.

BORKMAN: *(Raising an admonishing forefinger.)* Never be so mad as to doubt yourself!

FRIDA: But good lord—when nobody else knows?

BORKMAN: As long as you know, that's enough. Where will you be playing this evening?

FRIDA: Down at the lawyer's house. At the Hinkels'.

BORKMAN: *(Gives her a quick, searching look.)* You said the Hinkels'?

FRIDA: Yes.

BORKMAN: *(With a bitter smile.)* Do guests really come to that man's house? Can he get people to visit him?

FRIDA: Yes, a lot of people are coming, according to Mrs. Wilton.

BORKMAN: *(Heatedly.)* But what sort of people? Can you tell me that?

FRIDA: *(A little apprehensively.)* I really don't know. Except—well, I do know that young Mr. Borkman will be there.

BORKMAN: *(Stunned.)* Erhart? My son?

FRIDA: Yes, he's coming.

BORKMAN: How do you know?

FRIDA: He said so himself. About an hour ago.

BORKMAN: Is he out here today?

FRIDA: Yes, he's been at Mrs. Wilton's all afternoon.

BORKMAN: (Searchingly.) Do you know if he's been here, too? Has he been talking to anyone downstairs, I mean?

FRIDA: Yes—he was with Mrs. Borkman for a while.

BORKMAN: (Bitterly.) Ah, I should have known.

FRIDA: But there was also a strange lady with her, I think.

BORKMAN: Was there? Well, I expect people do come and visit her every now and then.

FRIDA: Should I tell young Mr. Borkman—if I see him later—to come up and see you?

BORKMAN: (Brusquely.) Don't say anything! I expressly forbid it. If people want to come up and see me, they can come of their own accord. I will not beg from anybody.

FRIDA: All right then, I won't say anything. Good night, Mr. Borkman.

BORKMAN: (Pacing and growling.) Good night.

FRIDA: Oh—do you think I could run down the spiral staircase? It's quicker.

BORKMAN: Good Lord, I don't care what stairs you run down. Good night to you!

FRIDA: Good night, Mr. Borkman. (She goes out through the little tapestry-door to the left.)

(BORKMAN, lost in thought, goes over to the piano to close it, but then stops. He looks at all the emptiness around him and starts to walk up and down, from the corner near the piano to the upstage right corner, continuing ill at ease and restless, back and forth. Finally he goes over to the writing table, listens in the direction of the sliding door, quickly takes up a hand mirror, looks in it and adjusts his cravat.

There is a knock on the sliding door. BORKMAN hears it, quickly looks in its direction, but remains silent. After a moment the knock is repeated, this time somewhat louder.)

BORKMAN: (Standing by the writing table, his left hand resting on it, his right hand thrust into the breast of his coat.) Come in!

(VILHELM FOLDAL comes cautiously into the room. He is a bent, worn-out man with mild blue eyes and thin, long gray hair hanging down over his coat collar. A portfolio under his arm. A soft felt hat in his hand and large, horn-rimmed glasses, which he pushes up on his forehead.)

BORKMAN: (Changes his posture and looks at the entering figure with a half-disappointed, half-satisfied expression.) Ah, only you.

FOLDAL: Good evening, John Gabriel. Yes, only me.

BORKMAN: *(With a severe glance.)* You're late, I think.

FOLDAL: Well, it's not exactly a short trip, you know. Especially when you have to go on foot.

BORKMAN: Why do you always walk, Vilhelm? The streetcar runs past your house.

FOLDAL: It's healthier—and then I save on the fare, too. So, has Frida been up to play for you lately?

BORKMAN: She left only a moment ago. You didn't run into her outside?

FOLDAL: No, I haven't seen her in the longest time. Not since she went to live with Mrs. Wilton.

BORKMAN: *(Sits on the sofa and motions with his hand to a chair.)* You might as well sit, Vilhelm.

FOLDAL: *(Sits on the edge of a chair):* Thank you very much. *(Looks at him dejectedly.)* Oh, you just can't imagine how lonely I am since Frida left.

BORKMAN: Why? You've got plenty more.

FOLDAL: Yes, God knows I have. Five of them. But Frida was the only one who understood me a little. None of the others do, not at all.

BORKMAN: *(Darkly, looking into space and drumming on the table.)* No, that's just it. The curse that we exceptional men, we chosen ones, have to bear. The multitude, the mob—the whole average herd—they can't understand us, Vilhelm.

FOLDAL: *(Resigned.)* It's not even understanding so much as—with a little patience you can always go on waiting for that a while longer— *(In a tearful voice.)* But there's something even more bitter.

BORKMAN: *(Fiercely.)* Nothing's more bitter than that!

FOLDAL: Oh, John Gabriel, yes there is. There's been an awful scene at home—just before I came here—

BORKMAN: Really? What about?

FOLDAL: *(Bursts out.)* My family—they despise me!

BORKMAN: *(Bristling.)* Despise—?

FOLDAL: *(Wiping his eyes.)* I've been feeling it for quite a while. But today it came out in the open.

BORKMAN: *(Pausing a little.)* There's no doubt you made a bad choice when you married.

FOLDAL: There wasn't really that much of a choice. Besides—you get anxious about getting married when you start getting on in years. And then, at that time, I was so poor, almost wiped out—

BORKMAN: *(Springing up wrathfully.)* Is this an accusation against me? A reproach—?

FOLDAL: *(Anxiously.)* No, John Gabriel, for God's sake—

BORKMAN: Oh yes, you're sitting there thinking that all the troubles that swept over the bank—

FOLDAL: *(Placating him.)* But I don't blame you for that! Heaven forbid!

BORKMAN: *(Growling, sits down again.)* Well, that's good, at least.

FOLDAL: And please don't think I'm complaining about my wife. She's not too refined or educated, poor thing, that's true—but all the same, she's a good soul. No, it's the children, you see—

BORKMAN: I might have guessed.

FOLDAL: Because the children are educated, and they expect more out of life.

BORKMAN: *(Looking compassionately at him.)* And so the young ones despise you, Vilhelm?

FOLDAL: *(Shrugs his shoulders.)* I haven't done much with my career, you know. I have to admit that.

BORKMAN: *(Comes nearer and places his hand on FOLDAL's arm.)* Don't they know you wrote a tragedy when you were young?

FOLDAL: Of course they know. But it doesn't seem to make any sort of impression on them.

BORKMAN: Then they don't understand. Because your tragedy is good. I absolutely believe that.

FOLDAL: *(Brightening.)* Yes, wouldn't you say there's quite a bit of good in it, John Gabriel? Lord, if I could only get it produced! *(Eagerly begins to open and leaf through this portfolio.)* Look! Here are some revisions I've been working on—

BORKMAN: You have it with you?

FOLDAL: Yes, I brought it along. I haven't read it to you in such a long time—and I thought it might be entertaining for you to hear an act or two—

BORKMAN: *(Stopping him as he stands.)* No, no, it can wait. Some other time.

FOLDAL: Oh, all right. As you wish.

(BORKMAN paces the floor, back and forth across the room. FOLDAL packs up his manuscript again.)

BORKMAN: *(Stopping in front of him.)* You were right just now—in what you said about your career. But I promise you this, Vilhelm: when my moment of redemption strikes—

VILHELM: *(Begins to rise.)* Oh, thank you—!

BORKMAN: *(Waves his hand.)* Please sit down. *(With mounting excitement.)* When my moment of redemption strikes—when they realize that they can't do without me—when they come up to me here, in this room—

and, bowing before me, beg me to take back the reins of the bank—the new bank they founded, and don't know how to run!— *(Stands as before, in front of the desk and strikes his chest.)* Here I'll stand to receive them! And all through the land they'll ask for the reports: what conditions does John Gabriel Borkman insist upon before he— *(Stops suddenly and stares at FOLDAL.)* You look dubious! Perhaps you don't believe they'll come? That one day they must, must, must come to me? You don't believe it?

FOLDAL: Yes, yes, God knows I do, John Gabriel.

BORKMAN: *(Sits on the sofa again.)* I believe it absolutely. My conviction is unshakable—they will come. Without that conviction, I'd have put a bullet through my head long ago.

FOLDAL: *(Fearfully.)* Oh, no, never that—

BORKMAN: *(Triumphantly.)* But they will come! Oh yes, they'll come! Just wait! Any day, any hour, I'm expecting them here. And, as you can see, I am ready to receive them.

FOLDAL: *(With a sigh.)* If only they'd come soon.

BORKMAN: Yes, my friend. Time passes; the years pass; life—uch, no—I don't dare think about it! *(Looks at him.)* Do you know how I feel—every now and then?

FOLDAL: No.

BORKMAN: Like some Napoleon who's been shot and wounded in his very first battle.

FOLDAL: *(Putting his hand on his portfolio.)* I know that feeling.

BORKMAN: Yes, well, no doubt you do—on a smaller scale.

FOLDAL: *(Quietly.)* My little world of poetry is very precious to me, John Gabriel.

BORKMAN: *(Heatedly.)* Yes—but I! Who could have created millions! All the mines I could have commanded! All the new shafts I could have sunk, in endless numbers. Waterfalls! Stone quarries! Shipping lines—trade routes across the whole wide world. This—all this—I should have created myself!

FOLDAL: Yes—don't I know! You'd have stopped at nothing.

BORKMAN: *(Wringing his hands.)* And instead, now I have to sit here, a wounded eagle watching while others sneak in and, piece by piece, steal my prey.

FOLDAL: That's just how I feel.

BORKMAN: *(Disregarding him.)* Think about it. I was so close to my goal. If I'd only been given eight days grace—all the deposits would have been redeemed—all the securities I'd played with so daringly would have been back in place, just like before. Gigantic stock companies—dizzying in their scale—were a mere moment away from coming into being. And no one would have lost a penny.

FOLDAL: God, yes—you were so incredibly close—

BORKMAN: *(With stifled rage.)* But treachery destroyed me! At the decisive moment. *(Looks at him.)* Do you know what I maintain is the most hideous crime a man can commit?

FOLDAL: No, tell me.

BORKMAN: Not murder. Not robbery. Not burglary in the middle of the night. Not even perjury. These are mostly committed against people you hate—or don't care about at all.

FOLDAL: So what's the most hideous of all, John Gabriel?

BORKMAN: *(With emphasis.)* The most hideous crime of all is to abuse a friend's trust.

FOLDAL: *(A little skeptically.)* Yes, but just listen now—

BORKMAN: *(Passionately.)* What are you trying to say? I can see it in your face—but it's not true. The people who had securities in the bank—they would have got them all back. Every penny. No—I'm telling you: the most hideous crime a man can commit is to reveal a friend's confidential correspondence—laying bare, for all the world to see, what was meant for one person only—in private—like a whisper in a dark, empty, locked room. A man who is capable of stooping to such means is infected—poisoned all through his being—the morality of a master criminal. I had a friend like that. And he crushed me.

FOLDAL: I can guess who you're talking about.

BORKMAN: There wasn't one detail of my business that I didn't share with him freely. And then, at the crucial moment, he turned against me the very weapons I'd placed in his hands.

FOLDAL: I never could understand why he—well, of course, there were all sorts of rumors at the time.

BORKMAN: What were the rumors? Tell me. I don't know anything. Because I went immediately to—into isolation. What did people say, Vilhelm?

FOLDAL: People said—you would have been named a cabinet minister.

BORKMAN: That was offered to me. But I declined.

FOLDAL: So you weren't standing in his way.

BORKMAN: Oh no—that's not why he betrayed me.

FOLDAL: Then I've got no idea.

BORKMAN: I might as well tell you, Vilhelm.

FOLDAL: Yes.

BORKMAN: It was—something to do with a woman.

FOLDAL: A woman? No—but John Gabriel—

BORKMAN: *(Dismissively.)* Well, well, well—let's not say another word about these stupid old stories. And as it turned out, neither of us got a cabinet post.

FOLDAL: But he made it to the heights.

BORKMAN: And I, to the depths.

FOLDAL: It's a horrible tragedy.

BORKMAN: *(Nodding to him.)* Almost as horrible as your own, it seems, when I think about it.

FOLDAL: *(Innocently.)* Yes, at least that horrible.

BORKMAN: *(Laughing quietly.)* But really, if you look at it from another angle, it's a kind of comedy too.

FOLDAL: A comedy? This?

BORKMAN: Yes, in a way. The way it's turning out. Just listen to this—

FOLDAL: What?

BORKMAN: You say you didn't meet Frida when you came in?

FOLDAL: No.

BORKMAN: While the two of us sit here, she's down there playing dance music in the house of the man who crushed me.

FOLDAL: I had no idea.

BORKMAN: Yes, she took her music and left me. For that high and mighty household.

FOLDAL: *(Apologetically.)* Well, well, the poor child—

BORKMAN: And just guess who she's playing for—among others.

FOLDAL: Who?

BORKMAN: For my son.

FOLDAL: What!

BORKMAN: Yes, what do you think of that, Vilhelm? My son, down there among the dancers tonight. Doesn't that sound like a comedy, as I said?

FOLDAL: Yes, but he doesn't know—

BORKMAN: Know what?

FOLDAL: Surely he doesn't know how he—how this man—

BORKMAN: Go ahead and use his name. I can bear to hear it now.

FOLDAL: I'm sure your son doesn't realize the connection.

BORKMAN: *(Gloomily, banging on the table.)* He knows it, as certainly as I'm sitting here.

FOLDAL: But how can you imagine he'd want to enter that house?

BORKMAN: *(Shaking his head.)* My son isn't likely to see things with the same eyes I do. I'd even swear that he's on my enemies' side. No doubt he thinks like they do—that as a lawyer, Hinkel was just doing his damned duty when he betrayed me.

FOLDAL: But my dear John Gabriel, who could have made him think that way?

BORKMAN: Who? Did you forget who brought him up? First his aunt—since he was six or seven. Then after that—his mother!

FOLDAL: I think you're being unfair to them—

BORKMAN: (*Flaring up.*) I'm never unfair to anybody! The two of them have turned him against me, I'm telling you!

FOLDAL: (*Placating him.*) Yes, yes, yes, I suppose that's true.

BORKMAN: (*Resentfully.*) Women! They warp and mutilate life for us! Mangle our destinies—disrupt our march to glory!

FOLDAL: Not all of them!

BORKMAN: No? Name one who's worth anything!

FOLDAL: Well, that's the problem. The ones I know aren't worth much—

BORKMAN: (*Snorting scornfully.*) So what's the point? Such women may exist—but you never see them.

FOLDAL: (*Warmly.*) Oh yes, John Gabriel, there's still a point, you see—it's a joy, and a blessing, to think that out there beyond all of us, somewhere, the true woman can be found.

BORKMAN: (*Stirs impatiently on the sofa.*) Oh, cut the poetic slop.

FOLDAL: (*Looks at him, deeply hurt.*) You call my holiest belief poetic slop?

BORKMAN: (*Harshly.*) Yes I do! This kind of thing is the reason you haven't gotten further in the world. If you could get rid of all that garbage, maybe I could help you get on your feet—get you on your way.

FOLDAL: (*Seething inwardly.*) Ah, but you can't do that.

BORKMAN: I certainly *can*, when I get back into power.

FOLDAL: But the chances of that are pretty remote.

BORKMAN: (*Vehemently.*) Maybe you think it will never happen? Answer me!

FOLDAL: I don't know how to answer you.

BORKMAN: (*Rises, cold and superior, motioning with his hand to the door.*) Then I no longer have any use for you.

FOLDAL: (*Rising.*) No use—!

BORKMAN: Since you don't believe that my destiny will change—

FOLDAL: But I just can't believe something that's against all reason! Such a total redemption—

BORKMAN: Go on—go on—

FOLDAL: I never got my degree—but I've read enough to know—

BORKMAN: (*Quickly.*) Impossible, you mean?

FOLDAL: At least unprecedented.

BORKMAN: Exceptional men need no precedents.

FOLDAL: The law doesn't take that into account.

BORKMAN: *(Caustically.)* You're no poet, Vilhelm.

FOLDAL: *(Involuntarily clasping his hands.)* You say that in all seriousness?

BORKMAN: *(Turning away, not answering.)* We're just wasting time. It's best if you don't come here again.

FOLDAL: So you want me to leave you?

BORKMAN: *(Without looking at him.)* I have no use for you any more.

FOLDAL: *(Speaking gently and taking his portfolio.)* No, no—no, I suppose that's true.

BORKMAN: Here you've been lying to me, all this time.

FOLDAL: *(Shaking his head.)* Never lying, John Gabriel.

BORKMAN: Haven't you been sitting there lying about your faith in me— your hope, your confidence?

FOLDAL: It wasn't a lie, if you believed in my dream. As long as you believed in me, I could believe in you.

BORKMAN: Then we've been deceiving each other. And possibly ourselves as well.

FOLDAL: But isn't that how friendship works, John Gabriel?

BORKMAN: *(Smiling bitterly.)* Yes—deception— that's what friendship is. You're right about that. I've been shown that once before.

FOLDAL: *(Looking over at him.)* No gift for poetry. How could you say something so brutal to me?

BORKMAN: *(In a gentler voice.)* Well, I'm really not an expert in these things.

FOLDAL: More than you know, perhaps.

BORKMAN: I?

FOLDAL: *(Softly.)* Yes, John Gabriel. I've had my own doubts—every now and then, you know—this terrible doubt that I've wasted my life for the sake of an illusion.

BORKMAN: If you doubt yourself, you'll never stand on your own two feet.

FOLDAL: That's why it was so comforting to come here—for some support from you, who had faith. *(Takes his hat.)* But now you seem like a stranger to me.

BORKMAN: And you to me.

FOLDAL: Good night, John Gabriel.

BORKMAN: Good night, Vilhelm.

> *(FOLDAL leaves to the left. BORKMAN stands for a while, staring at the closed door; makes a move, as if to call back FOLDAL, but recollects himself and begins to pace up and down the room, his hands behind his back. Then he stops at the sofa table and turns off the lamp. The room is semi-dark.*
> *In a little while, there is a knock on the tapestry door in the background.)*

BORKMAN: *(By the table, starts suddenly, turns, asks loudly.)* Who is it, who's knocking?

(No answer, another knock.)

BORKMAN: *(Standing still.)* Who is it? Come in!

(ELLA RENTHEIM, with a lighted candle in her hand, appears in the doorway. She is wearing a black dress, as before, with her coat worn loosely over her shoulders)

BORKMAN: *(Staring at her.)* Who are you? What do you want with me?

ELLA: *(Closing the door behind her and approaching nearer.)* Borkman—it's me. *(She sets the candle on the piano and stands beside it.)*

BORKMAN: *(Stands as if struck by lightning, staring intently at her and whispering half aloud.)* Is it—is it Ella? Ella Rentheim?

ELLA: Yes, "your" Ella, as you used to call me. Once. Many, many years ago.

BORKMAN: *(As before.)* Yes, it *is* you, Ella—I can see it now.

ELLA: Do you still recognize me?

BORKMAN: Yes, I'm beginning to—

ELLA: The years have been hard on me, and it's autumn for me now. Wouldn't you say, Borkman?

BORKMAN: *(Evasively.)* You've changed a bit. At least at first glance—

ELLA: Those dark curls down the back of my neck are gone—those curls you loved to wind around your fingers.

BORKMAN: *(Quickly.)* That's it! Now I see, Ella. You've changed your hair style.

ELLA: *(Smiling sadly.)* That's right. It's all in the hair style.

BORKMAN: *(Changing the subject.)* I had no idea you were in this part of the country.

ELLA: I just got here.

BORKMAN: Why did you make the journey—now, in winter?

ELLA: You'll hear why.

BORKMAN: Is there something you want from me?

ELLA: That too. But if we're going to talk about that, I'll have to start a long way back.

BORKMAN: You seem tired.

ELLA: Yes, I'm tired.

BORKMAN: Won't you sit down? There, on the sofa.

ELLA: Thank you. I need to sit down.

(She goes over to the right and sits on the nearest corner of the sofa. BORKMAN stands by the table with his hands behind his back and looks at her. A short silence.)

ELLA: I can't conceive of how long it's been since we last met face to face, Borkman.

BORKMAN: *(Darkly.)* A long, long time. And all the horror in between.

ELLA: A whole lifetime in between. A wasted lifetime.

BORKMAN: *(Looking sharply at her.)* Wasted!

ELLA: Yes, absolutely wasted. For both of us.

BORKMAN: *(Coldly businesslike.)* I don't consider my life wasted yet.

ELLA: Then what about *my* life?

BORKMAN: You're responsible for that yourself, Ella.

ELLA: *(With a start.)* You can say that!

BORKMAN: You could have been happy without me, easily.

ELLA: You believe that?

BORKMAN: If you'd made up your mind to it.

ELLA: *(Bitterly.)* Yes, I'm only too aware that there was someone else standing by, ready to receive me.

BORKMAN: But you turned him away.

ELLA: Yes, I did.

BORKMAN: Time after time, you turned him away. Year after year—

ELLA: *(Scornfully.)* Year after year I turned away happiness, is that what you mean?

BORKMAN: You could easily have been happy with him. And it would have saved me, too.

ELLA: You—?

BORKMAN: Yes, you would have saved me then.

ELLA: What do you mean?

BORKMAN: He believed I was somehow behind your constant refusals. So he got his revenge. Which wasn't hard for him—with all my confidential letters in his possession. Then he made use of them—and that was the end of me. For the time being, at any rate. So you see, I owe it all to you, Ella.

ELLA: I see, Borkman. When it comes right down to it, perhaps *I* owe a debt to you.

BORKMAN: That's one way to put it. I know perfectly well how much I have to thank you for. You bought the estate, this whole property, at the auction. And then you put the house at my—and your sister's—disposal. You took Erhart in and cared for him in every way.

ELLA: For as long as I was allowed to—

BORKMAN: By your sister, yes. I've never gotten involved in these domestic issues. As I was saying: I know how much you've sacrificed for me and for your sister. You were in a position to do it. But remember, I put you in that position.

ELLA: *(Fiercely.)* You're completely wrong about that, Borkman! It was my feeling for Erhart—for you too—that made me do it!

BORKMAN: *(Interrupting.)* My dear, let's leave feelings out of it. I mean, of course, that when you acted as you did, I was the one who gave you the power to do it.

ELLA: *(Smiling.)* Hm—the power, the power.

BORKMAN: *(Heatedly.)* Yes, exactly—the power! When the great blow was about to be struck—at that critical moment when I couldn't spare family, friends, anybody—when the time came for me to seize control of the millions that were in my hands—I still spared everything of yours— everything you possessed—even though I could have taken it and used it too, just like all the rest.

ELLA: *(Coldly and calmly.)* That's certainly true, Borkman.

BORKMAN: Yes it is. And that's why—when they came for me—they found everything of yours untouched in the vault.

ELLA: *(Looking at him.)* I've thought a lot about that—why you spared everything of mine—and only of mine.

BORKMAN: Why?

ELLA; Yes, why. Tell me.

BORKMAN: *(Hard and scornful.)* You're thinking, possibly, so I could have a cushion in case everything failed?

ELLA: No, no—you didn't think like that in those days.

BORKMAN: Never! I was completely certain of victory.

ELLA: Well then—why?

BORKMAN: *(Shrugging his shoulders.)* Good lord, Ella—it's not that easy to recall motives from twenty years ago. All I remember is that when I wrestled with all the tremendous projects that were about to be launched—pacing alone, in silence—I imagined that I was some kind of captain of the sky—I walked the sleepless nights preparing my giant balloon for the battle, ready to sail out over an unknown, perilous sea.

ELLA: *(Smiling.)* You, who were so certain of victory.

BORKMAN: *(Impatiently.)* People are like that, Ella. They can doubt and believe, both at once. *(To himself.)* And that must have been why I wouldn't take you or your belongings with me in the balloon.

ELLA: *(Tensely.)* Why? Tell me why.

BORKMAN: *(Not looking at her.)* You don't take what's dearest to you on such a journey.

ELLA: But you *had* what was dearest to you on board already. Your whole future.

BORKMAN: Life isn't always the dearest thing.

ELLA: *(Breathlessly.)* So that was how you felt?

BORKMAN: It seems that way now.

ELLA: You thought I was the dearest—

BORKMAN: So it would appear.

ELLA: But that was years and years after you'd betrayed me—and married—someone else.

BORKMAN: Betrayed, you call it? You know very well that I was driven by higher motives—well, *other* motives, anyway. Without his support, there was no way I could have proceeded.

ELLA: *(Controlling herself.)* And so you betrayed me in service of—higher motives.

BORKMAN: I couldn't do without his help. And you were the price for that help.

ELLA: And you paid the price. In full. Without demurring.

BORKMAN: I had no other choice. It was victory or defeat.

ELLA: *(In a trembling voice, looking at him.)* Is what you're saying true—that I was, at that time, the dearest thing in the world to you?

BORKMAN: Then and later—for a long time after.

ELLA: And even so you bartered me—traded away your rights in love—sold my love to another man so you could run a bank.

BORKMAN: *(Gloomy, bowed.)* It was necessary.

ELLA: *(Rising from the sofa, passionate and trembling.)* Criminal!

BORKMAN: *(Starting, but controlling himself.)* That's a word I've heard before.

ELLA: Don't think for a minute that I'm talking about whatever laws you might have broken—what you did with all those stocks and securities, or whatever they were—do you think I care about that? If I'd been permitted to stand by your side, when everything came down around you—

BORKMAN: *(Tensely.)* What then, Ella?

ELLA: Believe me, I would gladly have borne it all with you. The shame, the ruin, I'd have helped you through everything.

BORKMAN: You would have? Could you have?

ELLA: Yes I could. Because I didn't yet know about your great and terrible crime—

BORKMAN: What crime? What do you mean?

ELLA: I mean the crime for which there is no forgiveness.

BORKMAN: *(Staring at her.)* You must be out of your mind!

ELLA: *(Coming closer.)* Murderer! You've committed the great, mortal sin.

BORKMAN: You're raving, Ella!

ELLA: You've killed my ability to love. *(Approaching him.)* Do you understand what that means? The Bible speaks of a mysterious sin for which there can be no forgiveness. I've never been able to grasp what that could be.

But now I see. The great, unforgivable sin is to murder someone's ability to love.

BORKMAN: And you say I've done that?

ELLA: That's what you've done. I never understood what happened to me until tonight. When you deserted me and turned instead to Gunhild—I thought it was just ordinary weakness on your part, and heartless scheming on hers. And I almost think I despised you a little, in spite of everything. But *now* I see it! You betrayed the woman you loved! Me, me, me! You were ready to trade the thing you held dearest for the sake of profit. And so you've committed a double murder! Your own soul—and mine!

BORKMAN: *(Cold, controlled.)* I recognize that uncontrolled passion of yours, Ella. No doubt it's natural for you to see things as you do. You're a woman. And so, you don't recognize anything in the world other than your feelings.

ELLA: That's right, I don't.

BORKMAN: What your own heart tells you—that's all.

ELLA: That's all! That's all! You're right.

BORKMAN: But remember that I'm a man. You were the dearest thing in the world to me—as a woman. But when it comes right down to it, one woman can always be replaced by another.

ELLA: *(Looks at him, smiling.)* Was that what you discovered when you took Gunhild as your wife?

BORKMAN: No—but my calling helped me to bear *that* as well. I wanted to command all the sources of power in this land. From earth and sea— forest and mountain—all the hidden hoards of this world—I wanted to carve out a kingdom for myself—to bring them all into submission, and in so doing, create well-being for thousands and thousands of others.

ELLA: *(Lost in memories.)* I know. So many evenings when we talked about your plans—

BORKMAN: Yes, I could talk with you, Ella.

ELLA: I teased you, and asked you if you hoped to awaken all the slumbering gold-spirits.

BORKMAN: *(Nodding.)* Yes, I remember the phrase. All the slumbering gold-spirits.

ELLA: But you didn't take it as a joke. You said, "Yes, Ella—yes, that's precisely what I want."

BORKMAN: And it was. All I needed was a leg up—and that was all dependent then on one man. He was willing and able to get me that key position in the bank—if I, for my part—

ELLA: Exactly. If you, for your part, gave up the woman you loved, and who loved you so inexpressibly in return.

BORKMAN: I knew how all-consuming his passion was for you. Knew that he'd never—for any other consideration—

ELLA: And so you came to terms.

BORKMAN: *(Vehemently.)* Yes I did, Ella! Don't you see? The hunger for power was so overwhelming in me. So I came to terms. I *had* to do it. And he helped me up, halfway to those heights that beckoned to me, that I longed for. And I climbed and climbed. Year after year I climbed and climbed.

ELLA: And I was erased from your life.

BORKMAN: And in the end, he cast me back into the abyss. Because of you, Ella.

ELLA: *(After a short, thoughtful silence.)* Borkman—don't you think there's been a curse on our whole relationship?

BORKMAN: *(Looks at her.)* A curse?

ELLA: Yes, don't you think so?

BORKMAN: *(Uneasily.)* Yes. But why—? *(Cries out.)* Oh, Ella, I don't know who's right any more—you or I!

ELLA: You are the one who sinned. You caused the death of all my human joy.

BORKMAN: *(Anguished.)* Don't say that, Ella!

ELLA: All my joy as a woman, at least. Since that time, when your image began to fade for me, I've lived my life as if I were under a total eclipse of the sun. Year after year it became harder—and finally it was impossible—for me to love any living creature. Not humans, nor animals, nor plants—only that one alone—

BORKMAN: Which one?

ELLA: Erhart, of course.

BORKMAN: Erhart—?

ELLA: Erhart. Your son, Borkman.

BORKMAN: Has he really claimed such a warm place in your heart?

ELLA: Why else do you think I took him in? And kept him as long as I could? Why?

BORKMAN: I thought it was out of compassion. Like everything you did.

ELLA: *(With strong inner emotion.)* Compassion, you say! *(Laughs.)* I haven't known a moment's compassion—since you betrayed me. I have no such feeling. If a poor, hungry child found its way into my kitchen, shivering and crying and begging for a scrap of food, I let the cook take care of it. I never felt the urge to bring the little child to me, warm it by the fire, and look on with pleasure while it ate its fill. Now I had never been like that when I was younger; I remember that so distinctly. It's *you* who've made this barren desert inside me—and outside, too.

BORKMAN: Except for Erhart.

ELLA: Yes, except for your son. But for everything else, everything that stirs with life—you've taken from me a mother's joy, and a mother's sorrows and tears as well. And *that*, perhaps, is my dearest loss.

BORKMAN: Can you mean that, Ella?

ELLA: Who can say? My mother's sorrows and tears might have helped me most of all. *(In strong agitation.)* But I *couldn't* accept my loss! And so I took Erhart to me. Won him completely. Won every part of his warm, trusting, child's heart—until—ah!

BORKMAN: Until what?

ELLA: Until his mother—his natural mother—took him away from me again.

BORKMAN: He had to leave you. To come here to town.

ELLA: *(Wringing her hands.)* But I can't bear the desolation, Borkman—or the emptiness. Or the loss of your son's heart.

BORKMAN: *(With a malignant look in his eyes.)* Hm. I doubt you've lost it, Ella. A heart's not easily lost to anyone down below—on the ground floor.

ELLA: I've lost Erhart here. *She's* won him back. Or someone has. That's clear enough from the occasional letters he writes to me.

BORKMAN: Have you come here, then, to take him home with you?

ELLA: Yes, if that were actually possible.

BORKMAN: It's possible, if you really want it. Your claim on him is first—and best.

ELLA: Oh, claims, claims! What good are claims in this case? If I don't have him of his own free will—I don't have him at all. And I must have my child's heart, whole and undivided.

BORKMAN: You must remember that Erhart's already in his twenties. You can't count on having his whole and undivided heart, as you put it, for very long.

ELLA: *(With a heavy smile.)* It wouldn't have to be for very long.

BORKMAN: Oh no? I'd have thought that when you craved something this much, you'd want it for the rest of your life.

ELLA: So I do. That's why it wouldn't have to be for long.

BORKMAN: *(Startled)* What do you mean by that?

ELLA: Of course you know that I've been ill these last years.

BORKMAN: You have?

ELLA: You didn't know?

BORKMAN : Not really.

ELLA: *(Looking at him, surprised.)* Erhart never told you?

BORKMAN: I can't really remember right now—

ELLA: Maybe he hasn't spoken of me at all?

BORKMAN: Yes, I'm sure he's talked about you. But then, I so seldom get to see anything of him. Almost never. Someone below keeps him away from me. Far away, you understand?

ELLA: Are you certain of that, Borkman?

BORKMAN: Yes, I'm quite certain. *(Changes his tone.)* So, Ella, you've been ill.

ELLA: Yes, I have. And then this autumn, when it got so much worse, I had to come to town to consult some specialists.

BORKMAN: And you've already seen them?

ELLA: Yes, this morning.

BORKMAN: What did they say?

ELLA: They completely confirmed what I had suspected for a long time—

BORKMAN: And?

ELLA: *(Calmly and evenly.)* I have a mortal illness, Borkman.

BORKMAN: Oh, Ella, you mustn't believe that.

ELLA: An illness for which there's no help, or cure. The doctors don't have a remedy for it. They have to let it take its course. They can't do anything to stop it. Just make things a little easier, I guess. And that's good, at least.

BORKMAN: Oh, but it could be a long while yet, believe me.

ELLA: I was told I might last the winter.

BORKMAN: *(Unthinking.)* Well, the winter's quite long.

ELLA: *(Quietly.)* Anyway, it's long enough for me.

BORKMAN: *(Evasively lively.)* But how on earth could you have come down with this illness? You—who've always lived such a healthy and regular life—? Do you know how it happened?

ELLA: *(Looking at him.)* The doctors think that perhaps, at some time in the past, I went through an extreme emotional crisis.

BORKMAN: *(Flaring up.)* Emotional crisis! Aha—I understand. I'm to bear the blame.

ELLA: *(Mounting agitation.)* It's too late for that now! But I must have my heart's child, my one and only child, before I pass away! It is so painful for me to think that I'm going to lose everything alive here—lose the sun, the light, the air, without leaving behind anyone who'll think of me, remember me with warmth and sadness—as a son remembers the mother he has lost.

BORKMAN: *(After a short silence.)* Take him, Ella. If you can win him.

ELLA: *(Animated):* You give your consent? *Can* you, Borkman?

BORKMAN: Oh yes. It's not such a great sacrifice, you know. Because I have no hold on him in any case.

ELLA: Thank you, thank you for the sacrifice all the same. But now I have just *one* thing to beg of you. A great thing for *me*, Borkman.

BORKMAN: Well, say it.

ELLA: You'll probably think it's childish of me—perhaps you won't understand it at all—

BORKMAN: Say it—say it, then!

ELLA: When I pass on from here—I will leave behind a substantial—

BORKMAN: So I imagine—

ELLA: And my intention is to give it all to Erhart.

BORKMAN: Well, you really don't have anyone closer.

ELLA: *(Warmly.)* No, truly, there's no one closer to me.

BORKMAN: None of your own blood. You're the last.

ELLA: *(Nodding slowly.)* Yes, that's it exactly. When I die, the Rentheim name dies, too. And that is an agonizing thought for me. Erased from the world—all the way down to my name.

BORKMAN: Ah. I see what you're getting at.

ELLA: *(Passionately.)* Don't let that happen! Let Erhart bear my name after me!

BORKMAN: *(Looking angrily at her.)* I understand you all too well. You'll spare my son from having to bear his father's name. That's what you want.

ELLA: Never! I would have borne that name with you defiantly—gladly. But a mother who soon must die—a name means more than you realize, Borkman.

BORKMAN: *(Cold and proud.)* Very well, Ella. I shall be man enough to bear my name alone.

ELLA: *(Grasping and shaking his hands.)* Thank you, thank you! Now everything is settled between us, completely. Yes, let it be. You've made amends as far as you could. For when I'm gone from this life, Erhart Rentheim will live on after me!

(The tapestry door is flung open. MRS. BORKMAN, her large shawl over her head, stands in the doorway.)

MRS. BORKMAN: *(Violently agitated.)* Erhart will never take that name—never in all eternity!

ELLA: *(Shrinking back.)* Gunhild!

BORKMAN: *(Hard and menacing.)* No one has permission to come up here!

MRS. BORKMAN: *(Advances a step.)* I give myself permission.

BORKMAN: *(Moves toward her.)* What do you want with me?

MRS. BORKMAN: To fight for you, struggle for you, protect you from evil powers.

BORKMAN: You'll find the darkest of those powers in yourself, Gunhild.

MRS. BORKMAN: *(Harshly.)* That's as may be. *(Threatening, arms up-stretched.)* But this is what I say: he will bear his father's name! And lift it high again, to honor! And I alone shall be his mother! I alone! My son's heart will be mine. Mine and no one else's. *(She goes out through the tapestry door and closes it behind her)*

ELLA: *(Shaken, distraught.)* Borkman—this storm will be the wreck of Erhart! You and Gunhild have got to come to an understanding. We must go down to her right now.

BORKMAN: *(Looking at her.)* We? I, as well, you mean?

ELLA: Both of us.

BORKMAN: *(Shaking his head.)* She's hard, you know. Hard as the metal I once dreamed of carving from the mountain.

ELLA: And now we'll see how hard that is.

(Borkman without answering, stands and looks uncertainly at her.)

F.ND OF ACT TWO

ACT THREE

MRS. BORKMAN's living room. The lamp is still burning on the table by the sofa. The garden room is completely dark. MRS. BORKMAN, with her shawl over her head, enters, in a state of high excitement, through the hall door. She goes to the window and pulls the curtain to one side. Then she crosses over to sit by the stove, but immediately springs up, goes over to the bell-pull, and rings. No one comes, and so she rings again, this time more violently. Soon after, the MAID comes in through the hall. She appears sulky and sleepy and seems to have dressed in a hurry.

MRS. BORKMAN: *(Impatiently.)* Where were you, Malene? I had to ring twice!

MAID: Yes, ma'am, I heard you.

MRS. BORKMAN: But even so, you didn't come.

MAID: *(Crossly.)* Well, I thought I ought to put on a few clothes, at least.

MRS. BORKMAN: Yes, get dressed properly. And then—right away—you'll run and get my son.

MAID: *(Stares in amazement at her.)* You want me to get Mr. Erhart?

MRS. BORKMAN: Yes. Just tell him that he has to come home to me at once, because I must speak with him.

MAID: *(Sullenly.)* Then I really ought to go and wake the coachman over at the manager's—

MRS. BORKMAN: Why?

MAID: So he can harness the sleigh. That's an awful snowstorm out there tonight.

MRS. BORKMAN: That's nothing. Hurry and go! It's just around the corner.

MAID: Oh, ma'am, it isn't, you know—it isn't just around the corner.

MRS. BORKMAN: Of course it is. Don't you know where Mr. Hinkel's is?

MAID: *(Sarcastically.)* Oh, I see. Is that where Mr. Erhart is tonight?

MRS. BORKMAN: *(Startled.)* Yes. Where else would he be?

MAID: *(Hiding a smile.)* Well, I just thought he was over there—where he usually is.

MRS. BORKMAN: Where do you mean?

MAID: Over at that Mrs. Wilton's—as they call her.

MRS. BORKMAN: Mrs. Wilton? My son doesn't go there regularly.

MAID: *(Half mumbling.)* Some would say he's over there every day.

MRS. BORKMAN: Idle talk, Malene. Now go on over to the Hinkels' and make sure you bring him back.

MAID: *(Tosses her head.)* Oh, God help us—all right, I'm going.

(She is about to go out through the hall, when the door is opened. ELLA RENTHEIM and BORKMAN are seen in the doorway.)

MRS. BORKMAN: *(Taking a step back.)* What does this mean?

MAID: *(Terrified.)* In Jesus' name!

MRS. BORKMAN: *(Whispers to the maid.)* Tell him he must come at once!

MAID: *(Softly.)* Yes, ma'am.

(ELLA and, behind her, BORKMAN come into the room. The MAID sneaks around in back of them and through the door, closing it after her. A short silence.)

MRS. BORKMAN: *(After recovering, turns to ELLA.)* What does he want down here with me?

ELLA: To try and come to an understanding with you, Gunhild.

MRS. BORKMAN: He's never tried before.

ELLA: Tonight he wants to.

MRS. BORKMAN: The last time we faced each other—was in court. When I was called upon to give an explanation- -

BORKMAN: *(Stepping closer.)* Tonight it's my turn to give an explanation.

MRS. BORKMAN: *(Regarding him.)* You!

BORKMAN: Not about how I broke the law. The whole world knows about that.

MRS. BORKMAN: *(With a bitter sigh.)* Yes, that's the truth. The whole world knows it.

BORKMAN: But they don't know why I broke the law. Why I had to break it. People don't see that I had to do it because I was myself—I was John Gabriel Borkman—and no one else. And that is what I want to try to explain to you.

MRS. BORKMAN: *(Shaking her head.)* No one is acquitted by intentions. Or impulses, either.

BORKMAN: In his own eyes, they can acquit him.

MRS. BORKMAN: *(With a gesture of dismissal.)* That's enough! I've thought over and over again about those dark actions of yours.

BORKMAN: And I as well. During those endless five years in my cell—and elsewhere—I had time for that. And for eight years up there in the salon, I've had even more time. I've retried the case again and again—held new hearings—for myself. Time after time I've tried it. I've been my own accuser, my own defender, and my own judge. And more impartial than anyone else could be—I'll dare say that. I've paced the floor up there, turning every one of my actions inside out. Examined them from every angle, front and back, as ruthlessly as any lawyer. And the verdict, every time, is the same: the only person I've injured is myself.

MRS. BORKMAN: What about me? And your son?

BORKMAN: You are both included when I say myself.

MRS. BORKMAN: And the hundreds of others? That people say you ruined?

BORKMAN: *(More fiercely.)* I had the power. And the irresistible urge inside. The imprisoned millions lay there, all over the land, deep inside the mountains, and called out to me. They cried, cried for freedom—but no one else could hear. Only I, alone.

MRS. BORKMAN: Yes, and ruined the name of Borkman.

BORKMAN: Who knows—if others had had the power, they might have done the same.

MRS. BORKMAN: No one—no one but you would have done it.

BORKMAN: Maybe not. They didn't have my abilities. And even if they had tried it, they wouldn't have done it the way I saw it could be done. The act itself would have been different. In short, I've acquitted myself.

ELLA: *(Softly imploring.)* Oh, how can you say that so confidently, Borkman?

BORKMAN: *(Nodding.)* Acquitted myself in that matter, I mean. But then comes the great, crushing self-indictment.

MRS. BORKMAN: What is that?

BORKMAN: I've walked back and forth up there wasting eight precious years of my life. The day I was set free, I should have walked out into reality—a reality hard as iron, free of dreams. I should have started at the bottom and swung myself up to the heights once more—higher than ever, in spite of all that came between.

MRS. BORKMAN: It would just have been the same life all over again, believe me.

BORKMAN: *(Shaking his head and looking at her meaningfully.)* Nothing new ever happens. But what has already happened doesn't repeat itself, either. The eye transforms the action. And so a newborn eye can transform an old action. *(Breaking off.)* No, you can't understand that.

MRS. BORKMAN: *(Curtly.)* No, I can't understand it.

BORKMAN: And there's my curse. I've never found understanding in a single human soul.

ELLA: *(Looking at him.)* Never, Borkman?

BORKMAN: Except one—perhaps—long, long ago. Back when I didn't think I needed understanding. But since then—never, and no one! No one there, alert and eager to encourage me, to ring for me like a morning bell, urging me on to great new works—and impressing on me that nothing I've done is beyond repair.

MRS. BORKMAN: *(Laughing scornfully.)* So, after all, you depend on outside impressions.

BORKMAN: *(Mounting anger.)* Yes, when the whole world, in chorus, hisses that I am so lost, so far beyond redemption, then there are moments when I come close to believing it. *(Raising his head.)* But then my inmost, invincible confidence rises up again. And it acquits me!

MRS. BORKMAN: *(Looks at him harshly.)* Why didn't you ever come to me and ask for what you call understanding?

BORKMAN: Would that have been of any use? Coming to you?

MRS. BORKMAN: *(With a dismissive gesture.)* You've never loved anything outside yourself—that's the heart of it.

BORKMAN: *(Proudly.)* I loved power!

MRS. BORKMAN: Power, yes!

BORKMAN: The power to create human happiness, in wider and wider circles around me.

MRS. BORKMAN: Once you had the power to make me happy. Did you use it?

BORKMAN: *(Not looking at her.)* When there's a shipwreck—often someone has to go under.

MRS. BORKMAN: And your son! Have you used your power—has your life's work made him happy?

BORKMAN: Him? I don't know him.

MRS. BORKMAN: No, that's true. You don't even know him.

BORKMAN: *(Hard.)* You've seen to that—his own mother.

MRS. BORKMAN: *(Looking at him with a triumphant expression.)* Oh, you don't know the half of what I've seen to.

BORKMAN: You?

MRS. BORKMAN: Oh yes, I.

BORKMAN: Well, say it then.

MRS. BORKMAN: I've seen to your obituary.

BORKMAN: *(With a short, dry laugh.)* My obituary? Well, well! It sounds as if I'm already dead.

MRS. BORKMAN: And so you are.

BORKMAN: *(Slowly.)* Yes, you may be right. *(Flaring.)* No, no! Not yet! I've been close to it—very close. But now I'm awake. Revived. Life still lies before me. I can see this new life—radiant, pulsating, waiting for me— And you'll get to see it too, you too—

MRS. BORKMAN: *(Raising her hand.)* Stop dreaming about life! Stay there where you lie, and keep quiet.

ELLA: Gunhild! Gunhild, how can you—!

MRS. BORKMAN: *(Not listening to her.)* I will raise a monument over the grave.

BORKMAN: A pillar of shame, you mean?

MRS. BORKMAN: Oh no—nothing made of stone or metal. No one will be able to carve their insults on this monument. It will be as if a dense thicket, a grove of trees and bushes encircled your living death. A canopy over everything that was once dark—hidden forever from human sight— John Gabriel Borkman!

BORKMAN: *(Hoarsely and bitterly.)* And *you'll* perform this labor of love?

MRS. BORKMAN: Not with my strength alone. I can't hope to do it. But I've raised a helper to devote his whole life to this one goal. His life will be lived in such purity, such grandeur and light, that your own life will sink into the dark shafts you dug in the earth, and be forgotten.

BORKMAN: *(Darkly and dangerously.)* If you're talking about Erhart, say it straight out.

MRS. BORKMAN: *(Looking at him straight in the eye.)* Yes, Erhart. My son. Whom you were willing to give up—in penance for your own crimes.

BORKMAN: *(With a glance at ELLA.)* In penance for my greatest sin.

MRS. BORKMAN: *(Dismissively.)* Against a stranger! Remember your sin against me! *(Looks triumphantly at them.)* But he won't listen to you! When I call out to him in my need, he'll come! Because he wants to be with me! With me, never anyone else— *(Suddenly listens, cries out.)* I hear him! There he is—there he is—Erhart!

(ERHART BORKMAN flings open the door and comes into the room. He is wearing an overcoat and a hat.)

ERHART: *(Pale and anxious.)* Mother—what in God's name—! *(He sees BORKMAN standing in the doorway of the garden room, starts, takes off his hat. Silence for a moment.)* What do you want, mother? What's happened here?

MRS. BORKMAN: *(Stretching her arms to him.)* I want to see you, Erhart. To keep you with me, always!

ERHART: *(Stammering.)* Keep me? Always! What do you mean by that?

MRS. BORKMAN: Keep you, keep you. I've got to. Because there's someone who wants to take you away from me.

ERHART: *(Retreats a step.)* Ah. Then you know about it.

MRS. BORKMAN: Yes. You know about it too?

ERHART: *(Surprised, looking at her.)* Do I know? Yes, of course—

MRS. BORKMAN: Aha—a conspiracy! Behind my back! Erhart!

ERHART: *(Quickly.)* Mother, tell me what you know.

MRS. BORKMAN: Everything. Your aunt has come here to take you back from me.

ERHART: Aunt Ella!

ELLA: First listen to me, Erhart.

MRS. BORKMAN: She wants me to give you over to her. She wants to take your mother's place, Erhart! She wants you to be her son, not mine, from now on. Inherit everything from her. To leave your own name behind and take hers instead.

ERHART: Aunt Ella—is all this true?

ELLA: Yes, it's true.

ERHART: I didn't know a word about this until now. Why do you want me back with you again?

ELLA: Because I feel I'm losing you here.

MRS. BORKMAN: You're losing him to me—yes! Just as it should be.

ELLA: Erhart, I can't risk losing you. You should know that I'm lonely—and dying.

ERHART: Dying?

ELLA: Yes, dying. Will you come and stay with me to the end? Bind yourself to me completely, like my own child.

MRS. BORKMAN: *(Cutting in.)* And abandon your mother, and also perhaps your mission in life? Is that what you want, Erhart?

ELLA: I'm a condemned woman, Erhart. Answer me.

ERHART: *(Warmly, moved.)* Aunt Ella, you've been so indescribably good to me. With you, my childhood was filled with all the carefree, joyful feelings that anyone could wish for—

MRS. BORKMAN: Erhart!

ELLA: Oh, bless you that you can still see it like that.

ERHART: But I can't sacrifice myself to you now. It's just not possible for me to be a son to you, honestly and completely—

MRS. BORKMAN: Ah, I knew it! You can't win! You can't win, Ella.

ELLA: *(Sadly.)* I see that. You've won him back.

MRS. BORKMAN: Yes, yes—he's mine, and mine he'll stay! Erhart—isn't that right—we two still have a stretch of road to cover together.

ERHART: *(Struggling with himself.)* Mother, I might as well come right out with it—

MRS. BORKMAN: *(Tensely.)* Well?

ERHART: It's a short stretch of the road, mother.

MRS. BORKMAN: *(Stands as if struck.)* What are you trying to say?

ERHART: *(Gathering courage.)* Good Lord, mother—I'm still young! I feel like the air in here is smothering me.

MRS. BORKMAN: Here with me?

ERHART: Yes, Mother.

ELLA: Then come home with me, Erhart.

ERHART: Oh, Aunt Ella—it's no better with you. Life is different there, but no better. Not for me. It's still roses and lavender—the air of stale rooms, just like here.

MRS. BORKMAN: *(Shaken, but with self-control.)* In your mother's house, you say?

ERHART: *(With rising impatience.)* Yes, I don't know what else to call it. All this sickly pampering and—and idolizing. I can't stand it any more.

MRS. BORKMAN: *(Looking at him with deep seriousness.)* Are you forgetting what you've dedicated your life to, Erhart?

ERHART: *(Vehemently.)* You mean what you've dedicated it to! You, have been my will! While I've never been allowed to have one. But now I can't wear this harness any longer. I'm young! Just remember that, mother. *(With a respectful, considerate glance at BORKMAN.)* I can't dedicate my life to atone for someone else. Whoever that might be.

MRS. BORKMAN: *(Gripped by growing dread.)* Who is it who's changed you, Erhart?

ERHART: Who? Couldn't it be I myself who—?

MRS. BORKMAN: No, no, no! You've fallen under a strange power. Not your mother's any longer—or your—your foster mother's either.

ERHART: *(With forced defiance.)* I'm under my own power, Mother! And my own will, too.

BORKMAN: *(Stepping toward ERHART.)* Then perhaps my hour has come at last.

ERHART: *(Distantly polite.)* In what way—? What do you mean, Father?

MRS. BORKMAN: *(Scornfully.)* Yes. That's my question too.

BORKMAN: *(Continuing undisturbed.)* Listen to me, Erhart. How would you like to join your father? A man can never recover from a fall through someone else's actions. That's a fable that's been spun around you down here in this stale air. You could live the holiest life in the world, and it would do me absolutely no good.

ERHART: *(Formal, respectful.)* What you say is true.

BORKMAN: Yes it is. And it wouldn't be any good, either, if I let myself fade away in penance, or get shattered to bits by remorse. I've been trying to live on dreams and hopes all these years. But these things are no good for me. And now I'm done with dreaming.

ERHART: *(Bowing slightly.)* Then—what do you intend to do?

BORKMAN: I intend to redeem everything. Start at the bottom again. Only through his present and his future can a man atone for his past. Through work—endless work for everything I once thought was life itself. But now it's a thousand times more exalted than it was then. Erhart—will you join me, and help me win this new life?

MRS. BORKMAN: *(Raising a warning hand.)* Don't do it, Erhart!

ELLA: *(Warmly.)* Yes, yes, do it! Oh, Erhart, help him!

MRS. BORKMAN: You can advise that? You—lonely and dying?

ELLA: It doesn't matter about me.

MRS. BORKMAN: That's right, as long as *I'm* not taking him from you.

ELLA: Precisely, Gunhild.

BORKMAN: Will you, Erhart?

ERHART: *(Very distressed.)* Father—right now, I can't. It's just not possible.

BORKMAN: Well, what do you ultimately want to make of yourself?

ERHART: *(Fervently.)* I'm young! I want to live my own life for once! To live my life!

ELLA: Can't you spare two short months to bring a little light into my last remaining days?

ERHART: Aunt Ella—I just can't, no matter how much I want to.

ELLA: Not even for someone who loves you so much?

ERHART: As true as I live, Aunt Ella, I can't do it.

MRS. BORKMAN: *(Looking sharply at him.)* And your mother no longer has any claim on you, either?

ERHART: I'll always love you, Mother. But I just can't go on living only for you. Because there's no life for me here.

BORKMAN: Then join with me! Because life —Erhart, life is work. Come— let's go forward, the two of us, into life and work together.

ERHART: *(Passionately.)* Yes, but I don't want to work now. I'm young! I've never understood it before. But now I feel it rushing through me, warm and urgent—I don't want to work. I want to live. Just live!

MRS. BORKMAN: *(Exclaims, suspecting.)* Erhart, what will you live for?

ERHART: *(With sparkling eyes.)* For happiness, mother!

MRS. BORKMAN: And where do you imagine you'll find it?

ERHART: I've already found it!

MRS. BORKMAN: *(Crying out.)* Erhart—!

(ERHART goes quickly to the hall door and opens it.)

ERHART: *(Calling.)* Fanny—you can come in now.

(MRS. WILTON, in outdoor clothes, appears in the doorway.)

MRS. BORKMAN: *(With clasped hands.)* Mrs. Wilton—!

MRS. WILTON: *(Somewhat shy, with a questioning glance toward ERHART.)* Can I then—?

ERHART: Yes, now you can come in. I've said everything.

(MRS. WILTON comes into the room. ERHART closes the door after her. She bows formally to BORKMAN who returns her greeting. Short silence.)

MRS. WILTON: *(In a low but firm voice.)* So the word's been spoken. I can well imagine that I stand here like one who has brought a great misfortune on this house.

MRS. BORKMAN: *(Slowly, regarding her stiffly.)* You've destroyed the last remnants of everything I've lived for. *(Erupting.)* But it's all so completely impossible —!

MRS. WILTON: I understand very well that it must strike you as impossible, Mrs. Borkman

MRS. BORKMAN: Yes, you must be able to see that for yourself—or can't you?

MRS. WILTON: I'd rather call it quite unusual. But, just the same, that's how it is.

MRS. BORKMAN: *(Turning.)* Are you really serious about this, Erhart?

ERHART: This is my happiness, mother. All the beauty, all the joy that life has to offer. That's all I can say.

MRS. BORKMAN: *(To MRS. WILTON, wringing her hands.)* Oh, how you've entangled and seduced my unlucky son.

MRS. WILTON: *(A proud toss of the head.)* That's not what I've done.

MRS. BORKMAN: You say you haven't?

MRS. WILTON: No. I didn't entangle him—or seduce him, either. Erhart came to me of his own free will. And of my own free will, I met him half way.

MRS. BORKMAN: *(Scornfully surveying her.)* Yes, you did! I can easily believe it.

MRS. WILTON: *(With restraint.)* Mrs. Borkman—there are forces in life that you don't seem to know very much about.

MRS. BORKMAN: Which, may I ask?

MRS. WILTON: Forces that urge two people to join their lives together—a bit rashly, perhaps, but also indivisibly.

MRS. BORKMAN: *(Smiles.)* I thought you were already indivisibly joined—to someone else.

MRS. WILTON: *(Brusquely.)* That someone left me.

MRS. BORKMAN: He's still living, they say.

MRS. WILTON: He's dead to me.

ERHART: *(Decisively.)* Yes, mother. To Fanny, he's dead. And anyway, this other man doesn't concern me.

MRS. BORKMAN: *(Regarding him severely.)* Then you already know—all this about the other man?

ERHART: Yes, mother. All about it.

MRS. BORKMAN: And still you say it doesn't concern you!

ERHART: *(Dismissively arrogant.)* All I know is that happiness is what I want. I'm young! I want to live!

MRS. BORKMAN: Yes, Erhart, you are young. Much too young for this.

MRS. WILTON: *(Firmly and seriously.)* Don't think, Mrs. Borkman, that I haven't told him the same thing. I've laid bare the whole story of my life to him. I've reminded him over and over that I'm a full seven years older than he is—

ERHART: *(Interrupting.)* There's no need, Fanny. I knew it all along.

MRS. WILTON: But nothing's worked. Nothing.

MRS. BORKMAN: Oh? Really? Why didn't you just send him away? Close your house to him? You certainly could have done that.

MRS. WILTON: *(Looking at her and speaking softly.)* I simply couldn't do it, Mrs. Borkman.

MRS. BORKMAN: Why not?

MRS. WILTON: Because my happiness also depended on this one here.

MRS. BORKMAN: *(Scornfully.)* Hm—happiness, happiness.

MRS. WILTON: I'd never known before what happiness could be in life. And I can't possibly turn it away just because it comes so late.

MRS. BORKMAN: And how long do you plan on this happiness lasting?

ERHART: *(Interrupting.)* Short or long, mother. It's all the same to me.

MRS. BORKMAN: As blind as you are, don't you see where all this is leading?

ERHART: I don't care about looking ahead all the time. I just want the right to live life for once.

MRS. BORKMAN: And you call this life, Erhart!

ERHART: Yes—can't you see how lovely she is?

MRS. BORKMAN: And I'll have to bear this crushing shame as well!

BORKMAN: *(In the background, hard and sharp.)* Ha! You're well practiced in bearing that sort of thing, aren't you, Gunhild!

ELLA: *(Pleading.)* Borkman!

ERHART: *(Similarly.)* Father!

MRS. BORKMAN: I'll have to go on, day in and day out, seeing my son together with a—with a—

ERHART: *(Breaking in harshly.)* You won't see anything like that, Mother. Don't even worry about that. I'm not staying here any longer.

MRS. WILTON: *(Quickly and firmly.)* We're leaving, Mrs. Borkman.

MRS. BORKMAN: *(Going pale.)* You're leaving too! Together, perhaps?

MRS. WILTON: *(Nodding.)* I'm traveling south, yes. Along with a young girl. And Erhart's coming with us.

MRS. BORKMAN: With you—and a young girl?

MRS. WILTON: Yes. It's little Frida Foldal, who I took into my house. I want her to go abroad, where she can really study her music.

MRS. BORKMAN: So you're taking her with you?

MRS. WILTON: Yes—I can't very well let the child loose down there on her own.

MRS. BORKMAN: *(Suppressing a smile.)* What do you say about that, Erhart?

ERHART: *(Somewhat embarrassed, shrugging his shoulders.)* Well, Mother—if that's how Fanny wants it—

MRS. BORKMAN: When does this distinguished company embark, if one may ask?

MRS. WILTON: We're leaving right away. Tonight. My sleigh is waiting down the road—at the Hinkels.

MRS. BORKMAN: *(Looks straight at her.)* Ah—so that was the party.

MRS. WILTON: *(Smiling.)* Yes, just for Erhart and me—and little Frida too, of course.

MRS. BORKMAN: Where is she now?

MRS. WILTON: Waiting for us in the sleigh.

ERHART: *(Painfully embarrassed.)* Mother, can't you understand—we wanted to spare you—everybody—all of this.

MRS. BORKMAN: You would have left without one word of goodbye?

ERHART: I thought that would be best. For both sides. We were packed and ready to go. But then I got your message—so— *(Reaches for her hand.)* Goodbye then, mother.

MRS. BORKMAN: *(Warding him off.)* Don't touch me!

ERHART: *(Gently.)* Is that your last word?

MRS. BORKMAN: *(Harshly.)* Yes.

ERHART: *(Turning.)* Good bye then, Aunt Ella.

ELLA: *(Pressing his hands.)* Good bye, Erhart. Live your own life, and be as happy—as happy as you possibly can be.

ERHART: Thanks, Aunt Ella. *(Bowing to BORKMAN.)* Goodbye, Father. *(Whispers to MRS. WILTON.)* Let's get out of here, the sooner the better.

MRS. WILTON: *(Quietly.)* Yes, let's.

MRS. BORKMAN: *(Smiling malignly.)* Mrs. Wilton. Do you think it's a good idea to take this young girl along with you?

MRS. WILTON: *(Returning the smile, half ironic, half serious.)* Men are so unpredictable, Mrs. Borkman. Women too. When Erhart's done with me—and I with him—it will be good for both of us, if he, poor man, has someone to fall back on.

MRS. BORKMAN: What about yourself?

MRS. WILTON: Oh, let me assure you, I can manage for myself. Well, goodbye, everybody!

(She nods and goes out through the hall doorway. ERHART stands for a moment, as if hesitating, then he turns and follows her.)

MRS. BORKMAN: *(Sinking down, hands clasped.)* Childless.

BORKMAN: *(As if awakening to a decision.)* I'm going into the storm alone! Hat! Coat! *(He walks quickly toward the door.)*

ELLA: *(Anxiously stopping him.)* John Gabriel, where are you going?

BORKMAN: Into the storm—out into life, don't you hear me? Let go, Ella.

ELLA: *(Holding fast to him.)* No, no, I won't let you go. You're ill. I can see it.

BORKMAN: Let me go, I tell you! *(He tears himself loose and goes out through the hall.)*

ELLA: *(In the doorway.)* Help me hold him back, Gunhild!

MRS. BORKMAN: *(Cold and hard, standing in the middle of the room.)* I won't hold on to anything in the world. Not any more. Let them all leave me. The one, and the other. Both of them. As far as they want. *(Suddenly, with a rending shriek.)* Erhart, don't go!

(MRS. BORKMAN rushes with outstretched arms toward the door. ELLA stops her.)

END OF ACT THREE

ACT FOUR

Open courtyard outside the main building, which stands to the right. A corner of this with an entrance door and a flight of steps juts out. Along the background, almost into the courtyard, are steep slopes covered in spruce trees. A small wood begins to spread to the left. The snowstorm has stopped; but the ground is thickly covered with new-fallen snow. The spruce trees, heavy and bent, are similarly covered. Dark night sky. Drifting clouds. The moon is intermittently faintly visible. The surroundings are seen in the opaque light from the snow.

BORKMAN, MRS. BORKMAN, and ELLA are standing on the steps. BORKMAN is leaning, weak and tired, against the wall of the house. He wears an old-fashioned cloak thrown over his shoulders, holds a soft, gray, felt hat in one hand and a thick knotted stick in the other. ELLA carries her coat over her arm. MRS. BORKMAN's large shawl has slipped down below her neck so that her hair is uncovered.

ELLA: *(Standing in MRS. BORKMAN's path.)* Don't go after him, Gunhild.

MRS. BORKMAN: *(Violently agitated.)* Let go of me, Ella! He can't leave me!

ELLA: It's no use, I tell you. You won't catch him.

MRS. BORKMAN: Let me go, Ella. Let me go anyway. I'll cry out to him on the road. He'll have to hear his mother's cry.

ELLA: He can't hear you. By now he's already sitting in the sleigh—

MRS. BORKMAN: No, he can't be in the sleigh already!

ELLA: He's been sitting there for some time, believe me.

MRS. BORKMAN: *(In despair.)* If he's in the sleigh, then he's sitting with her, with her—her.

BORKMAN: *(Laughing sardonically.)* And he certainly won't hear his mother's cry.

MRS. BORKMAN: No—he won't hear it. *(Listening.)* Shhh. What's that?

ELLA: *(Also listening.)* It sounds like bells.

MRS. BORKMAN: *(With a muffled cry.)* Her sleigh.

ELLA: Or maybe someone else's.

MRS. BORKMAN: No, no, it's Mrs. Wilton's sleigh! I know those silver bells. Listen! Now they're driving right by here. Down below, on the hill.

ELLA: *(Quickly.)* Gunhild, if you want to call for him, do it now! Perhaps even now he can— *(The sound of sleigh bells passing close by, in the woods.)* Hurry, Gunhild—they're right below us now!

MRS. BORKMAN: *(Stands uncertain for an instant, then stiffens, cold and hard.)* No—I won't call for him. Let Erhart Borkman drive on past me. Far away, off to what he now calls happiness and life.

(The sounds are lost in the distance.)

ELLA: *(A moment later.)* No sound of them now.

MRS. BORKMAN: To me they sounded like funeral bells.

BORKMAN: *(With dry, quiet laughter.)* Ah—but they're not ringing for me just yet.

MRS. BORKMAN: But for me. And for him as well.

ELLA: *(Nodding thoughtfully.)* Who knows—they might be ringing in happiness and life for him after all, Gunhild.

MRS. BORKMAN: *(Starting, stares at her.)* Happiness and life?

ELLA: For a little while, at least.

MRS. BORKMAN: You'd wish him happiness and life—with her?

ELLA: *(Warmly and fervently.)* Yes, with all my heart and soul.

MRS. BORKMAN: *(Coldly.)* Then you must be richer in the power to love than I am.

ELLA: *(Looking into the distance.)* Perhaps the loss of love nourishes that power.

MRS. BORKMAN: *(Fastens her eyes on her.)* If that's true—soon I'll be just as rich as you, Ella. *(She turns and goes into the house)*

ELLA: *(Stands for a moment, looking anxiously at BORKMAN, then lays a hand gently on his shoulder.)* John, come on in now—you too.

BORKMAN: *(As if just awakening.)* Me?

ELLA: Yes. You can't take this sharp winter air. I can see that, John. So come with me. Inside, where it's warm.

BORKMAN: *(Angry.)* Up into that room again, you mean?

ELLA: Or the living room, with her.

BORKMAN: *(Erupting with anger.)* I will never set foot under that roof again.

ELLA: What are you going to do then? So late in the night, John?

BORKMAN: *(Putting on his hat.)* First of all, I'll go out and gaze upon all my hidden hoard of treasures.

ELLA: *(Looking anxiously at him.)* John, I don't understand you!

BORKMAN: *(With a laugh that becomes a cough.)* Oh, I don't mean buried loot. Don't worry about that, Ella. *(Stops and points.)* Do you see him there? Who is it?

(VILHELM FOLDAL, in an old, snow-spattered overcoat, with his hat pulled down and a large umbrella in his hand, appears around the corner of the house, awkwardly stumbling through the snow. He limps noticeably on his left foot.)

BORKMAN: Vilhelm! What brings you here again?

FOLDAL: *(Looking up.)* In heaven's name—is that you standing out here on the steps, John Gabriel? *(Bowing.)* And Mrs. Borkman too, I see!

BORKMAN: *(Curtly.)* This isn't my wife.

FOLDAL: Oh, excuse me. You see, I lost my spectacles in the snow. But here you—who haven't been outdoors—?

BORKMAN: *(Recklessly vivacious.)* It's about time I started being an outdoorsman again, wouldn't you say? Almost three years in custody—five years in the cell—eight years up there in the salon—

ELLA: *(Worried.)* Borkman, please!

FOLDAL: Ah, yes, yes, yes.

BORKMAN: Tell me now—what do you want with me?

FOLDAL: *(Remaining standing at the foot of the steps.)* I just needed to see you, John Gabriel. I felt I had to go up and see you in the salon. Oh God—that salon—

BORKMAN: You still wanted to visit me, after I'd shown you the door?

FOLDAL: Yes, in God's name, what does that matter?

BORKMAN: What have you done to your foot? You're limping.

FOLDAL: Yes, guess what—I've been run over.

ELLA: Run over!

FOLDAL: Yes, by a sleigh.

BORKMAN: Aha!

FOLDAL: With two horses. They came down the hill so fast, I couldn't get out of the way—so—

ELLA: So they ran you over?

FOLDAL: Drove right into me, Mrs.—or Miss. Right into me—knocked me over into the snow, so I lost my spectacles and broke my umbrella— *(Rubbing himself.)* And my foot's hurt a little, too.

BORKMAN: *(Laughing inwardly.)* Do you know who was riding in that sleigh, Vilhelm?

FOLDAL: No, how could I see? It was enclosed, and the blinds were pulled. And the driver didn't stop for so much as a second while I fell down and rolled around—but none of that matters a bit because— *(Bursts out.)* Oh, I'm so incredibly happy, you see!

BORKMAN: Happy?

FOLDAL: Well—I don't know exactly what I should call it. But "happy" is the closest thing that comes to mind. Because something truly wonderful has happened! So what else could I do? Of course, I had to come here and share my joy with you, John Gabriel.

BORKMAN: *(Gruffly.)* All right, share your joy.

ELLA: But first, take your friend inside with you, Borkman.

BORKMAN: *(Hard.)* I'm not going back in that house, I've told you.

ELLA: But you heard him—he's been run over!

BORKMAN: We all get run over, at least once in our lives. But you have to get right back up again, as if nothing happened.

FOLDAL: Those are profound words, John Gabriel. But I can tell you everything out here—it'll just take a moment.

BORKMAN: *(More gently.)* Yes, Vilhelm—please do.

FOLDAL: Well, just listen now! Imagine this: when I got home this evening, I found a letter. Can you guess who it was from?

BORKMAN: Possibly from your little Frida.

FOLDAL: Exactly! Imagine, you got it right away! Yes—it was a long—a fairly long letter from Frida. A servant brought it. Do you have any idea what she wrote?

BORKMAN: Could it be, by any chance, a goodbye to her parents?

FOLDAL: That's it! You're incredible, John Gabriel. Yes, she wrote that Mrs. Wilton had taken such a liking to her—and she wants her to go abroad with her—so that Frida can better study her music, she writes. And so Mrs. Wilton has arranged for a good tutor to join them on the trip. And study with Frida. Unfortunately she's a little behind in some areas, you see.

BORKMAN: *(Laughing inwardly to the point of shaking.)* Oh yes, oh yes. I see everything very clearly, Vilhelm.

FOLDAL: And just think—she only found out about this trip tonight. At the party you know about—hm! And she still took the time to write to me. And I have to say—the letter's so warm and kind, and so affectionate— not a trace of contempt for her father this time. What a fine thing to do, you know—that she wanted to say goodbye in writing, before she left. *(Laughing.)* But that's not going to be good enough for me!

BORKMAN: *(Looks inquiringly at him.)* How so?

FOLDAL: She writes that they'll be leaving early tomorrow. Very early.

BORKMAN: Well, well. Tomorrow? That's what she writes?

FOLDAL: *(Laughing and rubbing his hands.)* Yes, but just watch me—I'll pull a fast one on them. I'm on my way up to Mrs. Wilton's.

BORKMAN: Now? Tonight?

FOLDAL: Good heavens, yes—it's not all that late yet. And if the house is dark, I'll ring the bell. Won't hesitate. Because I've just got to see Frida before she leaves. Good night! *(He is about to go.)*

BORKMAN: Listen, Vilhelm. You can save yourself that hard stretch of road.

FOLDAL: Oh, you're thinking of my foot.

BORKMAN: Yes—and you won't get in to Mrs. Wilton's anyway.

FOLDAL: I certainly will. I'm prepared to keep pulling at that bell until someone comes and opens up. Because I'm going to see Frida, I've just got to.

ELLA: Your daughter has already left, Mr. Foldal.

FOLDAL: *(Stopping as if struck.)* Frida's already left! You know for sure? Where did you hear that?

BORKMAN: From her prospective tutor.

FOLDAL: Oh yes? Who is he?

BORKMAN: A student named Erhart Borkman.

FOLDAL: *(Beaming with delight.)* Your son, John Gabriel! Is he going with them?

BORKMAN: He's the one. He'll be helping Mrs. Wilton educate your little Frida.

FOLDAL: Well, thank God for that. So the child's in the best possible hands. Now—you're absolutely sure they've already left with her?

BORKMAN: They were in the sleigh that ran you over.

FOLDAL: *(Clasping his hands.)* Imagine—my little Frida in that elegant sleigh!

BORKMAN: *(Nodding.)* Ah yes, Vilhelm—your daughter's riding in high style now. And young Borkman, too. Well now—did you notice those silver bells?

FOLDAL: Yes, I—*silver* bells, did you say? They were silver bells? Real, genuine silver?

BORKMAN: You can count on it. Everything was genuine—outside and in.

FOLDAL: *(Moved.)* Isn't it wonderful, how fortune operates in human life! How my—my little gift of poetry has transformed itself into Frida's music. And so my being a poet wasn't in vain after all. Because she'll go forth into the great wide world I once had such beautiful dreams of seeing. Little Frida is riding in that lovely sleigh—with silver bells on the harness—

BORKMAN: And runs over her father—.

FOLDAL: *(Joyful.)* Oh, that! It doesn't matter about me—as long as the child— So, I'm too late after all. Well then. I'll go home and comfort her mother. She's been sitting in the kitchen, crying.

BORKMAN: She's crying?

FOLDAL: *(Laughing slightly.)* Yes, can you imagine? She was really crying her eyes out when I left.

BORKMAN: And you're laughing, Vilhelm.

FOLDAL: Yes, I really am. But she—poor thing doesn't know any better, you see. Well then. Goodbye! Good thing that streetcar's nearby. Goodbye, goodbye, John Gabriel. Goodbye, Miss—! *(He bows and limps back the way he came.)*

BORKMAN: *(Stands silent a moment and stares straight ahead.)* Goodbye,

Vilhelm! This isn't the first time in your life you've been run over, old friend.

ELLA: *(Looks at him with concealed anxiety.)* You're so pale, John—so pale.

BORKMAN: From the prison air up there.

ELLA: I've never seen you like this.

BORKMAN: I doubt you've ever seen an escaped convict before.

ELLA: Please come inside with me now, John!

BORKMAN: Stop trying to lure me inside. I've told you already.

ELLA: But now that I'm begging you so desperately? For your own sake—
    (The MAID comes out onto the steps.)

MAID: Excuse me, but madam says I'm to lock the front door now.

BORKMAN: *(Softly to ELLA.)* You hear that? Now they want to lock me in again.

ELLA: The President of the Bank's not feeling well. He wants some fresh air first.

MAID: Yes, but madam said—

ELLA: I'll lock the door. Leave the key in it, so—

MAID: All right. God help us. I'll do as you say. *(She goes back into the house.)*

BORKMAN: *(Listens silently for a moment; then quickly descends into the courtyard.)* Now I'm outside the walls, Ella. They'll never get a hold of me again.

ELLA: *(Joining him.)* You're a free man in there as well, John. You can come and go at will.

BORKMAN: *(Softly, as if in terror.)* Never under a roof again! Out here in the night—this is good. If I went back to that salon now, the ceiling and walls would crumple up and crush me—squash me flat as a fly.

ELLA: Where will you go then?

BORKMAN: Just go, and keep on going, and going. See if I can win my way forward to freedom again, to life and to humanity. Ella—will you go with me?

ELLA: Me? Now?

BORKMAN: Yes, yes, now. Right away.

ELLA: But how far?

BORKMAN: As far as I can.

ELLA: Think what you're doing! Out in this cold, wet, winter's night.

BORKMAN: *(With a hoarse guttural sound.)* Ah—ah—the lady's worried about her health. Yes, yes—it certainly is delicate, isn't it?

ELLA: It's yours I'm worried about.

BORKMAN: Ha ha ha! A dead man's health. I have to laugh at you, Ella! *(He goes farther.)*

ELLA: *(Following, clutching him.)* What did you say you were?

BORKMAN: A dead man. Don't you remember? Gunhild told me to rest in peace where I lay.

ELLA: *(Decided; wraps her cloak around her.)* I'm going with you, John.

BORKMAN: Yes, we belong together, we two—don't we, Ella. *(Goes farther.)* Come on then!

(They have meanwhile entered a small wood to the left, which little by little conceals them until they disappear. The house and courtyard disappear. The landscape, with its slopes and mountain ranges, changes slowly and steadily and gets wilder and wilder.)

ELLA'S VOICE: *(Heard in the woods to the right.)* Where are we going, John? I don't know where I am.

BORKMAN's VOICE: *(Higher up.)* Just keep to the snow tracks behind me.

ELLA'S VOICE: Why do we need to climb so high?

BORKMAN's VOICE: *(Nearer.)* We have to go up the twisting path.

ELLA: *(Still hidden.)* I can't manage much farther.

BORKMAN: *(On the edge of the wood to the right.)* Come on, come on! We're not far from the vista now. There used to be a bench there, in the old days.

ELLA: *(Seen coming through the trees.)* You remember that?

BORKMAN: You can rest there.

(They have emerged into a small clearing, high up in the woods. The slope rises steeply behind them. To the left, far below, a wide expanse of landscape with fjords and high mountain ridges towering one after the other. In the clearing to the left is a dead fir tree with a bench beneath it. The snow lies deep in the clearing. BORKMAN, and after him ELLA, wade with difficulty through the snow.)

BORKMAN: *(Stands by the vista, left.)* Come here, Ella, and you'll be able to see.

ELLA: *(Joins him.)* What do you want to show me, John?

BORKMAN: See how the land lies before us—free and open, far off into the distance.

ELLA: We used to sit there on that bench so often, gazing out, even farther beyond that.

BORKMAN: We were gazing into a land of dreams in those days.

ELLA: *(Nodding heavily.)* The land where our dreams lived, yes. And now that land is covered with snow—and the old tree is dead.

BORKMAN: *(Not hearing her.)* Can you make out the smoke from the great steamships out on the fjord?

ELLA: No.

BORKMAN: I can. They come and they go. They make one community of the whole wide world. Spreading light and warmth over human hearts in many thousands of homes. That was what I dreamt of doing.

ELLA: *(Quietly.)* And it stayed a dream.

BORKMAN: It stayed a dream, yes. *(Listening.)* And listen—down there by the river. The factories are working! My factories! All the ones I wanted to create! Listen now—listen to them go. They're on the night shift. Night and day they're working. Listen, listen! The wheels spinning, the gleaming cylinders pumping up and down! Can't you hear them, Ella?

ELLA: No.

BORKMAN: I hear them.

ELLA: *(Anxiously.)* I think you're mistaken, John.

BORKMAN: *(More and more fired up.)* But all these—are only the outworks around the kingdom, you understand.

ELLA: Kingdom, you say? What kingdom?

BORKMAN My kingdom, of course! The kingdom I was about to take possession of when I—when I died.

ELLA: *(Quietly, shaken.)* Oh John—John.

BORKMAN: And now there it lies—leaderless, defenseless, for bandits to sack and pillage— Ella! Can you see the mountain ranges there—far off? One behind the other. They reach upward. They tower. There's my deep, endless, inexhaustible kingdom.

ELLA: Ah—but an icy breath blows from that kingdom, John.

BORKMAN: That breath stirs in me like a gust of life. It carries greetings from the spirits that would serve me. I sense them, those captive millions. I feel the veins of iron ore stretching out their coiling, branching, alluring arms to me. I saw them before me like living shadows—that night I stood in the bank vault with a lantern in my hand. You were yearning to be set free. And I tried. But I wasn't strong enough. Your treasures sank back into the depths. *(With outstretched hands.)* But now I whisper to you here in the stillness of the night. I love you, lying there, quiet and still in the depths and the darkness. I love you, your riches struggling to be born—I see your shimmering processional of power and glory—and I love you, love you, love you.

ELLA: *(With quiet but mounting agitation.)* Yes—down there is where your love still lives, John. It's always been there. But up here in the daylight world was a warm, living, human heart that beat for you. And you crushed this heart. No, more than that. Ten times worse. You sold it for—for—

BORKMAN: *(Shivers, as if the cold went through him.)* For the kingdom, and the power, and the glory, you mean?

ELLA: Yes, that's what I mean. I've said it to you once before tonight. You have murdered the power to love in the woman who loved you. And whom you loved in return. As much as you could love anyone, that is. *(With upraised arm.)* And so I prophesy, John Gabriel Borkman: you will never win the prize you sought with that murder. You'll lead no triumphal procession into your cold dark kingdom.

BORKMAN: *(Staggers to the bench and sits down heavily.)* I almost fear your prophecy is right, Ella.

ELLA: *(Going to his side.)* Don't fear it, John. It's the best thing that could happen.

BORKMAN: *(With a cry, clutching his chest.)* Ah! *(Weakly.)* Now it's let me go.

ELLA: *(Shaking him.)* What is it, John?

BORKMAN: An ice-hand gripped my heart.

ELLA: John! So now you feel the ice-hand.

BORKMAN: *(Murmuring.)* No—not an ice-hand. A hand of iron ore. *(He slides down on the bench.)*

ELLA: *(Tearing off her coat and draping it over him.)* Stay quiet, right there. I'll go and get some help for you. *(She goes a few steps to the right; then stops, goes back, and slowly feels his pulse and face. Slowly and firmly.)* No. Better so, John Borkman. Much the best for you.

(She tucks the coat more tightly around him and sits down in the snow in front of the bench. Short silence. MRS. BORKMAN, wrapped in her overcoat, emerges through the wood on the right. In front of her, the MAID with a lighted lantern.)

MAID: *(Shining light on the snow.)* Yes, ma'am. These are their tracks all right.

MRS. BORKMAN: *(Searches around.)* Yes, here they are! Over there—sitting on the bench. *(Calling.)* Ella!

ELLA: Are you looking for us?

MRS. BORKMAN: *(Harshly.)* I had to do it.

ELLA: *(Pointing.)* See, Gunhild: here he lies.

MRS. BORKMAN: Sleeping!

ELLA: *(Nodding.)* A deep sleep, and a long one, I think.

MRS. BORKMAN: *(Exclaiming.)* Ella! *(Controls herself, and asks quietly.)* Did it happen—deliberately?

ELLA: No. It was an ice-cold hand of iron ore that gripped his heart.

MRS. BORKMAN: *(To the MAID.)* Get some help. Get some people from the farm.

MAID: Yes, ma'am. *(Softly.)* In Jesus' name— *(She goes through the wood on the right.)*

MRS. BORKMAN: *(Standing behind the bench.)* So—it was the night air that killed him.

ELLA: It seems that way.

MRS. BORKMAN: And such a strong man.

ELLA: *(Moving in front of the bench.)* Won't you even look at him, Gunhild.

MRS. BORKMAN No, no, no. *(Lowering her voice.)* The President of the Bank was the son of a mountain miner—and he couldn't survive the fresh air.

ELLA: More likely it was the cold that killed him.

MRS. BORKMAN: *(Shaking her head.)* The cold you say? The cold—killed him a long time ago.

ELLA: *(Nodding.)* And shaped the two of us as shadows.

MRS. BORKMAN: You're right about that.

ELLA: *(With a painful smile.)* A dead man, and two shadows—that's what the cold has created.

MRS. BORKMAN: Yes—coldness in the heart. And now we two can reach out our hands to one another, Ella.

ELLA: Now I think we can, Gunhild.

MRS. BORKMAN: We two twin sisters—over the man we both have loved.

ELLA: We two shadows—over the dead man.

(MRS. BORKMAN behind the bench, and ELLA, in front of it, reach out their hands to each other.)

END OF THE PLAY

NOTE

ACT ONE

[1] When the lamp is brought into the garden room, a whole "green world" is revealed, associated with Mrs. Wilton. She is described as *yppig,* which means both "buxom" and "lush" or "luxuriant," as of vegetation.

WHEN WE
DEAD AWAKEN

✦═ 1899 ═✦

CHARACTERS

PROFESSOR ARNOLD RUBEK, sculptor
MAJA RUBEK, his wife
SPA MANAGER, inspector of the baths
ULFHEIM, a landowner
A WOMAN TRAVELLER
A NUN
STAFF, GUESTS OF THE SPA, CHILDREN

TIME AND PLACE

The action of Act One takes place at a coastal spa. Acts Two and Three take place in the vicinity of a mountain sanatorium and the surrounding mountain landscape.

ACT ONE

Outside the spa hotel, with the main building partly seen to the right. An open, park-like space with a fountain, groups of large, ancient trees, and bushes. To the left is a little pavilion, almost covered with ivy and wild vine. A table and chairs stand in front of it. In the background a prospect over the fjord down to the sea, with promontories and small islands in the distance. It is a still summer morning in the warmth of the sun.

PROFESSOR RUBEK and his wife MAJA are seated in basket chairs at a table set for them on the lawn in front of the hotel. They are drinking champagne and seltzer and each has a newspaper. The PROFESSOR is an elderly, distinguished-looking man dressed in a black velvet jacket over light summer clothing. MAJA RUBEK is quite youthful, with a lively face with mischievous eyes, but with a trace of weariness. She is dressed in an elegant travelling dress.

MAJA: *(Sits for a while waiting for the PROFESSOR to say something. She lowers her paper with a sigh.)* Oh no, no—!

RUBEK: *(Looking up from his paper.)* Well, Maja? What is it that's bothering you?

MAJA Just listen to how silent it is here.

RUBEK: *(Smiling indulgently.)* And you can hear that?

MAJA: Hear what?

RUBEK: The silence?

MAJA: I most certainly can.

RUBEK: Well, you could be right, *mein Kind.* One really can hear the silence.

MAJA: Yes, God knows one can. When it's as overwhelming as it is here, then—

RUBEK: Here at the spa, you mean?

MAJA: Everywhere in this land of ours. In the city there was certainly enough noise and racket. But even there, I felt the noise and racket had something deathly about it.

RUBEK: *(With a searching glance.)* Then you're not all that happy, Maja, coming home again?

MAJA *(Looking at him.)* Are you happy?

RUBEK: *(Evasively.)* I—?

MAJA: Yes, you—who've been away so much longer than I have. Are you honestly happy—now that you're home again?

RUBEK: No, to speak frankly, not all that happy.

MAJA: *(Animatedly.)* No, it's plain to see! Wasn't that just what I predicted?

RUBEK: Maybe I've been away much too long. I feel so totally alien to all this—this provincial life.

MAJA: *(Eagerly, drawing her chair closer to him.)* There, you see, Rubek! Why don't we just go on our way again. As soon as we can!

RUBEK: *(A little impatiently.)* Yes, yes, that's the intention, Maja my dear. You know that.

MAJA: So why not take off now, right away? Imagine how snug and comfortable we'd be down there in our lovely new house—

RUBEK: *(Smiling indulgently.)* Shouldn't we say, our lovely new home?

MAJA: *(Curtly.)* I prefer "house." Let's leave it at that.

RUBEK *(His eyes dwelling on her.)* You really are a strange little person.

MAJA: Am I so strange?

RUBEK: Yes, I think so.

MAJA: But why is that? Maybe because I don't have any great urge to stick around traipsing about up here—?

RUBEK: Which of us made it such a life-and-death issue of coming up north this summer?

MAJA: It might well have been me.

RUBEK: Well, it definitely wasn't me.

MAJA; But, good lord—who could have guessed everything back here would have changed so much for the worse ? And all in so short a time! Imagine!— it can't have been more than four years since I left here—

RUBEK: To get married, yes.

MAJA: Married? What's that got to do with it?

RUBEK: *(Continuing.)* And to become *Frau Professor* and gain a splendid home—excuse me—a magnificent house, I ought to have said. And a villa on Lake Taunitz where the smartest folk now are to be found— Oh yes, it couldn't be finer or more impressive, I can vouch for that. And plenty of space, too—so there's no need for us to be falling over each other all the time—

MAJA: *(Unconcernedly.)* No, no—as far as house room's concerned, we've no shortage of that—

RUBEK: So now you find yourself enjoying a finer, more spacious style of living. And with a better social position than the one you were used to at home.

MAJA: *(Regarding him.)* Oh, so you think *I'm* the one who's done the changing?

RUBEK: Yes, Maja, that's what I think.

MAJA: Just me? Not the people here?

RUBEK: Well, yes—they too. Maybe a little. And not in the most amiable way—that I'll grant you .

MAJA: Yes, *that*, you must grant.

RUBEK: *(Changing the subject.)* You know what strikes me when I look at the way people live around here?

MAJA: No. Tell me.

RUBEK: I find myself recalling that night on the train coming up here.

MAJA: All you did was sit in the compartment, sleeping.

RUBEK: Not entirely. I noticed how silent it was at all the little stations where we stopped. Then I heard the silence—just like you, Maja—

MAJA: Hm—yes, just like me.

RUBEK: And that's how I realized we'd crossed over the border. Now, we were really home. Because at each little station stop the train would come to a halt—even though nothing was happening.

MAJA: Why did it stop, then. With nothing happening?

RUBEK: No idea. No traveller stepped out and none came aboard. And yet just the same, the train stood there, silently, seemingly forever. And at each station I could hear two railmen walking along the platform—one of them with a lantern in his hand—and they were talking to each other, softly, tonelessly, meaninglessly, in the night.

MAJA: Yes, you're right, in fact. There's always a pair of men walking by, speaking to each other—

RUBEK: About nothing. *(More animatedly.)* But only wait until tomorrow. Then we'll see the big luxurious steamer putting into the dock. We'll be boarding, to sail along the coast right to the north and into the Arctic Sea.

MAJA: Yes, but then you'll never get to see the real country at all—or the life there. And that was just what you came for.

RUBEK: *(Curtly dismissive.)* I've seen more than enough.

MAJA: So you really think a sea cruise will be better for you?

RUBEK: It's always a change.

MAJA: Oh, well—if it's what's best for you—

RUBEK: For me? Best for me?! There's not the slightest thing wrong with me!

MAJA: *(Getting up and going over to him.)* Yes, Rubek, there is. You must be aware of that yourself.

RUBEK: And what, my dearest Maja, might that be?

MAJA: *(Behind him, bending over the chair back.)* You tell me. You've begun wandering from place to place, neither calm nor content. You find nowhere to settle down, home or abroad. You've become completely unsociable of late.

RUBEK: *(Sarcastically.)* Really now—is that what you've noticed.

MAJA: It's hardly something anyone who knows you could miss. And then it's so sad to see you lose all interest in your work.

RUBEK: Have I done that, too?

MAJA: Think how you used to work, so furiously, from dawn to dusk.

RUBEK: *(Moodily.)* Yes, once. When—

MAJA: But right from the time your masterpiece passed from your hands—

RUBEK: *(Nodding reflectively.)* "Resurrection Day"—

MAJA: —that's travelled over the whole world. And made you famous—

RUBEK: Maybe that's been the misfortune, Maja.

MAJA: How could that be?

RUBEK: When I'd created this masterpiece of mine— *(A violent sweep of his hand.)* —because "Resurrection Day" *is* a masterpiece! Or was, to start with! No, it still is! It *shall*, it *must*, yes it *must* be a masterpiece!

MAJA: *(Staring at him in wonder.)* Yes, Rubek, of course it is. The whole world knows that.

RUBEK: *(Curtly dismissive.)* The whole world knows nothing! Understands nothing!

MAJA: Well, they're aware of something, in any case—

RUBEK: Something that's not there at all. Something that never even occurred to me. And see, it's *that* they're all going into ecstasies over! *(Growling to himself.)* There's no reward in sweating and straining for the mob—the masses—the "whole world."

MAJA: And you think it's any better—more worthy of you—just turning out portrait busts every now and then?

RUBEK: *(Smiling in satisfaction.)* They're not exactly portrait busts I set about modeling, Maja.

MAJA: But that's what they are, God knows—in these last two or three years. Ever since you were done with that big group and got it out of the house—

RUBEK: All the same, they're not exactly portrait busts, I'm telling you.

MAJA: What are they, then?

RUBEK: There's something ambiguous hidden behind those busts—something secret the public can't see—

MAJA: Really?

RUBEK: *(Continuing.)* Only I can see it. Which amuses me intensely. On the surface are those "striking likenesses" as they're called, which folk stare and gape and wonder at—*(Lowering his voice.)* But at the deepest level lurk the worthy, honorable horse faces, obstinate donkey snouts, flop-eared, low-browed skulls of dogs, greedy swine heads—with some flaccid, brutal visages of cattle thrown in as well—

MAJA: The dear, domestic zoo, in fact.

RUBEK: Just the domestic zoo, Maja. All the animals man has distorted into his own image. And which have distorted him in return. *(Emptying his champagne glass and laughing.)* And it's these two-faced works of art that our pillars of society commission from me—pay for in good faith—and pay amply, too. They're almost worth their weight in gold, as they say.

MAJA: *(Filling his glass.)* Really, Rubek! Drink now, and be happy.

RUBEK: *(Passing his hand over his brow repeatedly and leaning back in his chair.)* I *am* happy, Maja. Truly happy. That is, in a way. *(Is silent a moment.)* Because it's very lucky, really, to feel free and independent in every way. Having everything one can possibly wish for. Outwardly, that is. Don't you think so too, Maja?

MAJA: Oh yes, so far as it goes. It's fine enough, all right. *(Looking at him.)* But can you remember what you promised me that day we agreed on this difficult—

RUBEK: —agreed that we should marry. That wasn't easy for you was it, Maja?

MAJA: *(Continuing, untroubled.)* —and that I should travel abroad with you and stay there and have a good life. Can you remember what you promised me at the time?

RUBEK: No, I honestly can't. Well, what did I promise you?

MAJA: You said you would take me with you to the top of a high mountain and show me all the glory of the world.

RUBEK: *(Startled.)* Did I promise that to you as well?

MAJA: *(Looking at him.)* Me as well? Who else?

RUBEK: *(Casually.)* No, no, all I meant was, did I promise to show you—

MAJA: —all the glory of the world. Yes, that's what you said. And all that glory would be mine and yours, you said.

RUBEK: It's the kind of expression I would use at an earlier time.

MAJA: Only an expression?

RUBEK: Yes, something from my schooldays. The sort of thing I'd say to the other children when I wanted them to play in the forest, or in the mountains, with me.

MAJA *(Regarding him.)* Perhaps that's all you wanted from me—to go out with you and play .

RUBEK: *(Treating this as a joke)* Well, hasn't it been a pleasant enough game, Maja?

MAJA: *(Coldly.)* I didn't go away with you only to play.

RUBEK: No, no, that's true enough.

MAJA: And you've not taken me to any high mountain and shown me—

RUBEK: *(Irritated.)* —all the glory of the world? No, so I haven't. For I have to tell you, little Maja, you're not exactly made for mountain climbing.

MAJA: *(Trying to control herself.)* There was a time when you seemed to think so.

RUBEK: Four or five years ago, yes. *(Stretching in his chair.)* Four or five years—that's a long, long time, Maja.

MAJA: *(Regarding him with a bitter expression.)* Has that time seemed so very long to you, Rubek?

RUBEK: It's beginning to seem a little long now. *(Yawns.)* Every now and then.

MAJA: *(Returns to her chair.)* I won't bore you any longer. *(She sits in the chair, takes up her newspaper and leafs through it. Silence on both sides.)*

RUBEK: *(Leans on his elbows over the table and looks teasingly at her.)* Is the Professor's Wife offended?

MAJA: *(Coldly, not looking up.)* No, not at all.

(Guests of the spa, mostly women, singly or in groups, begin to cross the park from right to left. Waiters bring refreshments from the hotel, passing behind the pavilion. The SPA MANAGER, wearing gloves and carrying a stick, returns from his morning tour of the park, meets the guests, greeting them respectfully and exchanging words with one or two of them)

SPA MANAGER: *(Going over to PROFESSOR RUBEK's table and courteously raising his hat.)* May I wish you a good morning, Madam? Good morning, Professor.

RUBEK: Good morning, good morning, Inspector.

SPA MANAGER: *(Addressing MAJA.)* Might I ask, madam, if you enjoyed a restful night?

MAJA: Yes, thank you, quite remarkably so—on my part, at least. I always sleep like a stone at nights.

SPA MANAGER: Delighted to hear it. The first night in an unfamiliar place can be troublesome sometimes. And the professor?

RUBEK: Oh, my nights are in poor shape. Especially of late.

SPA MANAGER *(Showing sympathy.)* I'm sorry to hear it. But a few weeks stay here at the spa will set you right.

RUBEK: *(Looking at him.)* Tell me, Inspector, do any of your patients use the spa baths at night?

SPA MANAGER: *(Surprised.)* At night? No, I've never heard of anything like that.

RUBEK: You haven't?

SPA MANAGER: No, I know of no one here so sick they need do that.

RUBEK: Then is there someone who goes for a walk in the park at night?

SPA MANAGER: *(Smiling and shaking his head.)* No, Professor—that would go against regulations.

MAJA: *(Becoming impatient.)* Good lord, Rubek, it's just as I said this morning—it's something you dreamt.

RUBEK *(Dryly.)* Oh? Is that what I did? Thanks! *(Turning to the SPA MANAGER.)* You see, I happened to get up last night. I couldn't get to sleep. And I wanted to see what kind of night it was.

SPA MANAGER: *(Attentive.)* Yes, Professor? And so—?

RUBEK: So I looked out of the window—and then I caught a glimpse of a pale figure in among the trees.

MAJA: *(Smiling to the SPA MANAGER.)* And, the professor insists, this figure was wearing a bathrobe.

RUBEK: —or something of the sort, I said. I couldn't quite make out at that distance. But I saw that it was something white.

SPA MANAGER: How extraordinary. Was it a gentleman or a lady?

RUBEK: I'm almost certain it had to be a lady. But following behind her was another figure. And that was quite dark—like a shadow.

SPA MANAGER: *(Starting.)* A dark figure? Even black, maybe?

RUBEK: Yes, that's how it appeared to me.

SPA MANAGER: *(As if light is dawning.)* And following the one in white? Close behind her?

RUBEK: Yes. At a little distance.

SPA MANAGER: Ah! Then I think I can enlighten you, Professor.

RUBEK: So, what was it I saw?

MAJA: *(Simultaneously.)* Then the professor wasn't dreaming?

SPA MANAGER: *(Suddenly whispering while pointing to the background, right.)* Ssh! Just look over there— Let's keep our voices down for a moment.

A slender lady, clad in fine, cream-hued white cashmere, and followed by a deaconess in black with a silver cross hanging from a chain on her breast, emerges from behind the corner of the hotel and walks through the park over to the pavilion in the left foreground. Her face is pallid and drawn tight as if into a mask, the eyelids down, the eyes seeming to be sightless. Her dress reaches to her feet, falling in folds and close to her body. Over her head, neck, breast, shoulders, and arms she wears a large while shawl of crepe. She holds her arms crossed upward over her breast. This posture does not change. Stiff and measured pace while walking. The NUN's [1] bearing is similarly measured and is that of a servant. She follows the lady unwaveringly with her brown, piercing eyes. Waiters, with white napkins on their arms, emerge from the hotel doorway and glance curiously at the two strangers. These take no notice and, without looking about them, go into the pavilion.)

RUBEK: *(Has slowly risen involuntarily from his chair, staring at the closed pavilion door.)* Who was that lady?

SPA MANAGER: She's a visitor who's rented that little pavilion there.

RUBEK: A foreigner?

SPA MANAGER: Most likely. At any rate, both of them arrived here from abroad. About a week ago. She's never been here before.

RUBEK: *(Convinced, looking at him.)* It was her I saw in the park last night.

SPA MANAGER: Yes, it must have been her. I thought so straight away.

RUBEK: What is the lady's name, Inspector?

SPA MANAGER: She's signed in as "Madam de Satow with lady companion." We know nothing more than that.

RUBEK: *(Pondering.)* Satow? Satow—?

MAJA: *(With an ironic laugh.)* Do you know anyone of that name, Rubek? Well?

RUBEK: *(Shakes his head.)* No, no one at all. Satow? Sounds as if its Russian. Or Slavic, at any rate. *(To the SPA MANAGER.)* What language does she speak?

SPA MANAGER: When the two ladies are talking together, it's in a language I don't understand. But otherwise, she speaks perfectly good Norwegian.

RUBEK: *(Exclaiming in surprise.)* Norwegian! You're sure you're not mistaken?

SPA MANAGER: No, there's no way I could be mistaken.

RUBEK: *(Looks at him tensely.)* You've heard that yourself?

SPA MANAGER: Yes, I've personally spoken with her. On one or two occasions. Only a couple of words for the most part. She's very reserved. All the same—

RUBEK: All the same, she spoke Norwegian?

SPA MANAGER: Perfectly good Norwegian. Perhaps with a slightly northern accent.

RUBEK: *(Stares before him, moved, and whispers.)* That too.

MAJA: *(A little disconcerted and put out.)* Maybe the lady was one of your models at some time, Rubek? Think about it!

RUBEK: *(Glancing sharply at her.)* Models!

MAJA: *(With a teasing smile.)* Yes. In your younger days, that is. Because you must have had no end of models. Way back in the past, I mean.

RUBEK: *(In a similar tone.)* Ah no, my little Maja. In actuality, I've only ever had one single model—just the one—for everything I've created.

SPA MANAGER: *(Who has turned and is looking out to the left.)* Unfortunately, I must ask you to excuse me. Because now someone's approaching who's no overwhelming pleasure to keep company with. Especially when there are ladies present.

RUBEK: *(Looking out in the same direction.)* That hunter coming over there? Who is he?

SPA MANAGER: That's the big landowner, Ulfhejm.

RUBEK: Ah yes, Ulfhejm.

SPA MANAGER: The bear-killer, as they call him.

RUBEK: I know him.

SPA MANAGER: Yes, who doesn't know him?

RUBEK: Only very slightly, just the same. Has he become a patient here, at last?

SPA MANAGER: No, surprisingly enough—not yet. He just looks in here once or twice in the year—when he's on his way up to the hunting grounds. Excuse me, for the moment— *(He starts for the hotel.)*

ULFHEJM'S VOICE: *(From offstage.)* Hold it a moment! Stay there, for the devil's sake. Why are you always running away from me?

SPA MANAGER: *(Standing his ground.)* Not running, Mr. Ulfhejm, in the least.. *(ULFHEJM* [2] *enters from the left, followed by a servant leading a pair of leashed hounds. ULFHEJM is in hunting outfit, with high boots and a felt hat with a feather in it. He is a lean, tall, sinewy man with matted hair and beard, loud-voiced, of an age hard to discern from his appearance, but no longer young.)*

ULFHEJM: *(Heading straight for the SPA MANAGER.)* Is that the way you welcome visitors, eh? Slinking away with your tail between your legs—as if you had the devil at your heels?

SPA MANAGER *(Calmly, without answering.)* Did you come by the steamer, sir?

ULFHEJM *(Growling.)* I've not been granted sight of any steamer. *(His hands on his hips.)* Aren't you aware I sail in my own cutter? *(To his servant.)* Take good care of your fellow creatures, Lars. Make sure they stay ravenous, though. Fresh meat bones. But not too much meat. And raw and bloody, mind you. And get something into your own belly while you're at it. *(Aims a kick at him.)* Now, off to hell with you. *(The SERVANT goes off with the dogs behind the hotel.)*

SPA MANAGER: Will you be eating in the restaurant, sir?

ULFHEJM: In among all those half-dead flies and people? No thanks, that's not for me, Inspector.

SPA MANAGER: Well, suit yourself.

ULFHEJM: But let the maid lay out the usual spread. Plenty of food and a good supply of brandy! And tell her that either Lars or I will play the devil with her if she doesn't—

SPA MANAGER: *(Interrupts.)* We know all that from before. *(Turning.)* Is there anything I should tell the waiter to bring you? Or something for Mrs. Rubek?

RUBEK: No thanks, nothing for me.

MAJA: Nor for me, either.

(The SPA MANAGER goes into the hotel.)

ULFHEJM: *(Glares at them for a moment; then raises his hat.)* Well, hell and damnation—here am I, straight off the farm, landing right among tip-top society.

RUBEK: *(Looking up.)* What's that supposed to mean?

ULFHEJM: *(More restrained and polite.)* It seems I've run into no less than the great sculptor Rubek himself?

RUBEK: *(Nodding.)* We met a couple of times, socially, that autumn I last visited home.

ULFHEJM: Yes, but that's many years since. And that time you weren't as famous as you've become. In those days even a scruffy bear hunter dared approach you.

RUBEK: *(Smiling.)* I don't bite, even now.

MAJA: *(Regarding ULFHEJM with interest.)* Are you really and truly a bear hunter?

ULFHEJM: *(Sitting at an adjoining table, closer to the hotel.)* Bears by choice, ma'am. But otherwise I'll take whatever wild creatures come my way. Eagles, wolves, women, elk, or reindeer— So long as they're fresh and lively and full-blooded, then— *(He drinks from a pocket flask.)*

MAJA: *(Regarding him intently.)* But preferably bears?

ULFHEJM: Preferably, yes. Because then you can take a knife to them any time you're cornered. *(Smiling slightly.)* We both work on tough material— I and your husband. He hews away at his blocks of marble, as I imagine—and I hew at the taut and quivering sinews of bears. And we both force the material to yield to us. To become master and lord of it. We don't give up until we've triumphed over it, however toughly it resists.

RUBEK: *(Reflectively.)* There's some truth in what you say.

ULFHEJM: Yes, because the stone has something to struggle for, I'd say. It's dead and will use all its power and strength not to be hammered into life. The same way a bear resists anyone who comes poking at him in his lair.

MAJA: Are you going hunting now, up in the forests?

ULFHEJM: Yes, I'm heading way up high in the mountains. I dare say you've never been up high in the mountains have you, Mrs. Rubek?

MAJA: No, never.

ULFHEJM: Damnation, then see to it that you get up there, now, this summer. I'd be glad to take you and the professor.

MAJA: Thanks, but Rubek's thinking of a sea trip this summer.

RUBEK: Between the islands along the coast?

ULFHEJM: Puh! Why the devil do you want to mess around in those hellish, polluted channels. Just imagine it—drifting along in all that putrid local water—cloacal water,[3] it should be called.

MAJA: Did you hear that, Rubek?

ULFHEJM: No, instead, come with me up to the mountains. Where it's unsullied and unspoiled by humanity. You can't imagine what that means for me. But I suppose a fine lady like yourself— *(He pauses.)*

(The NUN comes out from the pavilion and goes into the hotel.)

ULFHEJM: Just cast your eyes on her. That black crow. Who's about to be buried?

RUBEK: I don't know of anyone here who's—

ULFHEJM: Well, someone here's soon going to give up the ghost. In some cramped cubicle or other. These who are sick and feeble should oblige us by getting themselves buried—the sooner the better.

MAJA: Have you ever been sick yourself, Mr. Ulfhejm?

ULFHEJM: Never. And then I wouldn't be sitting here. But my nearest and dearest—they've been sick, poor devils.

MAJA: And what did you do for those nearest and dearest?

ULFHEJM: Shot them, naturally.

RUBEK: *(Stares at him.)* You shot them?

MAJA: *(Drawing back her chair.)* You shot them dead?

ULFHEJM: *(Nodding.)* I never miss, ma'am.

MAJA: But how can you bring yourself to kill human beings?

ULFHEJM: I'm not talking about human beings.

MAJA: You said your nearest and—

ULFHEJM: —and dearest. My dogs, that's to say.

MAJA: And they are your dearest friends.

ULFHEJM: None more so. My honest, faithful, truly steadfast hunting comrades— Should one of them get sick and ailing then—bang! He's expedited—over to the other side.

(The NUN comes out from the hotel carrying a tray of bread and milk, and sets it down on a table outside the pavilion, which she re-enters.)

ULFHEJM: *(Laughing scornfully.)* See that—that's supposed to be food for human consumption! Skim milk and soft, mushy bread! You ought to see how my comrades feed. Would you like to see that?

MAJA: *(Getting up and smiling across to RUBEK.)* Yes, I'd love to.

ULFHEJM: You seem a lady who can cope with it. Come with me then. Be prepared for them gobbling down great, hefty knucklebones. Belching them up then gulping them down again. It's a real treat to see them. Come along and I'll show you. And let's talk a bit more about that mountain trip—

(He exits round the corner of the hotel. MAJA follows him. At the same moment the LADY comes out of the pavilion and sits at the table. She raises the glass of milk to drink but pauses and looks over to RUBEK with blank, expressionless eyes. RUBEK remains seated at the table staring gravely and intently at her. At last he gets up, takes a step toward her and stops.)

RUBEK *(Softly.)* I recognize you perfectly well, Irene.

THE LADY: You've guessed who I am have you, Arnold?

RUBEK: *(Not answering.)* And you've recognized me, I see.

THE LADY: With you it's a different matter.

RUBEK: Why should that be—with me?

THE LADY: Yes, you're still alive.

RUBEK *(Not understanding.)* Alive—?

THE LADY: *(After a moment.)* Who was that other? She you had with you at your table?

RUBEK: *(A little reluctantly.)* She? That was my—my wife.

THE LADY: *(Nodding slowly.)* Indeed. That's good, Arnold. Therefore, someone who's no concern of mine.

RUBEK: *(Uncertainly.)* No—you are right.

THE LADY: Someone you found for yourself after my lifetime.

RUBEK: *(Observing her intently.)* After your—? What are you saying, Irene?

IRENE: *(Not answering.)* And the child? It has a good life in this world. Our child lives on after me. In honor and glory.

RUBEK: *(Smiling, as at a distant memory.)* Our child? Yes, that's what we called it—at the time.

IRENE: In my lifetime, yes.

RUBEK: *(Trying cheerfully to let this pass.)* Yes, Irene, now you can be sure "our child" has become famous over the whole world. You'll have read about it, for certain.

IRENE: *(Nodding.)* And has made its father famous, too. That was your dream.

RUBEK: *(Softly, moved.)* It's you I owe everything to, Irene. Thank you for that.

IRENE: *(Sits reflecting for a while.)* If, at that time, I'd done what it was my right to do, Arnold—

RUBEK: Yes? What then?

IRENE: I should have killed that child.

RUBEK: Killed it, you say!

IRENE: *(In a whisper.)* Killed it—before I left you. Smashed it. Smashed it to dust.

RUBEK: *(Shaking his head reproachfully.)* You could never have done that, Irene. You hadn't the heart for it.

IRENE: No, at the time I hadn't that kind of heart.

RUBEK: But since then? Afterwards?

IRENE: Afterwards I killed it countless times. In daylight and darkness. Killed it in hatred—and revenge—and in agony.

RUBEK: *(Goes over to her table and softly asks.)* Irene—tell me now at last— after so many years—why did you leave me then? Taking flight and leaving no trace. Never to be found again—

IRENE: *(Slowly shaking her head.)* Oh Arnold, why tell you now—when I am on this other side.

RUBEK: Was there someone else you'd come to love.

IRENE: There was one, who had no use for my love. No use for my life, either.

RUBEK: *(Changing the subject.)* Hm—let's say no more about the past—

IRENE: No, no, say no more about that other world. Because it is a world beyond me, now.

RUBEK: Where did you go, Irene? You had vanished beyond all my efforts to find you.

IRENE: I passed into the darkness—while the child stood in the transfiguring light.

RUBEK: Did you travel much around the world?

IRENE: Yes, travelled through many lands and countries.

RUBEK: *(Regarding her with compassion.)* And how did you manage for yourself, Irene?

IRENE: *(Looking directly at him.)* Wait now, let me see— Ah yes, now I recall. I've stood on the revolving platform in variety shows. As a naked statue in living tableaux. Fetched in a lot of money. Which I never could with you—you never had any. And then I've gone with men I could drive demented. Once again, not something I could do with you. You held out better.

RUBEK: *(Hastily dropping that subject.)* And did you get married, as well?

IRENE: Yes, to one of them.

RUBEK: Who is your husband?

IRENE: He was a South American. A high diplomat. *(Staring out with a stony smile.)* I drove him out of his wits—incurably, irredeemably mad. Most enjoyable, I tell you—while it lasted. I could have laughed continually in my inmost self—if I'd had any inmost self.

RUBEK: And where does he live now?

IRENE: In a churchyard somewhere. With a tall, impressive monument over him. And with a lead bullet rattling in his skull.

RUBEK: He killed himself?

IRENE: Yes, he obligingly spared me the task.

RUBEK: You feel no grief for him, Irene?

IRENE: *(Uncomprehending.)* Grief? For whom?

RUBEK: For Herr von Satow.

IRENE: His name wasn't Satow.

RUBEK: No—?

IRENE: My second husband's name was Satow. He's a Russian.

RUBEK: And where is he?

IRENE: Far away in the Ural mountains. Among all his gold mines.

RUBEK: That's where he lives?

IRENE: *(Shrugs her shoulders.)* Lives? Lives? Actually, I killed him.

RUBEK: *(Starting.)* Killed—?

IRENE: Killed him with a fine, sharp dagger that I always have with me in my bed—

RUBEK: *(Vehemently.)* I don't believe you, Irene!

IRENE: *(Smiling gently.)* You may believe me all right, Arnold.

RUBEK: *(Regarding her sympathetically.)* Did you never have any children?

IRENE: Oh yes, I've had many children.

RUBEK: And where are these children, now?

IRENE: I killed them.

RUBEK: *(Firmly.)* You're sitting there lying to me!

IRENE: I killed them, I tell you. With my whole heart I murdered them. As soon, just as soon as they came into the world. No, long, long before then. One after the other.

RUBEK: *(Somberly and sadly.)* There's something hidden behind all that you're saying.

IRENE: How can I help it? Every word I speak to you is being whispered in my ear.

RUBEK: I believe I'm the only person who could fathom their meaning.

IRENE: You should be the only one.

RUBEK: *(Pressing his hands on the table and looking probingly at her.)* Some chord in you has snapped in two.

IRENE: *(Gently.)* It's what always must happen when a young, full-blooded woman dies.

RUBEK: Oh, Irene, put aside these desperate imaginings—! You're alive! Alive, alive!

IRENE: *(Slowly rises from her chair and says, trembling.)* I was dead for many years. They came and bound me. Lashed my arms together behind my back. Then they lowered me down into a tomb with iron bars for a cover. And with padded walls, so that no one on the earth above could hear the cries from the sepulcher. But now, in part, I'm beginning to rise from the dead. *(Resumes sitting.)*

RUBEK: *(After a pause.)* Do you see me as guilty of all this?

IRENE: Yes.

RUBEK: Guilty of—what you call your death?

IRENE: Guilty of this—that I had to die! *(Changes to a neutral tone.)* Why don't you sit, Arnold?

RUBEK: May I?

IRENE: Yes. You needn't be afraid of shivering with cold. I don't believe I'm entirely turned to ice just yet.

RUBEK: *(Draws up a chair and sits at the table.)* There, Irene. Now we're sitting together as we did in the old days.

IRENE: A little distant from each other. Also as in the old days.

RUBEK: *(Moving closer.)* It had to be that way, then.

IRENE: Had to be?

RUBEK: *(Insistently.)* There had to be a distance between us—

IRENE: There really had to be, Arnold?

RUBEK: *(Continuing.)* Do you remember what you answered when I asked if you would follow me out into the world?

IRENE: I raised three fingers in the air and vowed I'd follow you to the end of the world, the end of life itself. And that I'd serve you in all things—

RUBEK: As model for my art—

IRENE: In free and utter nakedness—

RUBEK: And you did serve me, Irene—bravely, gladly, and unhesitatingly.

IRENE: Yes, with all the throbbing blood of my youth I served you!

RUBEK: *(Nodding, with a glance of gratitude.)* That you can truly claim.

IRENE: Fell at your feet and served you, Arnold! *(Raising clenched fists against him.)* But you, you—you—!

RUBEK: *(Warding her off.)* I never wronged you. Never, Irene!

IRENE: Yes, you did! You wronged the very source of my existence.

RUBEK: *(Recoiling.)* I—!

IRENE: Yes, you! I stood in free and utter nakedness for you to behold— *(More softly.)* And never once did you touch me.

RUBEK: Irene, couldn't you understand there were days and days when I was nearly driven out of my mind with your beauty.

IRENE: Just the same, if you'd once touched me, I think I would have killed you on the spot. For I kept a sharp needle with me. Hidden in my hair.

(Reflectively stroking her forehead.) No, but yet—even so—that you could—

RUBEK: *(Looking at her pointedly.)* I was an artist, Irene.

IRENE: *(Darkly.)* Yes. Precisely. Precisely.

RUBEK: First and foremost an artist. And I was sick with desire to create the supreme work of my life. *(Lost in recollection.)* It was to be called "Resurrection Day." To be sculpted in the likeness of a young woman awakening from the sleep of death—

IRENE: Our child, yes—

RUBEK: *(Continuing.)* Awakening as the noblest, purest, most ideal of women, that's what she was to be. Then I found you. You embodied all I needed. And you agreed so joyfully and willingly. So you then left home and followed me.

IRENE: It was the resurrection of my childhood, when I followed you.

RUBEK: That was why I could use you above all. You and no one else. You were for me a holy creature, to be touched only by thoughts of the purest adoration. I was still a young man at the time, Irene. A superstitious dread possessed me that to touch you, to desire you sensually, would so defile my spirit I would be incapable of giving final form to what I was striving after. And I believe, to this day, there was some truth in that.

IRENE: *(Nodding with a touch of contempt.)* The work of art comes first—and then the human child.

RUBEK: Yes, you can condemn that if you want. But I was in complete thrall then to my artistic calling. And felt so exultantly fortunate in it.

IRENE: And you triumphantly fulfilled your calling, Arnold.

RUBEK: Thanks and praise to you—I fulfilled my calling. I wanted to shape the pure woman as I envisioned she must appear awakening on Resurrection Day. Not marveling over anything new, or unknown, or unimagined. But filled with a holy joy at discovering herself unchanged—she, a woman of the earth, in this higher, freer, happier region—after the long, dreamless sleep of death. *(Speaking more softly.)* That's how I shaped her. In your image I shaped her, Irene.

IRENE: *(Lays her hands flat on the table and leans backward in her chair.)* And then you were through with me.

RUBEK: *(Reproachfully.)* Irene!

IRENE: Had no further use for me.

RUBEK: And you can say that!

IRENE: Began to cast around for other ideal forms.

RUBEK: I found none. None after you.

IRENE: No other models, Arnold?

RUBEK: You were not a model to me. You were the source of my creative vision.

IRENE: *(Is silent for a moment.)* What poems have you created since? In marble, I mean. After that day I went from you?

RUBEK: I've created no poems since then. Just puttering around, modeling portraits.

IRENE: And that woman you're living with now—

RUBEK: *(Vehemently interrupting.)* Let's not talk of her. It cuts to the heart.

IRENE: Where are you planning to go with her.

RUBEK: *(Listless, weary.)* On some tediously long trip north up the coast.

IRENE: *(Looking at him with an almost imperceptible smile, and whispering.)* Travel instead high up into the mountains. As high as you can reach. Higher, higher—always higher, Arnold.

RUBEK: *(Tensely expectant.)* Are you going there?

IRENE: Do you have the courage to meet me one more time?

RUBEK: *(Struggling, uncertain.)* If only we could—ah, if only we could!

IRENE: And why can't we—if that's what we want? *(Looks at him and whispers entreatingly, clasping her hands.)* Come, Arnold, come! Come up to me—!

(MAJA enters around the corner of the hotel, flushed with happiness and hurries to the table where they previously had sat.)

MAJA: *(Still by the corner, not looking about her.)* Well, you can say what you will, Rubek, but— *(Stops as she catches sight of IRENE.)* Oh, excuse me, you've made a new acquaintance, I see.

RUBEK: *(Curtly.)* Renewed an acquaintance. *(Standing.)* What did you wish to say to me?

MAJA: It was only this—you can do what you please—but I am not coming with you on that disgusting steamer.

RUBEK: Why ever not?

MAJA: Because I want to go up into the mountains and the forests, that's why. *(Ingratiatingly.)* Oh, you must give me leave to do it, Rubek! I'll be so good, ever so good, after.

RUBEK: Who's put these ideas into your head?

MAJA: He has. That horrid bear killer. Oh, you can't imagine all the wonders he's been describing about the mountains. And about the life up there! They're hideous, revolting, and odious, the things he lies about. Yes, because I'm almost certain he's lying. But it's wonderfully alluring, just the same. Do I have leave to go with him? Only to see if what he's saying is true, you understand. Can I do it, Rubek?

RUBEK: Yes, that's fine with me. Just go up into the mountains—as far and as long as you like. I may be taking the same trip myself.

MAJA *(Quickly.)* No, no, no—you don't need do that! Not for my sake!

RUBEK: But I want to go to the mountains. My mind's made up.

MAJA: Oh, thank you, thank you. May I go and tell the bear killer at once?

RUBEK: Tell our bear killer whatever you like.

MAJA: Thank you, thank you. *(About to grasp his hand. He evades her.)* How sweet and kind you are today, Rubek! *(She runs into the hotel.)*

(At the same moment the pavilion door gently and soundlessly opens a little. The NUN is seen in the door opening, standing, and observing. No one sees her.)

RUBEK: *(Resolved, turning to IRENE.)* So we're meeting up there, then?

IRENE: *(Slowly rises.)* Yes, we shall indeed. I've searched for you so long.

RUBEK: When did you begin to search for me, Irene?

IRENE: *(With a suggestion of bitter irony.)* From the moment it dawned on me I'd given you something quite irreplaceable, Arnold. Something one should never part with.

RUBEK: *(Lowering his head.)* Yes, that's painfully true. You gave me three to four years of your young life.

IRENE: More, more than that, I gave you. Prodigal as I was in those days.

RUBEK: Yes, you were prodigal, Irene. You gave me all your naked loveliness—

IRENE: To contemplate—

RUBEK: And to consecrate—

IRENE: Yes, to consecrate for yourself. And for the child.

RUBEK: For you, also, Irene.

IRENE: But you have forgotten my rarest gift.

RUBEK: The rarest—? What gift was that?

IRENE: I gave you my young, living soul. After, I became empty inside. Soulless. *(Stares fixedly at him.)* That's when I died, Arnold. *(The NUN opens the door wide and stands aside for her. She goes into the pavilion)*

RUBEK: *(Stands staring after her. Then he whispers.)* Irene!

END OF ACT ONE

ACT TWO

High up, near a mountain sanatorium. The landscape stretches away across a bare, treeless plateau and toward a long mountain lake. On the other side of the lake a range of mountain peaks rises with blue-tinted snow in the crevasses. In the foreground to the left a stream ripples and divides over a steep face of rock and from there flows placidly across the plateau to the right. Scrub trees, plants, and boulders line the stream. In the foreground to the right a small knoll with a stone bench on its top. It is a summer evening just before sunset.

On the far side of the plateau beyond the stream a group of small children are playing and dancing, some in town clothes, others in traditional country dress. Their happy laughter can be heard, muted, during the following scene.

PROFESSOR RUBEK is sitting on the bench with a plaid over his shoulders, watching the children playing. After a moment MAJA comes making her way through some clumps of bushes to the left middle distance and peers about with her hand shading her eyes. She wears a flat tourist hat, a short, gathered-up skirt that reaches halfway down her legs, and high, sturdy, laced boots. In one hand she carries a long alpenstock.

MAJA: *(Catches sight of RUBEK and calls.)* Hallo! *(She crosses the plateau, then springs over the stream with the help of her alpenstock. She climbs the slope of the knoll.)*

MAJA: *(Panting.)* I've been hunting high and low for you, Rubek!

RUBEK: *(Nodding indifferently.)* Did you come up from the hotel?

MAJA: Yes, I just left that flytrap.

RUBEK: *(Briefly regarding her.)* You weren't at lunch, I noticed.

MAJA: No, we had our lunch under the open sky.

RUBEK: "We"? Who are we?

MAJA: Myself—and that odious bear killer.

RUBEK: I see. Him.

MAJA: Yes. And tomorrow early, we're going out again.

RUBEK: After bears?

MAJA: Yes. We're off to kill Bruin.

RUBEK: Have you found tracks of any?

MAJA *(Superior.)* You don't find bears up here above the treeline, do you?

RUBEK: Where then?

MAJA: Way below. On the wooded slopes in the thickest part of the forest. Where it's completely impenetrable to ordinary town folk.

RUBEK: And that's where the pair of you will be going tomorrow?

MAJA: *(Flings herself down in the heather.)* Yes, that's what we've planned. Or we might start out already this evening—if you don't raise any objection—

RUBEK: I? No, far from it—

MAJA *(Hurriedly.)* Lars will be coming along as well, naturally. With the dogs.

RUBEK: I've not the slightest interest in Mr. Lars and his dogs. *(Changing the subject.)* But wouldn't you rather sit up properly, here on the bench?

MAJA: *(Drowsily.)* No thanks. It's so pleasant, lying here in the soft heather.

RUBEK: I can tell by looking at you, you're tired.

MAJA:. *(Yawning.)* Yes, I rather feel I'm beginning to be.

RUBEK: That usually follows—once the excitement's over.

MAJA: *(Sleepily.)* Yes, I'll just lie here and close my eyes.

(A short silence.)

MAJA: *(Suddenly impatient.)* Ugh, Rubek, how can you bear to sit there listening to those children screeching? And watching all their goatish antics?

RUBEK: There's something harmonious—almost a kind of music—in their movements—every now and then. In the middle of all their ungainliness. And those rare moments are delicious to sit and wait for, when they happen.

MAJA: *(Somewhat scornfully.)* Always and forever the artist, aren't you, Rubek?

RUBEK: It's what I hope I'll continue to be.

MAJA: *(Rolling over onto her side and turning her back to him.)* He hasn't a trace of the artist in him.

RUBEK: And who might he be—this man who's no artist?

MAJA: *(Again in a sleepy tone.)* Him—the other one.

RUBEK: Our shooter of bears, you mean?

MAJA: Yes. Not a trace of the artist. Not a trace.

RUBEK: *(Smiling.)* No, I imagine you're on solid ground there.

MAJA: *(Vehemently, without stirring.)* And then he's so ugly, he really is! *(Pulling at a tuft of heather and throwing it aside.)* So ugly, so ugly! Ecch!

RUBEK: And for that reason you're ready to go off with him—out into the wilderness?

MAJA: *(Curtly.)* I don't know. *(Turning toward him.)* You're ugly too, Rubek.

RUBEK: You've only just discovered that?

MAJA: No. I've noticed it for some time.

RUBEK: One grows old, Maja. One grows old.

MAJA: No, I don't mean in that way. But you've acquired such a wearied, such a resigned look in your eyes. That is, when you deign to look at me—once in a while.

RUBEK: You believe you can see all that?

MAJA: *(Nodding.)* Little by little you've taken on this baleful look in your eyes. It's almost as if you were plotting some harm against me.

RUBEK: Really? *(Amiably, but serious.)* Come up here and sit beside me, Maja. Then we can have a little talk together.

MAJA: *(Half rising.)* Will you let me sit on your knee then? Like in the old days.

RUBEK: No, you mustn't do that. People can see us, down there in the hotel. *(Shifting a little.)* But you can sit here next to me on the bench.

MAJA: No thanks. I'd rather go on lying here where I am. I can hear just as well. *(Looking inquiringly at him.)* Now what was it you wanted to say to me?

RUBEK: *(Beginning slowly.)* What do you think was the real reason I agreed to our going on this summer trip?

MAJA: Well, among other things, you were pretty insistent it would do me a world of good. But—

RUBEK: But—?

MAJA: But now I don't believe for a moment that was why—

RUBEK: Why was it then, do you think?

MAJA: I now think it was because of that pale lady.

RUBEK: Because of Mrs. von Satow?

MAJA: Yes, she who's always on our heels wherever we go. Last evening she showed up here, too.

RUBEK: But what on earth—!

MAJA: Well, you've certainly known her intimately before. Long before you knew me.

RUBEK: I'd also forgotten her again—long before I knew you.

MAJA *(Sitting up.)* Do you forget so easily, Rubek?

RUBEK: *(Curtly.)* Yes, exceedingly easy. *(Gruffly adding.)* When I want to forget.

MAJA: Even a woman who has stood as a model for you?

RUBEK: *(Dismissively.)* When I've no more use for her, then—

MAJA: One who's stripped herself naked for you?

RUBEK: That means nothing. Not to us artists. *(Shifting to another tone.)* And how—might I venture to ask—could I have guessed she was here in this country?

MAJA: Well, you could have read her name in a visitors' list. In one of our newspapers.

RUBEK: Ah, but I had no idea of the name she now goes by. I've never heard tell of any Herr von Satrow.

MAJA: *(Pretending boredom.)* Oh well, God knows, I suppose you had some other reason for travelling.

RUBEK: *(Seriously.)* Yes, Maja—there was another reason. A totally different one. And it's this that we two need to discuss together.

MAJA: *(Stifling a burst of laughter.)* Oh lord, how solemn you look!

RUBEK: *(Eyeing her distrustfully.)* Yes, maybe more solemn than strictly called for.

MAJA: Well, what—?

RUBEK: And that's no doubt best for both of us.

MAJA: You're beginning to get me curious, Rubek.

RUBEK: Only curious. Not the least uneasy?

MAJA: *(Shaking her head.)* Not a trace.

RUBEK: Good. Listen then. The other day, down at the spa, you said you thought I'd become very irritable of late—

MAJA: Yes, so you have, too.

RUBEK: And what do you think could be the cause of that?

MAJA: How should I know? *(Quickly.)* Maybe you're bored living forever with me.

RUBEK: Forever—? Say, rather, everlastingly.

MAJA: Every day together, then. We've gone on, in that world down there, we two solitary people, for about four or five years, with hardly an hour apart from each other. We two, completely alone.

RUBEK: *(Now interested.)* Well then? And so—?

MAJA: *(Slightly emphatically.)* You're hardly a sociable man, Rubek. You're completely wrapped up in yourself and your own thoughts. And I've no way of talking with you properly about your concerns. All that about art and suchlike— *(A gesture with her hand.)* And God knows, I don't care much about it, either.

RUBEK: True enough. Which is why we mostly find ourselves sitting by the fire chattering about your concerns.

MAJA: Oh, lord—I've no concerns to chatter about.

RUBEK: No, maybe they're trivia. But in any case, that's how time passes for both of us, Maja.

MAJA: Yes, you're right there. Time passes. It's passing you by, Rubek! And no doubt *that* is what's making you so uneasy—

RUBEK: *(Nodding emphatically.)* And so restless. *(Writhing on the bench.)* No, I can't go on with this pathetic life much longer.

MAJA: *(Gets up and stands a moment looking at him.)* If you want to be rid of me, just say so.

RUBEK: What kind of talk is that? Want to be rid of you.

MAJA: Yes, if you want to be quit of me, then just say it straight out. And I'll go right away.

RUBEK: *(Smiling almost imperceptibly.)* Is that meant to be a threat, Maja?

MAJA: I don't imagine it can be any kind of threat for you.

RUBEK: *(Getting up.)* No, you're absolutely right, there. *(A moment later, adding.)* You and I can't possibly go on living together like this—

MAJA: Well then—!

RUBEK: Not "well then." *(Emphasizing the words.)* Just because we two can't go on living together by ourselves—doesn't mean that we should divorce.

MAJA: *(Smiling scornfully.)* Just separate a little, you mean?

RUBEK: *(Shaking his head.)* That's not necessary, either.

MAJA: It isn't? Say straight out what you want to do with me.

RUBEK: *(A little uncertainly.)* What I feel so desperately—even painfully— that I need, is someone by me who can enter into and share my innermost needs

MAJA: *(Interrupting tensely.)* And I don't do that, Rubek?

RUBEK: *(Evasively.)* Not in the way I mean. I must be able to share my life with someone who can complete me, make me whole, be one with me in all I'm striving after.

MAJA: *(Slowly.)* Yes, in weighty things like that I could never be much use to you.

RUBEK: No, it's best you let such things alone, Maja.

MAJA: *(Vehemently.)* And God knows, I've no inclination for it, either.

RUBEK: As I'm painfully aware. And it certainly wasn't what I had in view when I married you.

MAJA: *(Observing him.)* I can see you've someone else in mind.

RUBEK: Really? I've never noticed before that you were a mind reader. And you also can see who it is?

MAJA: Yes, I can. Oh, I know you so well, Rubek. So well!

RUBEK: Well then perhaps you'll have the goodness to—

MAJA: You're thinking all the time of that—that model that you once used for— *(Abruptly dropping that train of thought.)* I suppose you know people down at the hotel think she's mad?

RUBEK: Oh? And what do those same people down at the hotel think about you and your bear killer?

MAJA: That's got nothing to do with it. *(Returning to her previous train of thought.)* But it was that pale lady you were thinking about?

RUBEK: *(Frankly.)* About her—exactly! About when I no longer had any use for her— And when she, on her part, walked out on me—vanished—so that no longer—

MAJA: And so you took me up as some kind of consolation prize, I suppose?

RUBEK: (*Inconsiderately.*) Something like that, little Maja, to tell the truth. For a year and a half I'd gone on alone, brooding and putting the last, the final finishing touches to my work. "Resurrection Day" then went out all over the world bringing me fame—and all the other glory that goes with that. (*More warmly.*) But I no longer loved my own work. The public bouquets and incense only drove me, in nausea, into the depths of the forest. (*Looking at her.*) You, being a mind reader, can you guess what then occurred to me?

MAJA (*Casually.*) Sure. It occurred to you to make portrait busts of ladies and gentlemen.

RUBEK: (*Nodding.*) On commission, yes. With animal faces behind the masks. They got those gratis—a bonus, you might say. (*Smiling.*) But that's not exactly what I meant.

MAJA: What then?

RUBEK: (*Serious again.*) Just this: this whole business about the artist's calling and the artist's vision—and suchlike—began to pall on me and to strike me instead as something empty and hollow and meaningless.

MAJA: What would you put in its place?

RUBEK: Life, Maja.

MAJA: Life?

RUBEK: Yes. Isn't life in sunshine and beauty altogether more worthwhile than wasting one's days in a raw, damp cellar, working away until tired to death at lumps of clay and blocks of stone?

MAJA: (*With a little sigh.*) Yes, it's what I've always thought.

RUBEK: And then I'd become wealthy enough to live in luxury in the lazily shimmering sunlight. I was able to build myself a villa by Lake Taunitz— and the palace in the capital. And all the rest of it.

MAJA: (*Taking up his tone.*) And then, as the icing on the cake, you had the means to buy me. And gave me leave to make use of your riches.

RUBEK: (*Jokingly deflecting the talk.*) And didn't I promise to take you with me up a high mountain and show you all the glory of the world?

MAJA (*With a gentle expression.*) You may have brought me up a tolerably high mountain, Rubek, but you've not shown me all the glory of the world.

RUBEK: (*Laughing irritably.*) How impossible you are to please, Maja! How impossible. (*Vehemently.*) But do you know what it is that really drives me to despair? Can you guess?

MAJA: (*In quiet defiance.*) Yes, what else but that you now have to go about tied to me for life.

RUBEK: I wouldn't have put it quite so heartlessly.

MAJA: But the meaning would have been just as heartless.

RUBEK: You really have no clear notion of how an artist's mind works.

MAJA: *(Smiles and shakes her head.)* Good lord, I don't even have a clear notion of how my own mind works.

RUBEK: *(Continuing unaffected.)* I live so intensely, Maja. That's how we artists live. For my part I've been through a whole lifetime in the few years we've known each other. And I've come to see it's just not in my nature to find happiness in a life of leisure. That's not how life can be lived for me and my kind. I have to keep active—bringing work after work into being—up to the day I die. *(With difficulty.)* For that reason, I can't go on with you any longer, Maja— No longer with you alone.

MAJA: *(Calmly.)* Why not say, in simple language, you've grown tired of me?

RUBEK: *(Vehemently.)* Yes, I'm saying that! I've grown tired of you—intolerably tired and bored and worn-out from living with you. Now you know. *(Controlling himself.)* Those are ugly, brutal words I'm saying. I feel that all too keenly. And you're in no way at fault in this. I'm the one, no one else, who's undergone a transformation—*(Half to himself.)* an awakening to what my own life truly is about.

MAJA: *(Involuntarily clasping her hands.)* Then why on earth don't we just go our separate ways?

RUBEK: *(Looking astonished at her.)* You could agree to that?

MAJA: *(Shrugging her shoulders.)* Yes—if there's nothing else for it, then—

RUBEK: *(Animatedly.)* But there is something else. Another way out—

MAJA: *(Raising her forefinger.)* Now you're thinking about the pale lady again.

RUBEK: Yes. If the truth be told, I'm thinking of her ceaselessly. Ever since I met her again. *(A step closer.)* For now I must confide something to you, Maja.

MAJA: Well?

RUBEK: *(Tapping his chest.)* Inside here, you see—here I've a tiny little casket with a secret lock. And in that casket all my visions lie in safekeeping. But when she departed from me without a trace, the lock of the casket snapped shut. And she has the key and she took that with her. You, little Maja, you had no key. So everything inside there lies unused. And the years pass! And it's not possible for me to get at that treasure.

MAJA: *(Fighting a mischievous smile.)* So—get her to unlock it for you again.

RUBEK: *(Not understanding.)* Maja—?

MAJA: Well, isn't she here? And no doubt it's for the sake of the casket that she's come.

RUBEK: I've never mentioned a word of this to her.

MAJA: *(Looking innocently at him.)* But, my dear Rubek, is it really worth making all this fuss and bother over something so straightforward.

RUBEK: So you think this is so straightforward?

MAJA: Yes, I really think so. Simply go with whomever you most need. *(Nodding to him.)* I'll always end up with a place for myself.

RUBEK: What do you mean?

MAJA: *(Unconcerned, evasive.)* Well—I could always move out to the villa if that should be necessary. But there should be no need for that. Our house in town is large enough—and with a little good will, there's room enough for three.

RUBEK: *(Uncertainly.)* And do you think that would last long?

MAJA: *(Her tone light.)* Good lord, if it doesn't, it doesn't. There's no more to be said.

RUBEK: And then what do we do, Maja—if it doesn't work out?

MAJA: *(Cheerfully.)* Then we two should simply get out of each other's way. Split up completely. I'll always be able to find myself something new somewhere in the world. Where I'll be free. Free! Free! You needn't worry yourself on my account, Professor Rubek! *(Suddenly pointing to the right.)* Look! There she is!

RUBEK: *(Turning.)* Where?

MAJA: Over that open ground. Pacing along—like a marble statue. She's coming this way.

RUBEK: *(Stands gazing with his hand over his eyes.)* Doesn't she seem like the living image of Resurrection? *(To himself.)* To think I could have moved her to one side. Placed her in the shadow. Remodel her. What a fool I was!

MAJA: What's all that about?

RUBEK: *(Ignoring the question.)* Nothing. Not anything you could understand. *(IRENE approaches from the right over the plain. The children playing have already caught sight of her and run to meet her. She is now surrounded by the crowd of children, some seeming lively and trusting, others shy and fearful. She talks softly to them and indicates they should go down to the sanatorium. She herself wishes to rest a while by the stream. The children run off, down the slope, in midground left. IRENE goes over to the wall of mountain rock and lets the rivulets run coolly over her hands.)*

MAJA: *(Softly.)* Go down and speak with her alone, Rubek.

RUBEK And where will you go meanwhile?

MAJA: *(Looking meaningfully at him.)* Oh, I'm going my own way, from now on. *(She goes down the slope and leaps the stream with the help of her alpenstock. She stops before IRENE.)* Professor Rubek is standing up there waiting for you, madam.

IRENE: What does he want?

MAJA: He wants you to help with a casket that's snapped shut.

IRENE: Can I help with that?

MAJA: He believes you're the only one who can.

IRENE: Then I must try.

MAJA: Yes, madam, you really must.

> (*She goes down the path to the sanatorium. Soon after, RUBEK descends to IRENE but stays so that the stream is between them.*)

IRENE: (*After a short pause.*) She—that other one—said you were waiting for me.

RUBEK: I've been waiting for you year after year—without knowing it myself.

IRENE: I couldn't come to you, Arnold. Lying down there as I was, and sleeping a long, dream-filled sleep.

RUBEK: But now you've awakened, Irene.

IRENE: (*Shaking her head.*) My eyes are still filled with that heavy, deep sleep.

RUBEK: You shall see the light of day dawn for both of us.

IRENE: Don't ever believe that.

RUBEK: (*Insistently.*) I do believe it! And I know it! Now that I've found you again—!

IRENE: Risen.

RUBEK: Transfigured!

IRENE: Only risen, Arnold. Not transfigured.

> (*RUBEK balances his way across the stepping stones beneath the waterfall toward her.*)

RUBEK: Where have you been all day, Irene?

IRENE: (*Pointing outward.*) Far, far way, in the vast land of the dead.

RUBEK: (*To distract her.*) You don't have your—your friend with you today, I see.

IRENE: (*Smiling.*) My friend keeps a sharp eye on me, just the same.

RUBEK: Can she?

IRENE: (*Glancing about her.*) You can be sure she can. Wherever I am or go. Never lets me out of her sight— (*Whispers.*) Until one fine, sunny morning I shall murder her.

RUBEK: You want to do that?

IRENE: With all my heart. If only I could.

RUBEK: Why would you wish to do that?

IRENE: Because she's gone over to the powers of darkness. (*Secretively.*) Imagine, Arnold, she's made herself into my shadow.

RUBEK: (*Seeking to calm her.*) Well, well, well—we all must accept our shadows.

IRENE: I am my own shadow. (*Cries out.*) Don't you understand that?

RUBEK: *(Somberly.)* Yes, yes, Irene—I understand well enough. *(He sits on a stone beside the stream. She stands behind him, leaning against the rock face.)*

IRENE: *(After a pause.)* Why do you sit there with your eyes turned away from me.

RUBEK: *(In a hushed voice, shaking his head.)* I dare not—dare not look at you.

IRENE: Why don't you dare to any more?

RUBEK: You have a shadow that tortures you. And I have the weight of my conscience.

IRENE: *(With a joyful cry of liberation.)* At last!

RUBEK: *(Leaping up.)* Irene—what is it?

IRENE *(Warding him off.)* Keep calm, calm! *(Breathes deeply and speaks as if freed of a burden.)* There. They've let go of me. For the time being. Now we can sit and talk as we used to once—in life.

RUBEK: Ah, if only we could talk as we used to.

IRENE: Sit where you were. I'll sit here beside you.

(He sits down again. She sits on another, nearby stone.)

IRENE: *(After a short silence.)* Now I've come back to you, Arnold, from the most distant regions.

RUBEK: Yes, without doubt from an infinitely long journey.

IRENE: Come home to my lord and master.

RUBEK: To our—our own realm, Irene.

IRENE: Have you waited for me every day?

RUBEK: How could I dare wait for you?

IRENE *(With a sidelong glance.)* No, of course you didn't dare. Because you understood nothing.

RUBEK: Wasn't it really for someone else's sake you left me as suddenly as you did?

IRENE: Couldn't it as well have been for your sake, Arnold.

RUBEK: *(Looking at her uncertainly.)* I don't understand—

IRENE: When I'd served you with my soul and with my body—and the statue stood finished—our child as you called it—then I laid at your feet the most precious sacrifice of all—by erasing myself for all time.

RUBEK: *(Bowing his head.)* And laid waste my life.

IRENE: *(Suddenly flares up.)* *That* was exactly what I intended. That you should never, never create anything again—once you had created that only child of ours.

RUBEK: Was it jealousy driving your thoughts?

IRENE: I think it was closer to hatred.

RUBEK: Hatred? Hatred for me?

IRENE: *(Again fiercely.)* Yes, for you—for the artist who so indifferently and unfeelingly took a warm-blooded body, a young human life, and tore the soul out of it. Because you could use it to create a work of art.

RUBEK: And you can say that—? You who shared in my labor with such radiant passion, such high and holy yearning. In that work where we would join each morning as at a sacrament?

IRENE: *(Coldly, as before.)* There's one thing I must tell you, Arnold.

RUBEK: Well?

IRENE: I never loved your art before I met you. Nor since, either.

RUBEK: But—the artist, Irene?

IRENE: I hate the artist.

RUBEK: The artist in me, also?

IRENE: In you most of all. When I stripped myself naked and stood there before you, I hated you, Arnold.

RUBEK: *(Vehemently.)* No you did *not* Irene! That isn't true!

IRENE: I hated you because you could stand there completely unmoved.

RUBEK: *(Laughs.)* Unmoved? You believe that?

IRENE: So despicably self-controlled then. And because you were an artist, only an artist—not a man! *(Changes to a warmer, more intense tone.)* But that statue in wet, living clay, *that* I loved, as she rose up there, a human child filled with soul, formed from those raw, shapeless masses. Because *that* was *our* creation, our child. Mine and yours.

RUBEK: *(Sadly.)* And so it was, in spirit and truth.

IRENE: You see, Arnold, it's for our child's sake I've taken on this long pilgrimage.

RUBEK: *(Suddenly attentive.)* For that marble statue—?

IRENE: You call it what you will. I call it our child.

RUBEK: *(Uneasy.)* And now you wish to see it? Completed? In that marble that you always thought so cold. *(Eagerly.)* Maybe you don't know it's standing in a great museum somewhere—far from here?

IRENE: I've heard some such story.

RUBEK: And you always loathed museums. You called them sepulchers.

IRENE: I want to go on a pilgrimage there where my soul and my soul's child lie buried.

RUBEK: *(In alarm and dread.)* You must never look on that statue again! Do you hear, Irene? I implore you—! Never, never, look on it again!

IRENE: You think I might die a second time?

RUBEK: *(Clenching his fists.)* I don't know myself what I think! But how could I imagine you'd cling so obsessively to that image? You who went away from me—before it was completed.

IRENE: It *was* completed. And so I could go from you, leaving you alone.

RUBEK: *(Sitting, his elbows on his knees, rocking his head from side to side, his hands over his eyes.)* It was not then what it later was to become.

IRENE: *(Silently and swift as lightning, half draws a thin, sharp knife from her breast and whispers hoarsely.)* Arnold—have you done some harm to our child?

RUBEK: *(Evasively.)* Some harm? I cannot say for sure what you might call it.

IRENE: *(Breathless.)* Tell me right away—what have you done to the child?

RUBEK: I will tell you if you will sit and listen calmly to what I say.

IRENE: *(Hiding the knife.)* I will sit and listen as calmly as a mother can when she—

RUBEK: *(Interrupting.)* And I don't want you looking at me while I tell you.

IRENE: *(Moves over to a stone behind his back.)* I'll sit here behind you. So, tell me!

RUBEK: *(Takes his hands away from his eyes and stares ahead.)* When I discovered you I knew at once how I would use you for my masterpiece.

IRENE: You called it "Resurrection Day." I call it our child.

RUBEK: I was young then. With no experience of life. The Resurrection, I believed, could be most beautifully represented as a young and pure woman—innocent of all earthly experience—and awakening to light and glory with nothing ugly or tainted to shed.

IRENE: *(Quickly.)* Yes, and that's how I'm standing now in our work?

RUBEK: *(Hesitantly.)* Not altogether quite like that, Irene.

IRENE: *(In mounting tension.)* Not quite—? Am I not standing exactly as I stood for you?

RUBEK: *(Not answering.)* I got to know more about the world in the years that followed, Irene. "Resurrection Day" became a more—a more multilayered conception in my mind. The little round base on which your image stood erect and isolated—that didn't allow enough room for more images I now wanted to add—

IRENE: *(Groping for the knife, but stops.)* What more images? Tell me!

RUBEK: I re-envisaged it after what I saw with my own eyes in the world around me. It was what I had to do. There was no other way, Irene. I widened the base until it was large and spacious. And on that I laid a section of the arching, bursting earth. And up through the fissures in its crust there now swarmed human figures with secret animal faces. Women and men exactly as I new them from life.

IRENE: *(In breathless anticipation.)* But right at the center of that mass stands the young woman radiant with joy? Don't I, Arnold?

RUBEK: *(Evasively.)* Not quite at the center. Unfortunately I had to shift the statue back somewhat. For the sake of the composition, you understand. Otherwise it would have dominated it too much.

IRENE: But my face is still transfigured by the radiant light of joy?

RUBEK: It still is, Irene. In a sense, that is. A little subdued, perhaps. As my later conception required.

IRENE: *(Silently rises.)* That image expresses life as you know see it, Arnold?

RUBEK: Yes, that's what it does.

IRENE: And in that image you have shifted me back—a bit faded—as a background figure—in a group. *(She draws out the knife.)*

RUBEK: Not some background figure. Let's rather say a shape in the middle ground—something like that.

IRENE: *(Whispers hoarsely.)* Now you've pronounced judgment on yourself! *(About to stab him.)*

RUBEK: *(Turning and looking up at her.)* Judgment!

IRENE: *(Quickly hiding the knife and speaking in a voice choked with grief.)* My whole soul—you and I—we—we and the child—was in that solitary figure.

RUBEK: *(Intensely, pulling off his hat and wiping drops of sweat from his brow.)* Yes, but now hear how I have portrayed myself within the group. In the foreground, by a stream—just like here—sits a man weighed down by guilt, who cannot work his way free from the earth's crust. I call him remorse for an unrealized life. He's sitting there, dipping his fingers in the rippling water—to make them clean—and he's ravaged and tormented with the knowledge that he'll never never succeed. Never, through all eternity, will he free himself to a resurrected life. He must sit there, forever, in the hell of his own making.

IRENE: *(Hard and cold.)* Poet!

RUBEK: Why poet?

IRENE: Because you're slack and sickly and full of self-forgiving for all your life's sins—for all those you've committed and all those you've thought. You murder my soul— then model yourself in remorse and penance and contrition— *(Smiling.)* and with that, your account's settled, you assume.

RUBEK: *(Defiantly.)* I am an artist, Irene. And I'm not ashamed of the frailties I might bear about me. Because I was born to be an artist, you understand? I can't be anything but an artist, whatever the cost.

IRENE: *(Regarding him with a veiled, evil smile, speaking softly and gently.)* Poet—that's what you are, Arnold. *(Lightly stroking his hair.)* You big, dear, aging child—you can't even see it.

RUBEK: *(Annoyed.)* Why do you keep calling me a poet?

IRENE: *(A sly expression in her eyes.)* Because in that word lies something that extenuates and condones, my friend. Something self-justifying that spreads a cloak over every failing. *(Suddenly changes her tone.)* But I was a human being—then! And I also had a life to live—and a human destiny to fulfill. See, all that I let go—gave it all up to make myself serve your ends. Oh, that was suicide—a mortal sin against myself. *(In a half whisper.)* And that sin I can never atone for.

(She sits down beside him near the stream, watching him unnoticed while at the same time absentmindedly plucking some flowers from the bushes around them.)

IRENE: *(Seemingly self-controlled.)* I should have brought children into the world. Many children. Real children, not the kind hidden away in sepulchers. That should have been my calling. I never should have served you—Poet!

RUBEK: *(Lost in memories.)* Yet, they were beautiful times, Irene. Incredibly beautiful times—when I think back on them.

IRENE: *(Looking at him gently.)* Can you remember a little word you used when you were through—through with me and with our child? *(Nodding to him.)* Can you remember that little word?

RUBEK: *(Looks inquiringly at her.)* I said a little word then that you still remember now?

IRENE: Yes, you did. You can't remember it now?

RUBEK: *(Shaking his head.)* No, I honestly can't. Not just at this moment, anyway.

IRENE: You took both my hands and pressed them warmly. And I stood there in breathless expectation. And then you said: I thank you Irene, with all my heart. This has been a marvellous episode for me.

RUBEK: *(Looking doubtful.)* Did I say episode? It's not a word I'm given to using.

IRENE: You said episode.

RUBEK: *(With feigned unconcern.)* Yes, well—come to that, it *was* an episode.

IRENE: For that word, I left you.

RUBEK: You take everything so painfully to heart, Irene.

IRENE: *(Passing her hand over her brow.)* You could be right. Let us shake ourselves free of sorrows that lie deep in the heart. *(Plucks some petals from a mountain rose and strews them onto the stream.)* Look, Arnold, there are our birds, swimming.

RUBEK: What birds are they?

IRENE: Can't you see? They're flamingos, of course. Because they're rose-red.

RUBEK: Flamingos don't swim. They only wade.

IRENE: Then they aren't flamingos. They're gulls.

RUBEK: Yes, they could be gulls with red beaks. *(Plucking broad green leaves and tosses them after.)* Now I'm sending my ships after them.

IRENE: There must be no huntsmen on board.

RUBEK: No, there aren't any huntsmen. *(Smiling at her.)* Can you remember that summer we sat like this outside the little farmhouse on Lake Taunitz?

IRENE: *(Nodding.)* Saturday evenings, yes—when we'd finished the week's work—

RUBEK: And travelled out there by train. And stayed over Sunday.

IRENE: *(With an evil, hate-filled gleam in her eyes.)* It was an episode, Arnold.

RUBEK: *(As if not hearing.)* There, too, you sent your birds swimming in the stream. They were water lilies that you—

IRENE: They were white swans.

RUBEK: I meant swans. And I remember how I fastened a large downy leaf to one of the swans. A dock leaf, it must have been.

IRENE: Then it became Lohengrin's boat—with the swan leading it.

RUBEK: How happy you were with that game, Irene.

IRENE: We played it again and again.

RUBEK: Every Saturday, I think. All through the summer.

IRENE: You said I was the swan that drew your boat after.

RUBEK: Did I say that? Yes, it could well be. *(Engrossed in the game.)* But just look how your gulls are swimming downstream.

IRENE: *(Laughing.)* And all your ships have run aground.

RUBEK: *(Casting more leaves into the stream.)* I've enough ships in reserve. *(Following the leaves with his eyes, launches more leaves and, after a pause, says.)* Irene, I bought that little farmhouse on Lake Taunitz.

IRENE: You bought it then? You often said you would when you had the means to.

RUBEK: Since then I acquired the means. So I bought it.

IRENE: *(A sidelong glance at him.)* Are you living there now—in our old house?

RUBEK: No, I had it torn down long ago. Since then I've built a big, splendid, comfortable villa in its place—with a park around it. There's where we usually— *(Stops and corrects himself.)* where I usually spend the summer.

IRENE: *(Controlling herself.)* So you and—and that other one are staying there now?

RUBEK: *(A little defiantly.)* Yes. When my wife and I aren't travelling—as we are this year.

IRENE: *(Gazing far in front of her.)* Lovely, lovely was that life on Lake Taunitz.

RUBEK: *(As if searching within himself.)* And yet, Irene—

IRENE: And yet the two of us let slip by all that loveliness.

RUBEK *(Quietly and importunately.)* Has our repentance come too late?

IRENE: *(Not answering him but sitting silently awhile, then she points across the plateau.)* Look there, Arnold. The sun's going under behind those peaks. Just see how red it's glowing, that slant of light over the tufts of heather.

RUBEK: *(Looking outward, too.)* It's been long since I saw a sunset over the mountains.

IRENE: Or a sunrise?

RUBEK: A sunrise—? I don't think I've ever seen that.

IRENE: *(Smiling as if lost in memory.)* I once saw an incredibly beautiful sunrise.

RUBEK: You did? Where was that?

IRENE: High, high up on a dizzying mountain top. You lured me up there and promised I should see all the glory of the world if I would only—

RUBEK: If you would only—? Well?

IRENE: Do as you commanded. Follow you up to the heights above. And there I fell upon my knees—and worshiped you. And served you. *(Silent a moment, then says softly.)* Then I saw the sunrise.

RUBEK: *(Hesitantly.)* Couldn't you bring yourself to come and live with us in the villa down south?

IRENE: *(Regarding him with a scornful smile.)* Together with you and that other lady?

RUBEK: *(Pleading.)* Together with me—as in those days when we created together. Open up everything that's locked away in me. Couldn't you wish to do that, Irene?

IRENE: *(Shaking her head.)* I no longer have the key to you, Arnold.

RUBEK: You have the key! Nobody but you has it! *(Entreating, begging.)* Help me—so I can live my life over again!

IRENE: *(Impassive, as before.)* Empty dreams. Pointless—dead dreams. There can be no resurrection of our life together.

RUBEK: *(Abruptly, breaking off.)* So let's go back to our playing.

IRENE: Yes, playing, playing—nothing but playing.

(They sit strewing leaves and flower petals out into the stream, letting them swim and sail there. Over the steep slope to the left ULFHEJM and MAJA enter wearing hunting outfits. After them comes the SERVANT with the pack of hounds, which he leads out to the right.)

RUBEK: *(Sighting them.)* Look, there goes little Maja with her bear hunter.

IRENE: Your lady, yes.

RUBEK: Or the other's.

MAJA: *(Scanning the plateau as she goes, catches sight of the pair beside the lake and calls out to them.)* Good night, Professor. Dream of me. Now I'm off on an adventure.

RUBEK: *(Calling back.)* What kind of adventure is it going to be?

MAJA: *(Coming nearer.)* I'll be putting life before everything else.

RUBEK: *(Mockingly.)* Indeed, you're also going to do that, little Maja?

MAJA: Oh yes. And I've even made up a song about it. It goes like this:

> I am free! I am free! I am free!
> No more life in a mancage for me!
> I am free as a bird! I am free!
> Because, you see, I feel I've awakened now—at last.

RUBEK: So it would seem.

MAJA: *(Taking a deep breath.)* Oh, how heavenly light I feel, knowing I've awakened.

RUBEK: Good night, Maja—and good luck to you—

ULFHEJM *(Calling out to warn him.)* Shh. Quiet. The devil take your unlucky good wishes. Can't you see we're going hunting—

RUBEK: What will you bring home from the hunt for me, Maja?

MAJA: I'll get you a bird of prey for you to model. I'll wing it for you.

RUBEK: *(With a mocking, bitter laugh.)* Yes, winging, naturally of course by accident, that's long been your specialty, hasn't it?

MAJA: *(Tossing her head.)* Oh, just leave me to take care of myself— *(Nods and laughs roguishly.)* Goodbye—and enjoy a good quiet summer night on the mountain!

RUBEK: *(Cheerfully.)* And the worst luck in the world to both you and your hunting.

ULFHEJM: *(Roars with laughter.)* Now that's a wish I can live with!

MAJA: *(Laughing.)* Thank you, thank you, professor!

(They go over the visible part of the plain and out through the bushes on the right.)

RUBEK: *(After a short silence.)* A summer's night on the mountain. Yes, *that* would have been life!

IRENE: *(Suddenly, a wild expression in her eyes)* Is that what you want—a summer's night on the mountain—you and I?

RUBEK: *(Opens his arms wide.)* Yes, yes—come!

IRENE: You, my love, my lord and master!

RUBEK: Oh, Irene!

IRENE: *(Hoarsely, smiling and fumbling in her breast.)* It will only be an episode. *(Quickly, whispering.)* Shh, Arnold! Don't look round!

RUBEK: *(Likewise quietly.)* What is it?

IRENE: A face staring at me.

RUBEK: *(Involuntarily turning.)* Where? *(Starting.)* Ah—!

    (The NUN'S head has come halfway in view between the bushes by the pathway downward to the left. Her eyes are fixed unwaveringly on IRENE.)

IRENE: *(Rises and says, quietly.)* We must separate. No, you stay sitting. You hear me! You mustn't follow me. *(Bends over him and whispers.)* Till our meeting tonight. On the mountain.

RUBEK: Will you be there, Irene?

IRENE: I'll be there for certain. Wait for me here.

RUBEK: *(Repeats, as if dreaming.)* A summer night on the mountain. With you. With you. *(His eyes meet hers.)* Oh, Irene—that might have been our life. And we've thrown it away, you and I.

IRENE: We see what we've lost, irredeemably, only when— *(She breaks off.)*

RUBEK: *(Looks inquiringly at her.)* Only when—?

IRENE: When we dead awaken.

RUBEK: *(Dejectedly shaking his head.)* Yes, what do we see then?

IRENE: We see that we've never lived. *(She goes over across to the knoll and climbs down the hill. The NUN makes way for her and follows after. RUBEK remains sitting by the stream.)*

MAJA: *(Can be heard singing jubilantly in the mountains.)*

    I am free! I am free! I am free!

    No more life in a mancage for me!

    I am free as a bird! I am free!

END OF ACT TWO

ACT THREE

A wild landscape marked by crevices, with sheer precipices in the background. Snow-clad peaks soar to the right and lose themselves in drifting clouds above. To the left, on a slope of rock stands an old, half-collapsed hut. It is early morning. Dawn is breaking, but the sun has not yet risen.

MAJA enters, blushing red and in a furious temper, and clambers down the rocks. ULFHEJM follows after, half angry, half laughing, and holds her tightly by the arm.

MAJA: *(Trying to tear herself loose.)* Let go of me! Let go of me, I tell you.

ULFHEJM: Well, well. You look as if you're ready to bite. You're as feisty as a she-wolf.

MAJA: *(Hitting him on the hand.)* I said let me go! And behave yourself—

ULFHEJM: I'll be damned if I will.

MAJA: All right—then I'm not going another step with you. Do you hear—not another step—!

ULFHEJM: Ho ho! How do you think you'll escape from me on this wild mountain?

MAJA: I'll run down that rockface there if I have to—

ULFHEJM: To be smashed and mashed into dog meat—tasty and bloody— *(He lets go of her.)* There you are—go ahead. Run down the rock face if that's what you want. It's a dizzying drop. There's only one narrow path and that's nearly impassable.

MAJA: *(Brushes her skirt with her hand and glares at him in fury.)* You're a fine one to go out hunting with.

ULFHEJM: Say rather: to have some sport with.

MAJA: So this is what you call sport, is it?

ULFHEJM: Yes, I allow myself that liberty. It's the kind of sport I like best of all.

MAJA: *(Tossing her head.)* Well—I must say! *(After a moment, looking at him probingly.)* Why did you set the dogs loose up there?

ULFHEJM: *(Winking and smiling.)* So that *they* also could get to do a little hunting on their own.

MAJA: That's not true at all! It was not for the dogs' sake you let them go.

ULFHEJM: *(Still smiling.)* All right then, why did I let them loose? Let's hear it—

MAJA: You let them go because you wanted to get rid of Lars. He was to chase after them and bring them back, you said. And then meanwhile— Oh, that certainly was very charming of you!

ULFHEJM: And then meanwhile—?

MAJA: *(Cutting him short.)* Never mind about that.

ULFHEJM: *(In a confidential tone.)* Lars won't find them. You can count on that. He won't be back here with them until time's up.

MAJA: *(Looking furiously at him.)* No, I'm sure he won't.

ULFHEJM: *(Grabbing after her arm.)* Lars, you see, he knows my sporting habits.

MAJA: *(Eluding him and appraising him with her eyes.)* Do you know what you look like, Mr. Ulfhejm?

ULFHEJM: I imagine I look mostly like myself.

MAJA: You're perfectly right, there. Because you're the living image of a faun.

ULFHEJM: A faun—?

MAJA: Yes, a faun, exactly.

ULFHEJM A faun—isn't that some kind of monster? Or rather what's called a wood demon?

MAJA: Yes, that just the thing you are. With a beard like a goat and the legs of a goat. Oh yes—and the faun has horns, too.

ULFHEJM: Oh no! So *he's* got horns, too?

MAJA: A pair of beastly horns, just like you.

ULFHEJM: Can you see my unhappy little horns?

MAJA: I think I can see them quite distinctly.

ULFHEJM: *(Takes a dog leash from his pocket.)* Well then, I'd better set about tying you up.

MAJA: Are you completely mad? Tie me up—?

ULFHEJM: If I'm to be a devil then let me be a devil. Well now—so you can see the horns, eh?

MAJA: *(Placatingly.)* There, there, there—try to behave yourself, Mr. Ulfhejm. *(Breaking off.)* But where is this hunting lodge of yours you were bragging so much about. You said it should be somewhere around here.

ULFHEJM: *(Pointing grandly to the hut.)* Here it is, right before your eyes.

MAJA: *(Staring at him.)* That old pigsty there?

ULFHEJM: *(Laughing into his beard.)* It's housed more than one princess, just the same.

MAJA: Was it there that revolting man you told me about came in to the princess in the shape of a bear?

ULFHEJM: Yes, madam hunting comrade—here's the scene of the crime. *(With a gesture of invitation.)* If you would be so gracious as to step in—

MAJA: Isch! I wouldn't so much as set foot in there—isch!

ULFHEJM: Oh, a couple can sleep away a summer night comfortably enough in there. A whole summer, for that matter.

MAJA: Thanks! But one needs to acquire the taste for that. *(Impatiently.)* But now I'm bored, both with you and with this hunting trip. I want to go down to the hotel—now, before everyone wakes up.

ULFHEJM: And how do you imagine you're going to get down from here?

MAJA: That's your business. There must be some place or other here where we can find a path down.

ULFHEJM: (Pointing to the background.) To be sure there is—there's some sort of way down—right across that rock face there.

MAJA: There you are—with just a little good will—

ULFHEJM: But try finding out if you've got the nerve to go that way.

MAJA: (Hesitantly.) You don't think so?

ULFHEJM: Never in this world. That is, if I don't help you—

MAJA: (Uneasily.) Well then, come and help me. Why else are you with me?

ULFHEJM: Would you rather I set you on my back—

MAJA: Don't be absurd!

ULFHEJM: Or carried you in my arms?

MAJA: Let's not have any of that nonsense again.

ULFHEJM: (With inward resentment.) I once took a young urchin of a girl—lifted her out of the gutter and carried her in my arms. I handled her so gently. That's how I wanted to carry her all through life—so she'd never dash her foot against a stone. Because, when I found her, her shoes had worn so very thin—

MAJA: But all the same, you lifted her up and handled her gently like that?

ULFHEJM: Lifted her out of the mire and carried her as high and as gently as I could. (With growling laughter.) And do you know what I got for my pains?

MAJA: No. What?

ULFHEJM: (Smiling and nodding to her.) Horns—that's what I got. The horns you can see so distinctly. Now isn't that an amusing story, madam bear slayer?

MAJA: Oh yes, amusing enough. But I know another story that's even more amusing.

ULFHEJM: How does that story go?

MAJA: Like this. Once upon a time there was a foolish little girl who had both a father and a mother. But a somewhat impoverished home. And into this impoverished home there came a very powerful great lord of a man. And he took the little girl in his arms—just like you—and travelled far, far away with her—

ULFHEJM: Did she want so much to be wherever he was?

MAJA: Yes, for she was foolish, you see.

ULFHEJM: And he no doubt was truly a handsome figure of a man.

MAJA: Oh no, not so strikingly handsome as all that, either. But he got her to believe she would join him on the top of the highest mountain where everything would be bathed in light and sunshine.

ULFHEJM: So he was a mountain climber was he, this man?

MAJA: Yes, he was. In his way.

ULFHEJM: And so he took the wench up there with him—?

MAJA: *(Tossing her head.)* Oh for sure! He certainly took her with him, you can believe it. But not up. Ah no. He lured her into a cold, clammy cage where there was neither sunshine nor fresh air—or so it seemed to her— but just gilded walls lined with great ghosts of men and women turned to stone.

ULFHEJM: Well, what the devil—she deserved it!

MAJA: Yes, but isn't that quite an amusing story, just the same?

ULFHEJM *(Regarding her a moment.)* Listen to me, my fine hunting comrade—

MAJA: Well? Now what's it to be?

ULFHEJM: Shouldn't we two patch our tattered lives together?

MAJA: The squire wants to set up as a patchwork tailor?

ULFHEJM: Yes, that's what he wants to do. Can't we two try putting the pieces together here and there—and shape some kind of human life out of them?

MAJA: And when those wretched rags are thoroughly worn out—what then?

ULFHEJM: *(With a sweeping gesture.)* We'll then stand, fresh and free—just as we really are.

MAJA: *(Laughing.)* You with your goat legs, yes!

ULFHEJM: And you with your—well, let that pass.

MAJA: Then come—let's go.

ULFHEJM: Stop! Where to?

MAJA: Down to the hotel, of course.

ULFHEJM: And after that?

MAJA: So we'll take a pleasant farewell of each other and say "thanks for the company."

ULFHEJM: *Can* we separate, we two? You really believe we *can?*

MAJA: Yes, you never got round to tying me up, remember?

ULFHEJM: I can offer you a castle.

MAJA: *(Pointing to the hut.)* Looking like that one there?

ULFHEJM: It hasn't fallen apart like that.

MAJA: And all the glory of the world, perhaps?

ULFHEJM: A castle, I said—

MAJA: Thanks, but I've had enough of castles.

ULFHEJM: With splendid hunting grounds for miles around.

MAJA: Are there works of art in that castle, too?

ULFHEJM: (Slowly.) No, there are no works of art, but—

MAJA: (Relieved.) No, that's all to the good!

ULFHEJM: Then will you go with me, as far and for as long as I ask?

MAJA: There's a tame bird of prey keeping watch over me.

ULFHEJM: (Fiercely.) We'll put a bullet in his wing, Maja.

MAJA: (Looks at him a moment, then speaks resolutely) Come then, carry me through the depths below.

ULFHEJM: (Flings his arms around her waist.) It's high time we went. The mists are gathering round us.

MAJA: Is the way down fearfully dangerous?

ULFHEJM: The mountain mists are more dangerous.

(She breaks free, goes over to the chasm below but quickly draws back.)

ULFHEJM: (Goes laughing to meet her.) Makes your head swim a little, does it?

MAJA: (Weakly.) Yes, that too. But go take a look over there. Those two, climbing up.

ULFHEJM: (Goes across and leans out over the precipice.) It's only your bird of prey—and his strange lady.

MAJA: Can't we slip by them—without them seeing us?

ULFHEJM: Can't be done. The trail's much too narrow. And from here there's no other way down.

MAJA: (Bracing herself.) Oh well, let's face them here.

ULFHEJM: Spoken like a true bear hunter!

(RUBEK and IRENE climb into view from the chasm in the background. He has his plaid over his shoulders; she a fur cape thrown loosely over her white dress and a swansdown hood over her head)

RUBEK: (Still only half visible over the ridge.) What—Maja! Are we fated to meet yet again?

MAJA: (With feigned assurance.) At your service. Do come on up.

(RUBEK climbs up completely and reaches his hand to IRENE who also climbs fully into view.)

RUBEK: (Coldly to MAJA.) You've also been on the mountain all night, have you? Like us?

MAJA: I've been out hunting, yes. You did give me leave to go.

ULFHEJM: (Pointing toward the chasm.) Did you come up the path there?

RUBEK: You saw for yourself.

ULFHEJM: And the strange lady, too?

RUBEK: Yes, as you see. (With a glance at MAJA.) The strange lady and I plan never to go on separate paths from now on.

ULFHEJM: Didn't you know the path you took is a deadly one?

RUBEK: We two tried it, just the same. Because it didn't seem too bad at first.

ULFHEJM: No, nothing seems too bad at first. But then you come to a tight corner where there's no going forward or back. And there one is stuck fast, Professor! Rock trapped,[1] we hunters call it.

RUBEK: *(Smiling as he looks at him)* Are these meant for words of wisdom, Mr. Ulfhejm?

ULFHEJM: The lord forbid I should go in for words of wisdom. *(Urgently, pointing up to the peaks.)* But don't you see there's a storm gathering over our heads? Can't you hear the gusts of wind.

RUBEK: *(Listening.)* It sounds like the overture to Resurrection Day.

ULFHEJM: They're the storm blasts from the peaks, man! See how the clouds are convulsed, rolling and sinking. They'll soon be wrapping around us like a winding sheet.

IRENE: *(Starting.)* I know that winding sheet.

MAJA: *(Tugging at him.)* Let's see about getting down.

ULFHEJM: *(To RUBEK.)* I can't help more than one. Stay in the hut so long as—until the storm's over. I'll send people up to fetch you both—

IRENE: *(Crying out.)* Fetch us! No! No!—

ULFHEJM: *(Harshly.)* To take you by force, if necessary. It's now become a matter of life and death here. Now you know. *(To MAJA.)* Come then— and put your trust in your partner's strength.

MAJA: *(Clinging to him.)* God, if I manage to get down in my whole skin, I shall sing and dance for joy.

ULFHEJM: *(Begins the climb down and calls to the others.)* Make sure you wait there in the hut till the men come with ropes to fetch you.
(ULFHEJM with MAJA in his arms, clambers quickly but carefully down into the chasm.)

IRENE: *(Looking awhile with terrified eyes at RUBEK.)* Did you hear that, Arnold? Men are going to come and fetch me! Many men will come up here—

RUBEK: Just keep calm, Irene.

IRENE: *(In mounting fear.)* And she—the one in black—she'll be with them. For she must have missed me long ago. And then she will seize hold of me, Arnold! And put me in the straightjacket. Yes, because she keeps one with her in her box. I've seen it myself—

RUBEK: No one shall be allowed to harm you.

IRENE: *(With a manic smile.)* Ah no, I've my own remedy for that.

RUBEK: What remedy do you mean?

IRENE: *(Drawing out the knife.)* This!

RUBEK: *(Grabbing for the knife.)* You've a knife!

IRENE: Always, always. Both day and night. In bed, too.

RUBEK: Give me the knife, Irene!

IRENE: *(Hiding it.)* You're not having it. I may well find a use for it.

RUBEK: What would you want to use it for here?

IRENE: *(Looking fixedly at him.)* It was meant for you, Arnold.

RUBEK: For *me!*

IRENE: When we sat by Lake Taunitz last night.

RUBEK: By Lake Taunitz—?

IRENE: In front of the farmhouse. And we played with swans and water lilies—

RUBEK: And then? And then?

IRENE: And I heard you say, in a voice cold as ice, out of the grave, that I was nothing more than an episode in your life—

RUBEK: It was you who said that, Irene! Not I.

IRENE: *(Continuing.)* I had the knife out ready. I wanted to plunge it into your back.

RUBEK: *(Darkly.)* Then why didn't you?

IRENE: Because it became horribly apparent to me you were already dead—had been dead a long time.

RUBEK: Dead?

IRENE: Dead. Dead. You as well as I. There we sat, by Lake Taunitz, we two clammy corpses, playing games with each other.

RUBEK: I don't call that dead. But you don't understand me.

IRENE: Where is that burning desire for me that you strove and fought against when I stood freely before you as the woman risen from the dead?

RUBEK: Our love is not dead, Irene.

IRENE: That love that belongs to the life of earth—that beautiful, miraculous earthlife, so full of mysteries—*that* is dead in both of us.

RUBEK: *(Ardently.)* I tell you, that same love seethes and burns in me now as fiercely as ever it did before.

IRENE: And I? Have you forgotten what I am now?

RUBEK: You can choose to be whoever and whatever you want with me. For me, you're the woman I dream of you being.

IRENE: I've stood on the stage—naked— And showed myself before hundreds of men—after you.

RUBEK: It was I who drove you onto that stage—blind as I was at the time! I set that dead image of clay above the joy of life and of love.

IRENE: *(Eyes downcast.)* Too late. Too late.

RUBEK: Everything that lies between then and now has not lowered you a hair's breadth in my eyes.

IRENE: *(Her head raised.)* Nor in mine, either.

RUBEK: Well then! So we are free. And there's still time for us to live our lives, Irene!

IRENE: *(Regarding him sadly.)* The desire for life died in me, Arnold. Now I am risen. And I search for you and find you. And then discover that both you and life lie dead—just as I lay dead.

RUBEK: Oh, you are deluded! Life within us and around us still seethes and surges as it ever did!

IRENE: *(Smiling and shaking her head.)* Your young woman risen from the dead sees the whole of life as laid out in a morgue.

RUBEK: *(Throws his arms ardently around her.)* Then let us two dead souls live life to the full for once—before we go down into our graves again!

IRENE: *(With a cry.)* Arnold!

RUBEK: But not here in this half light. Not here with this hideous, wet grave cloth flapping about us—

IRENE: *(In mounting passion.)* No, no—up into the light glittering in all its glory. Up to the promised mountain peaks.

RUBEK: And up there we'll celebrate our marriage feast, Irene—my beloved.

IRENE: *(Proudly.)* The sun will look gladly on us, Arnold.

RUBEK: All the powers of light may look gladly on us. And those of darkness, too. *(Grasping her hands.)* Will you now follow me, my bride, redeemed and blest?

IRENE: *(As if transfigured.)* Gladly and willingly, I follow my lord and master.

RUBEK *(Leading her.)* First we must go through the mist, Irene, and then—

IRENE: Yes, through all the mists. And then right up to the top of the tower that gleams in the sunrise.

(The clouds of mist closes densely over the landscape. RUBEK and IRENE hand in hand, climb up over the snowfield to the right and soon disappear into the lower clouds. Sharp gusts of wind swirl and whine through the air. The NUN comes up over the rock slope to the left. She remains standing there, peering about silently.)

MAJA: *(Can be heard joyfully singing from far below.)*

I am free! I am free! I am free!

No more life in a mancage for me!

I am free as a bird! I am free![2]

(Suddenly, a sound like a thunderous roar is heard from above the snowfield. It rushes down, whirling at a terrifying speed. RUBEK and IRENE are obscurely glimpsed, whirled in the mass of snow and buried in it.)

THE NUN: *(Lets out a shriek, reaches out her arms toward them, and cries.)*
Irene! *(She stands silently awhile, makes the sign of the cross in the air in front of her and says.)* Pax vobiscum!
(MAJA's rejoicing and song continue from farther down the mountain.)

END OF PLAY

NOTES

ACT ONE.

[1] Nun. She is named a *diakonisse*— deaconness—throughout the play.

[2] Ulfhejm. Wolfhome.

[3] Ulfhejm's wordplay in the original (*brakvandet, braekvandet* means "brackish or vomit water") is the occasion for much desperate ingenuity on the part of translators.

ACT THREE.

[1] *Bergfast*. Mountain stuck.

[2] It is not clear if Maja's song sets off the avalanche, like Gerd's rifle shot in *Brand*.

BRIAN JOHNSTON has taught at universities in Britain, Norway, the Middle East, and the United States and is currently Associate Professor of Dramatic Literature at Carnegie Mellon University, Pittsburgh. He is the author of three highly acclaimed studies of Ibsen's drama: *To The Third Empire: Ibsen's Early Drama* (University of Minnesota Press, 1980), *Text and Supertext in Ibsen's Drama* (1989) and *The Ibsen Cycle* (Revised Edition) (1992), the latter two published by the Pennsylvania State University Press.